D0336838

The Secret of Crete

THE SECRET
OF CRETE

HANS GEORG WUNDERLICH

Translated from the German by

Richard Winston

SOUVENIR PRESS

The Secret of Crete was originally published in German under
the title *Wohin der Stier Europa trug*
Published in America by
Macmillan Publishing Co., Inc.

First British Edition published 1975 by
Souvenir Press Ltd., 95 Mortimer Street, London W1N 8HP

ISBN 0 285 62164 5

Printed and bound in Great Britain by
REDWOOD BURN LIMITED
Trowbridge & Esher

Contents

Book Three ✺ **IN THE SHADOW OF THE MINOTAUR**

Foreword

In the year 1900 British anthropologist and archaeologist Arthur Evans began excavating a Bronze Age site near the city of Herakleion in Crete, and came upon a building with nearly twelve hundred rooms. No one had the slightest idea who had originally created this enormous structure. Evans associated it with the ancient Greek traditions of King Minos, who supposedly ruled the island capital of Knossos two generations before the Trojan War. According to the tales, Minos had constructed a mysterious labyrinth. Evans regarded the site as the remains of this ruler's former palace, and he coined the concept of a "Minoan" culture in Bronze Age Crete. Ever since, scholars have become accustomed to referring to the palace builders of early Crete as "the Minoans," although to this day no one knows what they called themselves, these odd people who in their frescos depicted their men with dense black hair and reddish skins, their women with black curls and white complexions.

Shortly afterward a German expedition under the noted archaeologist Eduard Meyer, while excavating tombs in the great necropolis of Thebes West in Upper Egypt, came upon paintings amazingly similar to those that had been brought to light in the Palace of Knossos. They showed processions of reddish, black-haired figures of strikingly "Minoan" appearance who were carry-

ing utensils typical of early Crete. Evidently these were envoys
from the distant island kingdom in the eastern Mediterranean,
representatives of those same peculiar palace builders whom
Evans, ignorant of their real name, had called Minoans.

The thirty-five-hundred-year-old figures in the mural paintings
of these ancient Egyptian tombs might be mute, but the accompanying hieroglyphic text could be read. And it gave the
name that Egyptian contemporaries used for inhabitants of
Bronze Age Crete: *Keftiu*. Who were these strange Keftiu, whose
culture seemed like nothing else in the ancient world? Why had
they built so extensive a palace? What strange end had they
come to, that the memory of them had been almost entirely
blotted out for more than three thousand years?

These questions form the subject of this book. We shall be
touching upon one of the most burning questions in European
ancient history and prehistory. For Crete is now regarded as
the center of an early flowering of culture on European soil. But
did this ancient Cretan culture of the Keftiu which, following
Evans, we usually call Minoan, actually fertilize subsequent
European cultures? Or, as Evans himself assumed and as a good
many other scholars believe to this day, was it so thoroughly
destroyed by a succession of natural disasters that only a shadowy ancient Greek tradition bears witness to it? Did this happen centuries before the golden age of Greece began to unfold
upon the mainland? Was Minoan culture the forgotten fore-
runner of Greek civilization, and thus of our entire present
Western world?

Today an answer to these questions cannot be sought solely
in archaeology or history. As a geologist, I have attempted to
revive the discussion by infusing new observations, methods and
considerations into it. These have led me to a surprising revision
of earlier views. It may be necessary to view the ancient world
of the eastern Mediterranean in a new and unaccustomed light,
but perhaps by that light connections previously hidden will be
revealed.

There is one school of popular writing on archaeology that
focuses on the adventures and the triumphs of the excavators,
summing up and setting forth in an appealing form the writings
of the specialists. By contrast, I am here venturing to write an

original scientific paper in sufficiently clear language to make it understandable to lay readers. In so doing I hope that I shall stimulate colleagues in as many other scholarly disciplines as possible to collaborate on the investigation begun here. I follow this procedure also in order to pay a debt of gratitude to the general public for its keen interest in and support of my scientific work, and for the innumerable suggestions that have come to me from far and near, without which the writing of this book would not have been possible.

Historical accuracy would call for using the terms "Keftiu" and "Keftiu culture" in the following pages. But the fantasy names "Minoans" and "Minoan culture" are still too solidly established in general use to be relinquished, although there is no historical evidence to support them.

H. G. Wunderlich

Introduction:
Myths and Antimyths

The Minotaur, that monster of Greek legend, was half
bull and half man. According to the tales of the ancients, every
seven or nine years (or, some say, annually) he devoured seven
Athenian youths and seven virgins. Theseus, the Athenian hero
of royal blood, finally overcame and killed the beast. With the
aid of the Cretan king's daughter he escaped from the Minotaur's labyrinthine palace. Thereafter his native city was released from its gruesome tribute to the ruler of Crete.

Such was the story the Greek bards recited in the marketplaces
of the islands and the mainland. But could they be believed?
Surely these were fables and fantasies. Or was there a germ of
truth underlying the legend of the Minotaur?

The scholars of northern lands were not disposed to think
so. To the enlightened minds of later centuries, human sacrifice
and grotesque creatures of dual nature such as the Minotaur
did not fit in with that ideal Greek world they had conceived for
themselves. They quickly reinterpreted the ancient legend as a
symbolic account of how higher Hellenic culture overcame the
non-Greek bull cult of the ancient Cretans. The human sacrifices could never really have happened. The Minotaur was merely
a symbol for the Cretan god Zeus Asterios. And the labyrinth
where this god resided must surely be a pure fiction of the highly

imaginative Greek poets. Thus the Minotaur legend was stripped of its barbarousness. In the interpretation offered by enlightened humanists it faded into an intriguing, pretty metaphor.

So it remained until Arthur Evans came to Crete to find pre-Phoenician writings and began digging a few kilometers south of the capital city of Herakleion. Evans, born in 1851 in Nash Mills, England, graduate of Harrow, Oxford and Göttingen, was only after inscriptions, clay tablets and pieces of sculpture. What he actually brought to light, in decades of self-sacrificing labors, was nothing less than the labyrinth of ancient myth, the legendary palace of the Minotaur.

The monster of legend could be seen again in innumerable images of bulls, in bas-reliefs, small sculptures, bull-shaped vessels, seals and imprints of seals, and stylized bulls' horns. But once again the sinister shadows of legend were banished from the labyrinth, this time by the scientifically schooled archaeologist. From the remains of nearly twelve hundred deviously interconnected rooms, stairways, corridors, warehouses, colonnaded halls and cellars grouped around a great interior court, and from the fragmentary remains of wall paintings showing bull games, animal scenes, processions and portraits, as well as from clay and bronze utensils in a multitude of forms, Evans reconstructed Minoan culture. He extracted such a wealth of parallels to *fin de siècle* European civilization that all doubts were drowned in wonderment at the cultural and technological achievements of that early period in human history.

It now seemed clearer than ever that the Greek bards were terrible frauds who had peddled all kinds of nonsense about the gay and graceful island kingdom of the ancient Minoans. The innumerable portrayals of Theseus' battle with the Minotaur on classical vases, murals, mosaics, reliefs, gems and coins, and even as statues such as those from the Villa Albani near Rome, were evidently based on pure imagination. Even Homer could not be trusted. Had he not charged his blond hero Achilles, favorite of gods and men, with making twelve human sacrifices during the funeral ceremonies for his friend and comrade Patroclus, who had fallen in the struggle for Troy? Not to speak of the phantasmagoria with which *The Odyssey* swarmed. Why put any faith in fabulous tales when the evidence of archaeological excavation was becoming available?

Most specialists, as well as laymen, took that view. To be sure, some questions were raised about the methods of Evans's reconstructions. But these involved form, style and iconographic motifs. Hardly anyone doubted that the excavated labyrinth was indeed the Palace of Knossos, the celebrated residence of the ancient Cretan royal house. And almost everyone was impressed by the high culture and civilization of the Minoan period. Drainage systems, baths, frescos in the style of the turn of the century, women in striking toilettes, in the makeup and poses of Parisian ladies of the *belle époque,* undefended country estates instead of frowning citadels—surely the Minoan period of ancient Crete, from four thousand to thirty-five hundred years ago, must have been a golden age. What happy, carefree people, devoted to art, to sports, to love. How favorably this sunny realm of King Minos contrasted with the dark realities of the twentieth century, where in a Europe of nation-states men were slaughtering each other by the millions.

Only one man ventured to express reservations about this happy vision of the past. Oswald Spengler, perhaps the foremost German cultural philosopher of the first half of this century, had something to say about the Cretan question in his *World History of the Second Millennium B.C.,* published in 1935. Starting from an analysis of concepts of the hereafter toward the end of the Bronze Age, he applied his critical faculties to the archaeological finds. The absence of any protecting wall around ancient Cretan palaces and country estates, the pictures of bulls so reminiscent of the ancient Minotaur legend and that peculiar king's throne in the Palace of Knossos, which in his view would be more suitable "for a votive image or a priest's mummy," prompted Spengler to ask: "Were the 'palaces' of Knossos and Phaistos temples of the dead, sanctuaries of a powerful cult of the hereafter? I do not wish to make such an assertion, for I cannot prove it, but the question seems to me worthy of serious consideration."

The opportunity to pursue his question was not given to him, for he died the following year. "Is it not extraordinary that this suggestion of Spengler's was overlooked by a whole generation of archaeologists?" writes Z. Silberstein of Haifa, to whom I am indebted (together with Dr. B. Ascher of Haifa University College) for the reference to this passage in Spengler. In fact Spengler's farsighted hint seems to have had no influence whatsoever on Minoan archaeology.

In a way Spengler was simply again invoking the shadow of the man-eating Minotaur. But the beast emerged only for a brief moment. It was quickly repressed into the unconscious and consigned to oblivion. There was no room for such images while the world grappled with the daily problems of a bloodily combative modern age. When the Second World War was finally over and European mass tourism began to conquer the shores of the Mediterranean bay by bay and island by island, people were more reluctant than ever to be reminded of old horrors, whether of the most recent or of the most ancient times in the history of man. Life was to be placid, comfortable, devoted to amenities. Vacationers laid claim to undisturbed holidays. They needed those weeks of relaxation to recover from the harried dailiness of modern industrialism. Had not the ancient Cretans provided an example of a carefree way of life that could be happily imitated? It seemed as if four thousand years ago these people had found the secret of unthreatened peace and a high level of general prosperity. Surely what a monarchy of the Bronze Age had accomplished ought to be within the capacities of a modern democracy.

Thus the myth of the Minotaur, with its theme of human sacrifice, remained banished to regions of the unconscious where the spirits of the past await their hour to walk abroad. Then they burst forth, seize upon those who have bottled them up and force them to bloody acts in the name of ideologies, races or religions, urge them to *auto-da-fés*, show trials and concentration camps. Let us not deceive ourselves. Even in the most enlightened of centuries the heritage of the Stone Age still dwells within men. And it does not help at all to drive this sinister legacy into the abysses of the human psyche.

No such thoughts weighed upon me when I set out for Crete. I was not concerned with archaeology or cultural philosophy, but with recent mountain formation—orogeny. I had come to the conclusion some years earlier, on the basis of geological and geophysical indications, that such mountain formation was continuing in certain parts of the Mediterranean region right up to the present. This process included such phenomena as earthquakes, volcanic eruptions, recent elevations of the coastline and subsidences of the sea floor in certain basins of the Mediterranean. Indeed, Minoan archaeologists such as Evans, Marinatos and Nicolas Platon had repeatedly cited geologic events whenever they tried to explain the downfall of Minoan civilization.

BOOK ONE

Alabaster

1

The First Comer

In 1669 Candia, the last great bastion of Catholic Christendom on the island of Crete, fell to the Turks. Central Europe had not yet recovered from the aftereffects of the Thirty Years' War, which had devastated cities, villages and countrysides and reduced the population by a fourth. In Western Europe Louis XIV, the Sun King, was beginning his wars of conquest. The Signoria of Venice, which ruled the island of Crete, was engaged in a hopeless struggle against the victorious Turks, who only fifteen years later would be threatening the imperial city of Vienna.

In 1645 the Turks had landed at Gonia on Crete and in swift succession had conquered Canea and Rethymnon in the west. In May 1648 they had begun the siege of Candia, present-day Herakleion. Already they had occupied large parts of the island. The Greek Orthodox population had watched the Venetian garrisons depart without regret—in religious matters the Venetians were scarcely tolerant—and had bowed to the yoke of their new masters. Only the capital city of Candia, engirt by the mighty defenses constructed by the Venetian military architect Sanmicheli, and the forts of Spinalonga, Souda and Gramboussa, seemed impregnable. After eighteen long years of unsuccessful siege Hussein Pasha, the Turkish commander, was ordered home to Constantinople where he was executed. The situation changed after his successor, Grand Vizier Kiouprouli, took over. In a bloody struggle lasting three years, and at a cost of 140,000 dead, the heroically defended city of Candia was forced to capitulate. The garrison that had been reinforced by volunteers from many European countries and constantly resupplied by sea now was left with no choice. In return for unhindered withdrawal the keys of the city were handed over—a pure formality, since the doors, gates, houses, casemates and outworks that Commandant Francesco Morosini's eighty-seven keys once fitted had long since been shattered. Back in Constantinople the Turkish sovereign, Mohammed IV, did not hear that Candia had fallen until years later, and then by chance. In understandable vexation at the long and fruitless siege he had ordered under penalty of death that the word "Candia" was no longer to be mentioned at court, and this edict had been taken so literally that no one had dared report the final victory to him. Even so, the last Venetian garrison held out in the fortress of Spinalonga at the eastern end of the island until 1715.

The story goes that the pope eloquently lamented the loss of the diocese of Candia. For Venice, the loss of valuable trade connections must have been equally lamentable. As far back as the golden age of Greece the island of Crete had been famed for its wine, its olive oil and its honey. Honey and other sweets from Crete were so highly esteemed in Europe that the word *candy* survives to remind us of the city and the island. According to the philosopher Plato (427–347 B.C.), candied fruits, preserved by soaking them in crystallized honey, were favorite sacrificial gifts to the gods in ancient times, until men themselves gradually became more and more attached to this expensive food.

After the fall of Candia Cretan honey, mixed with meringue, almonds and nuts, became Turkish delight. Europe, however, had to look around for other sources of sweetening. Cane sugar from the Caribbean islands, especially Haiti and Cuba, replaced the Cretan product. There was one last vain attempt by Venice in 1692 to recapture the island of Crete. Afterward the islanders were abandoned to their fate for more than two centuries, during which time they engaged in an obstinate struggle against the Turkish garrison and despotic Turkish rule. Rebellions con-

stantly flared and died. The merchants in the counting houses
of Europe, meanwhile, had come to realize that the cost of
liberating Crete from the Turkish yoke would be greater, in
spite of all the profits to be derived from trade in Cretan sweets,
than the cost of the perilous voyage to the West Indies and the
rising colonies of the New World. And so for a long period
Europe forgot the island in the eastern Mediterranean to which
she owed her name. For it had been a Cretan queen, the legendary Princess Europa, daughter of Agenor and Telephassa of
Phoenicia and wife of the Cretan King Asterios, who gave her
name to this contentious and bellicose continent.

Not until the Greek struggle for liberation during the years
1821–1829 did the people of Europe once again turn their attention to their cultural motherland. Great Britain, France and Russia supported the Greeks until, in the Peace of Adrianople and
the London Protocol of February 3, 1830, the independence of
Greece was acknowledged by Turkey. The protective powers decided that Epirus, Thessaly, Samos, Chios and Crete would not
be annexed to the Kingdom of Greece. In a *firman* (decree) of
December 20, 1832, Sultan Mahmud II confirmed the cession
of Crete to Egypt. Under the Albanian ruler of Egypt, Mustafah
Pasha, Crete enjoyed a short period of felicity. In 1840, however,
the island, now under another Albanian usurper in Egypt,
Mohammed Ali, was once more taken by the Turks. Three more

FIG. 1 Hieroglyphic seals (*galopetres*).

bloody uprisings of the Cretans, in 1866, 1878 and 1897, forced
the European Great Powers to intervene. On November 14, 1898,
the last Turkish troops left Crete. But the foreign garrisons did
not depart until 1908, when Crete was united with the Kingdom
of Greece. Turkey, after losing the First Balkan War, was forced
in the London Peace of May 30, 1913, to consign Crete defini-
tively to Greece.

   With the withdrawal of the Turks the way was clear for one
of the most magnificent discoveries of the twentieth century in
the field of archaeology.

Fig. 2   Linear B. tablets, Knossos.
Upper: Evans *Scripta Min.* T, 49 No. 684
Lower: Horsehead tablet KN Ca 895.

   "A small, dreadfully nearsighted man who always carried a
small cane in order to feel his way along"—thus C. W. Ceram in
The March of Archaeology described Arthur Evans, the versatile, enterprising and wealthy scientist who was responsible for
those sensational discoveries. Evans had first found his way to
that part of the world some decades earlier, when he had been
the Balkans correspondent for the *Manchester Guardian* and had
supported the Slavs in their struggle to throw off Austrian rule.

Deported by the Austrians, he traveled in Greece and visited the excavations of Heinrich Schliemann, the German amateur archaeologist who had discovered Troy and excavated Mycenae and Tiryns. In 1893 hieroglyphic seals with pre-Phoenician inscriptions of unknown meaning lead Evans to Crete. There he found such seals being worn as amulets by the native women; they were called *galopetres* (milkstones) and were believed to increase the flow of mother's milk. Soon Evans became dissatisfied with those he could buy. He decided that he wanted to dig himself in order to obtain more of these curious seals from the pre-Greek period. In 1896 he published *Cretan Pictographs and Prae-Phoenician Script*. Now he wanted to pursue the subject. For this purpose Knossos, some 5 kilometers south of the capital city of Herakleion on the slope of the Kairatos Valley, seemed to him the most promising site. As it happened, Director Joubert of the French Archaeological Institute in Athens also wanted to dig there, but Evans, acting quickly and with innate commercial canniness, bought part of the hill. He used his own fortune for the purchase and appointed himself representative of a hitherto nonexistent Cretan Exploration Fund. Now that he owned the land he was secure against interference from other archaeologists. He would have begun digging as early as 1895 except for one obstacle: the highest Turkish authority on Crete refused the necessary *firman* (permit) for the excavations.

But good luck attended Arthur Evans and political circumstances soon favored his project. Within two years there was another uprising on the island. Europe, in fact the entire world, took the part of the long-oppressed Cretans, and with the onset of the new century the island at last became free. On March 23, 1900, Evans began the actual digging. Only a week later he already held in his hands the first newly discovered clay tablets with ancient Cretan inscriptions, and on April 15, after only three weeks of labor, he was able to report proudly to his father:

> The great discovery is whole deposits, entire or fragmentary, of clay tablets analogous to the Babylonian but with inscriptions in the prehistoric script of Crete. I must have about seven hundred pieces by now. It is extremely satisfactory, as it is what I came to Crete years ago to find, and it is the coping-stone to what I have already put together.

This fine, rapid success naturally encouraged Evans to push further. After five years he found himself in possession of no less than twenty-eight hundred inscribed tablets which had turned up in nearly fifty different places among the extensive ruins of the palace.

Knossos continued to obsess him. He dug and dug, devoting all his strength and financial means to the task. He discovered a new, hitherto unknown ancient Cretan culture. At his own expense he reconstructed the buildings he unearthed. In his four-volume opus, *The Palace of Minos* (1922–1935), he painted an impressive picture of life in the palace of the Bronze Age kings of Crete. The scholarly world hailed his work; as early as 1911 he was knighted for his achievements. He held a distinguished post at Oxford, where he lived until past his ninetieth year. All in all, his was a scholar's life rich in impressions and successes, of great importance and influence. Only one thing was missing which would have made his triumph complete; one failure marked a career otherwise rich in fulfillment. For although a kindly destiny had early enabled Evans to find the extensive archives of clay tablets in Knossos, and although his long life allowed him ample time for studying them, he was never able to penetrate the secrets of the scripts that had brought him to Crete as a young man.

It was probably his dearest wish to crown his lifework by deciphering the ancient Cretan scripts, by reanimating the language and the lives of those Cretan kings whose palace he had restored with such care. But that wish was not to be granted. Several times he began publication of the ancient Cretan writings. In 1909, for example, he brought out the *Scripta Minoa I*, printing the so-called hieroglyphic finds and a number of tablets in what were known as the Linear A and Linear B scripts. But at his death by far the largest part of his hoard was unpublished, and not even put into order—after he had "withheld the finds from science for a whole generation," as Werner Ekschmitt complained with some justice.* Nevertheless, we should not overlook the profoundly tragic aspect of his situation: this otherwise so fortunate man failed precisely where he had been most de-

---

* *Die Kontroverse um Linear B*, Munich, 1969.

termined to succeed. It is understandable that he would not
allow others to attempt to decipher Cretan writing as long as
there was some prospect that he himself might do it. As we
shall see, the decipherment of the Linear B texts began a decade
after Evans's death and depended on a hypothesis Sir Arthur
would have rejected out of hand: that the language of these
texts might be an ancient Greek dialect. Given Evans's view of
Cretan culture as "Minoan," as pre-Greek in essence, this possibility was beyond his grasp.

How was it that as early as 1895 Evans was so sure of where
he wanted to dig that he had bought the property? Was it sheer
luck? Had he intuitively selected the right spot or acted out of
superlative insight? Nothing of the kind. The site of Knossos was
already well known. The remains of walls could be recognized
in the hilly terrain before Evans began his dig, and potsherds
and bits of worked stone were commonly found. A Greek busi-
nessman from Herakleion had begun prospecting there as early
as 1878. His name—testimony to the living Cretan tradition that
had persisted down the millennia in legends, in names and occasionally in physiognomy—was Minos Kalokairinos. In the palace
area Kalokairinos exposed the first of the storerooms. At the turn
of the century the islanders knew quite well where to look for
ancient Knossos, where some success in finding "milkstones"
could be expected and where to direct the amiable gentleman
from distant England who was interested in seals and such.

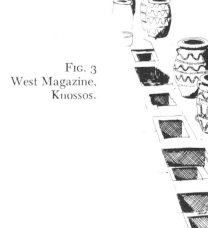

FIG. 3
West Magazine,
Knossos.

Heinrich Schliemann, the great amateur archaeologist, was also fairly certain, several years before Evans, where to dig. In a letter of January 1, 1889, he wrote:

> I should like to complete my life's labors with a great work, the excavation of the age-old, prehistoric palace of the kings of Knossos in Crete, which I believe I discovered three years ago. Unfortunately, however, for this purpose I must buy a whole estate which includes the site of Knossos, for I cannot reach my goal in any other way.

And on March 17, 1889 (in a letter to the great pathologist Rudolf Virchow):

> The palace is 55 meters long, 43.30 meters wide, and I am persuaded that I could . . . comfortably excavate it in a week with a hundred workmen. But not only 100,000 francs or 80,000 marks, even 40,000 francs or 32,000 marks are too much for me to throw away on labors completed in a week whose results— down to the very last potsherd . . . would benefit the museum in Herakleion.

He made serious efforts to acquire the property and would have done so had not the Turkish landowners upped the price and, to make matters worse, tried to cheat him on the survey of the area under negotiation. Schliemann, always thrifty and modest to the point of penuriousness in his personal life, decided against the purchase. Thus his associates lost the chance to reap the glory that fell to Evans a short while afterward. Nor would Schliemann himself have been able to supervise the excavations in Knossos. Less than two years after he wrote the letters quoted above he collapsed on a street in Naples. He was so poorly dressed that he was taken for an indigent, and by the time he was recognized and medical help was brought, it was too late.

Such was the death, at the age of sixty-nine, of the man who had defied the professional archaeologists of his day to carry out a childhood dream of rediscovering the buried sites of the heroic Trojans he had admired, and of bringing to light unsuspected treasures. Born in 1822 in Neu-Bukow, Mecklenburg, Heinrich Schliemann was introduced to the history and legends of antiquity in early childhood. When he read the description of Troy the boy found it impossible to believe that such mighty structures could have utterly vanished. He resolved that some day he would excavate Troy. But poverty compelled him to go to work instead of pursuing a classical education at the *Gymnasium.* When he was nineteen the ship on which he was a cabin boy was wrecked off the coast of Holland. There the young Schliemann remained and after a period of great poverty found a job in a commercial firm as correspondent and bookkeeper. He had fitted himself for the post by learning, in an astonishingly short time (with some languages only six weeks), English, French, Dutch, Spanish, Italian, Portuguese and Russian.

At the age of twenty-four he was sent to St. Petersburg, where for the first time he showed that acumen as a merchant that was to make him a fortune. After a visit to California in search of his missing brother (he acquired American citizenship because California entered the Union while he was there) he settled down in Moscow. By 1858 he had done so well in the indigo trade that he could retire from business. Meanwhile he had also learned Swedish, Polish, Latin, ancient and modern Greek, and had traveled through all of Europe, as well as Egypt and Asia Minor. He put in a few more years, however, in Russia and made additional millions by dealing in cotton and tea. After traveling around the world by way of Egypt, India, China, Japan and America he decided, in 1866, to give up business entirely and to devote himself to archaeology.

Travels to Greece and Asia Minor followed. In 1869 he astonished the professional archaeologists by asserting that Troy was to be found not near Bunarbashi, but on the hill known as Hissarlik (meaning "palace"). He maintained also that the graves of the Atrides, the legendary rulers of Mycenae, must lie inside rather than outside the walls of the citadel; he based this on the account of the ancient traveler Pausanias. In 1870–1873, 1878–1879 and from 1880 on he dug in Troy; in 1874 and 1876 in Mycenae; and after 1894 in Tiryns. On June 16, 1876, Schliemann discovered what he called "the treasure of Priam" in Troy, and in December 1876 the vast gold and silver hoards in the shaft graves of Mycenae. Altogether he found more than 15 kilograms of precious metals, chiefly gold. At the same time he received the degree of doctor of philosophy from the University of Rostock by writing a dissertation in ancient Greek. He defended his opinions against various critics and won the support of influential personages of the time, including Virchow. For his second wife he chose a Greek girl, Sophia Engastromenos, who was twenty-seven years his junior and who became his enthusiastic assistant. With her, he carried out excavations in Sicily and in Orchomenos in Greece.

It is hard to think of another man whose life contained as many amazing turns. We can only conclude from Schliemann's successes that he had extraordinary resourcefulness and intuition, for being an outsider was no advantage in archaeological enterprises. His work at Troy was severely criticized because he had the upper strata of the palace hill at Hissarlik removed before he had examined each layer in turn; he was in too much of a hurry to reach what he supposed to be the stratum of the Trojan War. In fact we know today that Schliemann's "Trojan" stratum was a thousand years older than the Ilion of the Trojan War. Nevertheless, it would be wrong to overlook his signal achievements. Moreover, Schliemann brought archaeology to the attention of the general public and in this way stimulated the support and funds without which modern archaeology would scarcely be conceivable.

Without Schliemann's vigor and enterprising spirit, without his conviction—not to say obsessiveness—without his physical and financial commitments and his finder's luck, Mycenaean civilization would not have been discovered, at least not at that time. Schliemann demonstrated that the age described by Homer in *The Iliad* and *The Odyssey* had in fact existed, though it dated back centuries before the first Homeric songs were written down. He showed what unsuspected ways and means were available to archaeology, and thus inaugurated the age of purposeful excavations. He recognized, in vague, general outline, the existence of a vanished but once coherent civilization in the Aegean region, one fundamentally distinct from the later Hellenic period, and he mused over the possible origins of this civilization. In the course of his reflections he was the first to point toward Crete, and thus inspired young Evans, who, as we have seen, visited Schliemann's excavations before he ever thought of embarking on any of his own.

But the first comer in Crete was Arthur Evans. He, too, was remarkably favored by fortune; he, too, was tremendously determined in pursuing his plans; and he, too, had the benefit of considerable private funds, although these were largely inherited rather than acquired. Fate withheld from both men the solution to a self-appointed problem that would have crowned their life-work. But despite such similarities, the differences between these two archaeological pioneers are striking. Compared to restive Schliemann—in Asia Minor today, the Peloponnesus tomorrow and Sicily the day after—a man who was forever hatching new ideas, plans and projects, Evans was a quiet, deliberate scholar. He devoted his entire life to a single goal: the excavation and reconstruction of the Palace of Knossos. And that is fortunate. Quite possibly Schliemann, with his hundred workmen, would have removed the remains of Knossos in a week as thoroughly as he did the upper strata of Troy. Or else he would have lost interest after a short while and begun digging somewhere else in the Mediterranean area.

Arthur Evans, less dynamic, was concerned about the smallest artistic detail and manifested great perseverance in fitting together shards and fragments of frescos. He was beyond a doubt the more suitable person for the problems presented by Knossos. Evans and Minoan civilization are so closely interwoven today that they are hard to separate. Just as Evans's life was determined by his encounter with the Minoan world, so the "Palace of Minos" has taken on the features that its discoverer saw in his mind's eye when he ordered restorations and reconstructions. And Knossos, the palace of King Minos, the labyrinth of Greek legend, has become the very essence of "Minoan."

Soon after Evans, French and Italian excavations brought to light similar structures. The French, worsted in their attempts to purchase the land at Knossos, turned to Mallia in the northeastern part of the island. The Italians went to Phaistos in the south. But no amount of effort on their parts could detract from the leading position of Evans's excavations in Knossos. Find after find was made, foundation upon foundation reconstructed. The museum in Herakleion filled. The island of Crete was still independent, had not yet been annexed to Greece, so that all the finds remained on Crete and were not transferred to the National Museum in Athens. At the time of the Italo-Turkish War for Rhodes and the Dodecanese, the *enosis* movement was led by

the Cretan politician Eleutherios Venizelos. By the Treaty of
London in 1913 Crete was annexed to Greece in order to forestall
Italian territorial claims. But by then the Herakleion Museum
had long since been established as the point of collection for
Minoan finds. Its situation is thus virtually unique; to this day
almost all Minoan remains are gathered together in the museum
of the capital, with the exception of those left at the site of
excavation. Thus there is no need to travel to Athens, London,
Paris and Rome (as is the case with so many other cultures, the
remains of which have been scattered to the four winds by the
zeal of collectors and the vagaries of the art trade) in order to
acquire an overview of Minoan civilization. The circumstances
could not be more favorable for anyone who wants to make an
intensive study of this fascinating and idiosyncratic culture. But
before we visit the museum let us set foot on the site of the
excavations at the Palace of Knossos.

2

Flight into the Past

✿

Above the waters of the Aegean the eye gazes far into the distance, unhindered by the mists and fogs of northern latitudes. Frequently the visibility is so good that you can look down on several of the widely scattered islands at the same time, although they are 50 kilometers and more apart. In the clear air white towers of cloud form in the thermal updrafts above the islands, suggesting the presence of land even when the island itself cannot immediately be discerned because of the shifting play of reflected gleams above the water.

The flight from the mainland to the largest island in the Aegean takes less than an hour. The coast of the Peloponnesus has barely vanished in the distance when the mountainous wall of the Lefka Ori, the White Mountains of western Crete that are covered with snow deep into summer, rises up before you. Then the island approaches rapidly; the plane loses altitude. Above the sheer cliffs of the steep northern coast around Amnissos the jet swings in a wide arc toward land. A series of lovely bays with deep-blue water flit by beneath the wings. You pass over light-gray cliffs with riblike ridges and barren limestone peaks, on one of which is a solitary broadcasting station. Even before you begin to worry whether the pilot can manage to land on that runway located on a narrow plateau extending from sheer rock, the fuselage quivers with the impact. You are in Nea Alikarnasos, New Halicarnassus, the airport of Herakleion.

It is 12 kilometers from the airport to the city. In summer you drive in heavy traffic along fiercely hot and dusty suburban roads with small houses to either side. The road winds through the imposing fortifications that surround the city, structures that date back to Venetian times, reminding us of the downfall of old Candia. Today, renamed Herakleion (Iraklion), the capital has conspicuously left behind its periods of decline; it is bustling with life. The name reminds us of Heracles, perhaps the best-known hero of Greek myth. Among his legendary deeds was the capture, binding and transporting to Mycenae of King Minos's terrifying bull. One wonders: Three thousand years ago how long would such a sea voyage have taken, with a wild bull on board no less, and then an overland journey at the end?

The towers and walls are not all that remind us of the four hundred years of Venetian rule in Herakleion. The lion of St. Mark still adorns the old citadel that dominates the entrance to the inner harbor. Further in toward the city the walls of the Venetian arsenal still frown above the water. To justify such structures Cretan trade must have yielded handsome profits to Venetian merchants, greater than those that could be made from the wine and olive oil that also flourished on Venetian *terra firma*. The excellent Cretan *sphakia* cheese, though highly appreciated in the Levant, also could not have been so profitable that it repaid decades of costly fighting. But it was a different matter with such articles as precious silk, honey and candied fruits, which delighted the hearts of the ladies of Western Europe.

The fountain in the heart of the city, dedicated by the Venetian governor Francesco Morosini in 1628 and adorned with lions and sirens, has survived the long siege and the period of Turkish rule. Hagios Markos, St. Mark's of Herakleion, stands diagonally across from it; after 226 years of service as a mosque it has recently been restored to its original early Venetian architecture. Nearby is the beautiful Venetian loggia of the town hall, erected as an armory shortly before the fall of Candia, and the sixteenth-century church of Hagios Titos, which was not converted to a mosque until 1862 when the building of the new cathedral in the southwestern part of the Old Town began.

The city no longer has many vestiges of Megalo Kastro, as Herakleion was known during the period of Turkish rule. In this respect it contrasts strongly with Rethymnon, where one may still see whole streets built in the old fashion, full of mosques and minarets. A German encyclopedia of 1888 says of Crete under Turkish rule: "Crafts, trade and shipping have sunk to a low ebb; the ports which so flourished under Venetian rule are almost all silted up; and most of the towns lie in ruins." But in recent times a veritable frenzy to build, partly stimulated by the tourist boom, has seized the inhabitants of Herakleion. The island's agricultural economy has benefited enormously by the influx of Greeks from Asia Minor who were resettled in Crete between 1922 and 1929—some thirteen thousand immigrants. As a result, there has been a dramatic rise in grape and raisin production; Crete's annual harvest now amounts to 3500 metric tons, putting it in the forefront of all the Greek provinces.

FIG. 4 Palace of Knossos: outline. The hatched area indicates the east wing, which lies one to two stories beneath the level of the central court.

But in Herakleion, whose thoughts would turn to trade and production? In Fodele, a small mountain village 20 kilometers west of the city, Domenikos Theotokopoulos, known as El Greco ("the Greek"), was born *ca.* 1541. Instructed by Michael Damaskinos in the strict painting techniques used for Byzantine icons, influenced further by Venetian and Roman masters, he became a Spanish painter famous for his own mannerist style, and died in Toledo in 1614. Herakleion itself was the birthplace of Nikos Kazantzakis, novelist of Cretan life and liberation, who won a world audience with his *Freedom or Death, Greek Passion* and *Zorba the Greek.* When he died in 1957 the city gave him its most beautiful grave site, the highest bastion of the encircling wall, from which it is possible to view both the crooked streets and roofs of the city and the gardens and vineyards of the coastal plain as far as the southern horizon, where the hills and mountain ranges fade into the far-off grayish-blue mists.

We drive 5 kilometers south by way of suburban streets with their scattered rows of houses, gardens, vineyards. The landscape is one of gentle slopes carved by deep ravines through which brooks flow most of the year but dry up in summer. We go a bit beyond the City Hospital and arrive at the parking place for the chief archaeological attraction of the island, the Palace of Knossos. Whole busloads of tourists throng the excavation area. What would a "tour of classical Greece" be without a visit to Knossos, the cradle of Western civilization! For the tourist trade it is a gift of the gods.

It is only a few steps from the entrance, with its inevitable postcard and souvenir stand, down shaded paths to the west forecourt of the palace, where we are greeted by a bust of the excavator, Sir Arthur Evans. Passing three deep, circular cisterns, their walls made of fieldstone, we turn to the west facade. It rises above the glacis of the forecourt in a series of mighty squared stone blocks. There are several projections, but no deep-cut window openings. The blocks are not crudely cut in cyclopean fashion, as at the citadel of Tiryns, but are carefully smoothed and fitted.

These enormous blocks rest upon a low, somewhat projecting foundation of limestone, which was evidently once stuccoed and

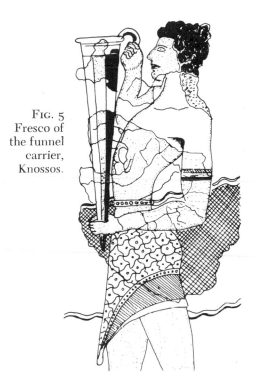

Fig. 5
Fresco of
the funnel
carrier,
Knossos.

painted. Only fragments of squared stone facade remain today; above it formerly rose an upper story that, according to
F. Matz,° must have been built of "rubble stone, set with mortar
in a timber frame." The ground floor alone is preserved, and that
only insofar as it was hidden underneath the surface of the hill
after the decay of the palace. Matz's surmise that "many windows, doors, loggias, verandas and balconies" must have existed
in the upper story is not justified by any of the finds on the
ground.

The west facade presents a rather forbidding aspect because
of the austere lines of those mighty squared blocks. Morover,
there is not a single doorway piercing it on ground level, nor is
there a staircase leading to the upper story. To enter the palace
one has to turn to the south, where in the projecting corner
between the main wing and a smaller side wing built onto the
southwest, a canopied entrance opens. The opening, which is
about 12 meters wide, is divided into two halves by a central

° "Die Agäis," *Handbuch der Archäologie* II (1950).

pillar of wood. The anteroom beyond terminates in two doors. One leads to a smaller room on the right which is called the room for the gate guards. The other opens into a doorless and windowless corridor 35 meters long and about 3.5 meters wide, which on the southern end abruptly turns in a right angle to the east. The anteroom was decorated by a painted stucco relief symbolizing the ancient Cretan mode of bullfighting, the *tauromachia*. The corridor shows an endless succession of lifesize figures in procession, who accompany the visitor into the interior of the palace. Russet figures with bare torsos, sparse skirts clothing their hips and black, curly hair, in postures of solemnity, carry variously shaped, artistically painted vases and jugs. One figure holds a blue funnel with handles three quarters of a meter long. It may be that similar live processions once took this route into the interior of the palace. Because of the frescos this corridor is generally referred to as the Procession Corridor.

After another right-angle turn the visitor reaches a small hall, divided up by wall buttresses and by supporting pillars. He finds himself at the foot of a broad staircase leading to the upper floor. Borrowing the term from the ancient Venetian *palazzi*, Evans speaks of the *piano nobile*, the *bel étage* of patrician houses in Venice, where the living and reception rooms were situated; these were above the storerooms where the Venetian merchants kept their wares. What this upper story of the palace may have looked like can scarcely be construed from the substructures of the lower floor. Besides this one staircase, a second of similar width led eastward and down into the great central court, and at several points there seem to have been light shafts or air shafts between the two stories.

Evans supports his theory that the upper story was the *piano nobile* by pointing out that the western sector of the lower story consists of more than twenty long, windowless storerooms, each accessible by only a single door. These rooms were partly brought to light as early as 1878 by Minos Kalokairinos. In the course of his excavation he found shards of thick-walled clay vessels, some of them as tall as a man. These so-called *pithoi* must once have been lined up close together, filling these rooms. Researchers have been able to reassemble the fragments, and the many rows of massive clay vessels in their long storerooms make as powerful an impression on the visitor as anything in the excavation site. This impression may also owe something to the authenticity of these chambers, for there has been little attempt at reconstruction here.

Anyone who has looked into the farms around the palace or elsewhere in the Mediterranean area and seen similar large clay jars used to keep olive oil will immediately be reminded of a large storehouse for wine, grain or olive oil. The magazines, however, did not serve solely as storerooms for these vessels. The floor, consisting of many neatly cut and carefully fitted gypsum slabs, has a long row of rectangular, shaftlike depressions running down the central line of the magazines. These depressions, too, were evidently once covered over with slabs. What sort of stores were kept in these trenches can no longer be determined; some have suggested grain, whereas others have suggested that the chambers were treasuries in which various types of precious articles were safely hidden.

Although the various magazines differ in length, toward the east they all terminate in a straight north-south corridor, so that the differences in length are marked on the west facade by numerous projections in the wall. Evidently interior construction rather than the external shape determined the plan, beginning with the grouping of the various rooms around the central court. But before we enter this court let us follow the long north-south corridor at the farther end of the magazines to its northern end, where it suddenly turns around and runs in the opposite direction. Such abrupt terminations and bends in the longitudinal corridors add to the labyrinthine quality of the entire layout, which is made even more complex by other features. For instance, at the bend two narrow corridors run parallel for from 12 to 15 meters, forcing everyone who wishes to go from the magazines to the central court (or vice versa) to make a detour of 25 meters, although it surely would not have been difficult to pierce the partition wall and thereby provide a shortcut to the central court. But evidently no one in the palace was especially interested in rapid and efficient work, an attitude that becomes even more clear when one notices that at the beginning of the eastern parallel corridor the way was blocked to prevent the continuous passage of traffic.

This is the decisive spot at which Arthur Evans, only a week after beginning his excavation, came upon that first deposit of clay tablets that prompted his enthusiastic letter to his father. And fifty more such hoards of clay tablets were to follow! No wonder Evans, with his passionate interest in the undeciphered scripts, concentrated the next forty years of his life on Knossos.

The storerooms and long corridors take up only the western half of the west wing. On the other side of the central court is a much less clearly arranged lower story whose uses appear to have been extremely variegated. Alongside the broad stair-case to the *piano nobile* lies a small Minoan "bath," adjacent to which is a "Greek temple." Toward the north runs the so-called Triple Shrine, the anteroom of which can be reached by way of the stairs from the central court. The adjacent western rooms are referred to as "cult pillar crypts" because their ceilings are supported by huge pillars and they are illuminated only by dim light from the central court.

The Triple Shrine is famous as the site of small, ancient statuettes that are among the most mysterious items turned up by the excavation of the palace. One of these, a female figure standing bolt upright in a long, artfully tiered skirt with wasp waist and open bodice, holds a small wriggling snake in each of her raised hands. Evans regarded this as either the image of an ancient Cretan snake priestess who served in this sanctuary or a snake goddess who was venerated here. We shall return to this graceful snake charmer in her topless garment.

Fig. 6
The "snake goddess,"
Knossos.

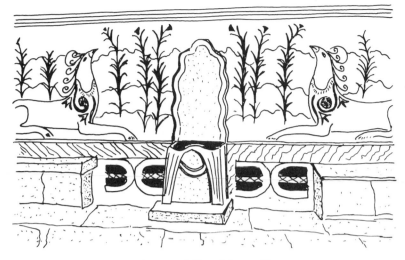

Fɪɢ. 7   Throne of King Minos, Knossos.

North of the second broad stairway leading from the *piano nobile* down into the central court is the so-called Throne Room, probably the room most often photographed. It cannot be reached from the interior of the building, but only from the open central court by way of an almost square anteroom. It receives only indirect light, through the doorways of the anteroom and a nearby light shaft. In the center of the long wall stands the throne of King Minos, made of fine-grained alabaster carved in curved lines, imitating a high-backed wooden chair. The wall behind it was decorated with pictures of kneeling griffins and stylized plants; this painting was apparently done in the Late Minoan period. The two griffins to the right and left of the throne have the heads of huge predatory birds and the sphinx-like bodies of big cats. A bold spiral band masks the place where bird's head and cat's body merge. Under the griffin fresco stone benches flank the throne. On the other side of the room several steps lead into a basinlike depression directly below the light shaft, which is believed to have been a sacred area: either a ritual bath, a pit for sacred snakes or possibly even an imitation of a Cretan cave sanctuary.

The Throne Room, which is smaller and lower than the antechamber outside the southwest portal, has a gloomy and oppressive air, which is scarcely alleviated by the bright colors of the

FIG. 8   Throne Room, Knossos.

griffin fresco. A warren of small, lightless rooms without any clearly visible function surrounds the Throne Room on the three sides that do not open onto the central court. Possibly these were "substructures," that is, basically underpinnings for the rooms above them. The adjacent rooms on the north appear to be similarly undifferentiated. Only two of these stand out from the rest: a complex close to the northwest corner of the palace, with another "lustral basin," and a segment in the vicinity of the central court which has been called, because of its shaftlike depressions, "the prison of Minos."

The section of the upper story restored by Evans had, to judge by the preserved bases of pillars, at least three rather sizable rooms supported on pillars: the "hypostyle," with three pillars and three piers; a "cult hall," which contains a number of pieces of built-in furniture of unexplained use; and the Great Hall, which extends above five of the magazines in the cellar. The area of the Great Hall was once supported by two wooden pillars. The dimensions and arrangement of the space in fact coincide well with the conception of a *piano nobile* with public rooms. But immediately adjacent to the Great Hall on the south are six storage magazines which (except for the shaftlike depressions in the floor) closely resemble those in the lower story below. Were these intended for storing wine jars so that the wine would be handy for official receptions?

Before we leave the upper story, the highest point in the whole complex, let us look around. Sunlight glitters upon the excavation area; its light-gray limestone walls and white alabaster slabs reflect the glare. Where somewhat higher remains of walls tower up, they cast deep shadows. A dark-green fringe of cypresses and stonepines encloses the site. The brightly dressed tourists being led in long lines by guides, or toiling alone through the tangle of corridors and stairs, make a curious contrast to the trees. Here, in the adjacent "cult hall," was found the fresco of a Cretan lady with curly black hair and a braided tress, with white complexion, large, expressive dark eyes and red-painted lips. Because of her "modern" appearance she has become known as "the Parisienne."

Beyond the tops of the pines the sun beats down mercilessly on the stony hills, whose higher elevations become more and more barren. Only the Kairatos Valley and the adjacent fertile plain at our feet are green with grapevines. The vineyard is called Castello Minos; it was planted by resettled Greeks from Asia Minor after the unfortunate war between the Greeks under Constantine I and the Turks under Mustafah Kemal (Ataturk) had been ended by the Treaty of Lausanne (1923), which initiated one of the major resettlements of this century. The grapes grow over a great expanse of historic soil; it is known that the excavated part of the palace constitutes only a fraction of the Minoan ruins on the slopes of the Kairatos Valley.

FIG. 9   "The Parisienne," Knossos.

As you raise your eyes you suddenly perceive the very odd nature of this site. From a ravine that narrows sharply toward the south, toward the interior of the island, the Kairatos River emerges into the fruitful coastal plain. In summer the river is very shallow. Along the flanks of the hills caves and tombs have been carved into the sinter-coated rock. The palace lies on the spur of a hill that slopes gently eastward to the river and is bordered on three sides by embankments. In the west this slope extends beyond the palace, joining the adjacent chains of hills. The location is remarkably exposed to be sure, and no provision was made to fortify it. The ashlar facade of the west is certainly massive, but would hardly have been enough to repel invaders. How could the peaceloving Cretans of the rather belli-cose second millennium B.C. afford to leave their most important royal residence unshielded by walls and gates? Did they have such confidence in their insular situation and their dominant position on the seas?

Above the hills to the south, in the direction of the distant Dikte Mountains which enclose the solitary but fruitful Lassithi Plain, huge clouds are massing. After the heat of the day a refreshing breeze blows in from the nearby sea. The shadows lengthen and the Minoan masonry glows with a warmer colora-tion. With surprising abruptness the bright day gives way to twilight. Today we have not visited even half of the excavated site; we have made only a first fleeting acquaintance with this remote world of the past. We can only wonder what impression the members of tours must have, who are hurried through the palace at half-hour intervals. We, who have spent an entire day, have seen only a part of the palace, and it has already given us plenty of material for meditation.

3

In the Heart of the Labyrinth

❀

The heart of the site is not the west wing of the palace, with its magazines, its cult and reception rooms. The center of the labyrinth is a large open area around which the chessboard patterns of the foundation walls close to form a great rectangle. The central court, barely 30 meters wide by somewhat more than 50 meters long, is the axis of the entire complex. It is what gives to the whole design a clarity that we otherwise rather painfully miss in the tangle of corridors. It imposes measure and direction upon the whole. After prolonged wanderings through cellars and stairways the confused visitor returns to the central court with a sense of relief. Here he can reorient himself and rest from the plethora of impressions.

The next morning finds us once more on the excavation site. In the bright light of the morning sun the shadowless rectangle of the central court lies spread out before us. It is not like an urban square in which streets from all sides terminate, nor a center for traffic and movement. Nor is it an accidentally empty lot in the midst of surrounding structures. It is the center around which the buildings are grouped, around which "everything revolves." But we wonder what may have taken place in this plaza. In appearance it resembles a soccer field, although it is only half the size in width and breadth. We recall the bas-relief of the bull game in the antechamber of the west portal. Was this court the area in which such ritual games took place? Or was it an arena for exuberant athletic competitions?

The facades of the east wing still lie in shade. But as the clock slowly approaches noon, the shade visibly brightens, and shortly after noon the rays of the sun fall in the same direction as the longitudinal sides. The central court is oriented by the sun! The long side runs fairly accurately in a north-south direction, the narrow side west-east. As a geologist I want to know precisely, and therefore I check with my compass. The interior facade of the west wing forms a fine straight base line. The compass shows 170°, that is a deviation from the strict north-south direction of 10°.

Immediately new questions arise. Were these people of four thousand years ago unable to determine south with more precision? That seems strange when we consider the straight lines of so many of the corridors in the palace and the numerous right angles. Or could south have changed its direction, either because of a shift in the earth's orbit or a rotation of the observation site? Both explanations seem improbable. The human race has been observing the course of the constellations for too long a period of time for such a shift to have gone unobserved; and movements of the earth's crust occurring with such speed as to produce a 10° rotation of the island of Crete in a mere four thousand years cannot be accepted as a tectonic possibility. I recall similar measurements that I carried out years ago on the positioned stones in Brittany. The rows of menhirs at Carnac, massive granite blocks set up in many endless parallel rows, likewise show a deviation of 10°. They do not run exactly east-west, but are set at 80°, slightly west-southwest to east-northeast. And further to the west, beyond the narrow peninsula of Quiberon which juts sharply to the south, the same spectacle is repeated in reverse: here we find rows of menhirs arranged in lines of 100° —that is, once again a 10° deviation from the east-west direction, but this time running slightly west-northwest to east-southeast.

There is no question that the ancients were quite able to take correct bearings. These deviations were not careless but deliberate. In Britanny the facts rule out an explanation by change of the astronomical elements of the orbit or by rotation of the observation site because in either case the deviation would be the same on both sides of the cape of Quiberon—which, curiously, points straight south. Evidently the direction of the rows of menhirs was determined on the basis of sunrise and sunset on a particular day in the year. The exact direction of south is determined by the highest point of the sun at noon and does not change in the course of the year. This southern direction corresponds precisely to the natural orientation of Cape Quiberon. The menhirs, however, are generally oriented in a west-easterly direction, by sunrise in the east and sunset in the west. Since the sun rises exactly in the east and sets exactly in the west only at the equinox, always deviating somewhat to the south at morning and evening during the six months of winter, the orientation of the menhirs must have been based on the summer months, when sunrise and sunset always deviate northward of the exact east-west line.

Many buildings in Egypt, Mesopotamia and Etruria were likewise oriented more or less strictly by the sun, although the direction was not the same in all cases. Depending on certain premises, at times the sunrise, the sunset or the noon zenith was the determining factor. The deviation in Knossos corresponds to that of the western rows of menhirs north of Quiberon, which were oriented by the sunset. Undoubtedly priests with astronomical expertise were at work when the central court was first measured and laid out.

Orientation was important not only for religious structures; it was also applied to secular urban buildings. We know, for example, what pains the Etruscans took (a thousand years after the end of Minoan rule on Crete) in planning and orienting the cities they founded. And the Roman legions, too, laid great stress on the formal arrangement of their campgrounds. Their practice was governed only in part by strategic considerations. The military tribune marked the center of the camp with a white flag. Here the commander's tent with the standards of the legion would be set up. From this point the layout of the camp streets followed the points of the compass precisely, and was the same in every Roman camp. The Greek historian Polybius, who came to Rome as a hostage, won the friendship of Scipio Africanus the Younger and took part in the Third Punic War as a military adviser, tells us that one axis, the *via principalis*, ran precisely north-south, and the second axis, the *via praetoria*, ran at right angles to it precisely east-west. These main streets of the camp intersected at the commander's tent (*praetorium*). The *via principalis* connected the south gate (*porta principalis dextra*) with the north gate (*porta principalis sinistra*), and corresponded to the *cardo*, the principal north-south street in Roman and Etruscan cities.

The east gate (*porta praetoria*), oriented toward the sunrise, was considered fortunate. The cohorts marched out to battle through this gate. The street corresponded to the *decumanus*, the main west-east street in Roman and Etruscan cities.

The opposite western gate (*porta decumana*), facing the sunset, was considered unlucky. Messengers bearing bad news entered through this gate; the dead were carried out of the camp there; and men condemned to death were led out through the west gate to the execution ground. No Roman officer or legionary would have indiscriminately used the west or the east gates, thus recklessly exposing himself to evil omens. We may ignore such "superstitions" nowadays but their significance was deeply rooted in the emotional life of the ancients, whose attitudes had been formed during the long millennia in which man was usually helplessly exposed to natural forces. Perhaps we may even venture the question: Have we not lost, along with any feeling for such ideas of outward orientation, a good measure of our inner orientation? And was it merely by chance that we entered the Palace of Knossos from the west yesterday, following the hordes of other visitors? For the palace, like a Roman camp and like many cities of antiquity, has four entrances, one for each cardinal direction.

The north approach is probably the most impressive. Once you pass through a narrow portal beside the northwest propylaeum, you enter a high columned hall, at the northern end of the palace, its ceiling supported by ten mighty orthostats. Evans called this room the Customs Station, probably theorizing that the goods for the palace storerooms were delivered here. A

FIG. 10   Palace of Knossos: portico with bull relief between the north propylaeum and the central court. In front of the portico a long gentle ramp leads to the central court. (The ramp is beyond the left margin of the picture.)

gently sloping ramp 20 meters long leads us to the higher level of the central court, past the elevated portico with the famous monumental bull relief that looms above the north entrance. Here we once more encounter the bull—was it an animal god, a sacrificial beast or an advertisement for the brilliant bull games held in the interior of the palace?

Outside the north gate, on the Sacred Way that leads to the west, is the "theatral area." It is a small rectangle with two sets of tiers at right angles to each other on the narrow eastern and the longer southern side. These tiers can have served no other purpose than to provide a sizable audience with a view of the rectangular area. Here arrivals approaching the palace by the Sacred Way from the west could be received solemnly and greeted before they continued on their way through the north or western portals into the interior of the palace. Possibly religious rituals or performances took place in this area.

The southern approach rises more steeply, since the land here drops to a deep hollow, one of the valleys bordering the Kairatos River. The ascent used to be made through a long roofed stairway which terminated in the south propylaeum. From here the visitor has to turn abruptly to the east. Through the southern corridor—which is about 50 meters long and runs parallel to the Corridor of the Procession visited yesterday, but without any direct connection to it—he reaches the southern section, which has two north-south corridors running through it that link it to the central court. Thus, whereas the western approach leads by way of the Corridor of the Procession into the interior of the west wing and by way of the broad stairway into the *piano nobile,* the route from the north and south portals does not really lead into the adjacent wings, but passes right through them to the central court. This direction corresponds to the *cardo,* the north-south axis with the two principal gates.

But while the main accesses to Roman camps and towns led in more or less straight lines to the center, the visitor to the Palace of Knossos is forced to change his direction several times. During our first visit yesterday we were struck by the curiously abrupt bends in the corridors, in both the Corridor of the Procession and the one outside the western magazines. None of the approaches to the palace was a straight line. It almost seems as if the intention was to leave the visitor in the dark about the actual direction of the access route. Anyone coming from the west would enter the palace either by a portal opening to the north and then by a corridor bent into a U shape, or by a north portal opening to the west, beyond which he is forced to turn south immediately. Anyone coming from the south likewise has to pass through two such bends at both ends of the southern corridor. Since the indications are that the Sacred Way from the west was much used in ancient times, perhaps it was especially important to diminish as far as possible the force of the evil omen attached to every western access. That is, making the route bend several times might have served to keep evil influences from the palace. The zigzags and seemingly arbitrary turns may, therefore, be understood as "directional locks" to bar such evil influences. Certainly they should not be construed as strategical devices to confound possible enemies, since the entire area—as we noticed with astonishment yesterday when we were looking out from the vantage point of the *piano nobile*—is wide open to attack from all directions.

FIG. 11   Palace of Knossos: zigzag corridors.

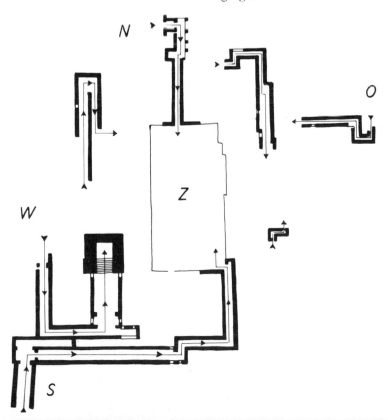

We have now visited the *porta decumana* on the west, the *porta principalis sinistra* on the north and the *porta principalis dextra* on the south. There remains only the last, the lucky *porta praetoria* on the east.

In Knossos this entrance is very different from the other three. On the western side of the palace a broad antechamber more than 12 meters wide opens to the visitor; on the north an impressive pillared hall receives him; on the south a roofed stairway leads to the southern propylaeum, and then the south corridor leads to the passageway with the "Priest-King," or "Young Prince," one of the finest frescos of the Minoan period. But on the eastern side we find only a hidden little door, without a portal or pillared hall, which leads by inconspicuous steep, crooked steps down into the Kairatos Valley. Instead of the expected *porta praetoria*, the east gate through which other ancient Mediterranean peoples ordained that good news should reach the city or camp, the gate through which the legions marched, trusting to its lucky auspices, the gate that faced the rising sun, symbol of life, we find only a secretive little back stairway.

How is it that these important rulers of Minoan civilization, priest-kings who carefully oriented their palace by the sun, so flouted the traditional meaning of the cardinal points that they did not open their palace wide to the east. To the lovely, fruitful river valley below, in order to allow beneficent influences to enter? Most visitors obviously came from the west, from the direction of the sunset, like messengers of ill fortune. Surely this was an anomaly for the ancient inhabitants of the Mediterranean region. We know from Polybius that the sturdy Roman legionaries and their officers regarded the omens of the cardinal points so seriously that they always carefully kept to the traditional directions. Perhaps the enlightened rulers of Knossos were far above such superstitions and auguries. But then why had they carefully oriented the palace by the sunset, instead of simply following the lay of the land?

Or had they taken over the site from early Stone Age inhabitants and merely continued an existing plan? But the layout is too strict in its rectilinear arrangement to have been the result of chance. The ancient Minoans seem to have known quite well what they were doing and why.

Fɪɢ. 12 Palace of Knossos: cyclopean eastern facade. The layout in
the interior is lightened by colonnaded halls and light shafts. The outside
facade, on the contrary, is rather forbidding with its austere and compact
structure, all the more so since the walls we see today have not been
carried up to their original height. Nevertheless these imposing walls
were not conceived as fortifications, as the more inviting structure in the
southeastern part of the excavation shows.

Moreover, what other meaning can we ascribe to the curious
bends in the corridors? If the Cretan king had been an enlightened monarch, not subject to the same superstitions as mega-
lithic, Egyptian or Etruscan-Roman priesthoods, or Roman legionaries, would he not have provided his palace with straight,
open, impressive entrances, without such twists and bends? But
so characteristic of Knossos are these zigzags that nowadays we
describe a maze of corridors that turn and wind in perplexing
ways as "labyrinthine"—that is, patterned on the Cretan palace.

It should not surprise us that the eastern facade above the
obscure eastern entrance does not present an inviting appear-

ance, with colonnaded arcades, loggias and terraces, but instead consists of windowless cyclopean masonry to a height of three stories. Of course, the upper part of this eastern facade is a reconstruction. Surely Arthur Evans would have had every inclination to restore pleasant open arcades, terraces or balconies looking down on the fruitful valley had there been the slightest indication of the presence of such agreeable structures. But in fact the palace's eastern facade, which is the best preserved of the entrances, presents that rather forbidding exterior we might have expected from the western facade.

There, from the fact that the ashlar masonry did not rise above the original surface of the hill, Evans had concluded that only the lower story had been made of such huge blocks and that it had been crowned by an upper story resting on columns. But since the blocks were made of a stone that slowly disintegrates under the open sky (we shall have much more to say on this later), it is understandable that the only portions of the western facade to be preserved would be those that had been protected from the weather over the millennia by being embedded in the earth.

The narrow, winding stairway at the east gate, below the cyclopean retaining wall, has a carefully fashioned drainage channel running beside the steps and faithfully following all the windings of the stairs. If we credit Evan's theory that this was the outlet for the palace's drains, the eastern entrance certainly could not have been welcoming to visitors. What would have been the point of constructing a drainage channel for sewage that carefully paralleled winding stairs, rather than disappearing underground as quickly as possible?

Let us follow this winding staircase on the eastern side of the palace. It leads down to the valley of the Kairatos River, which is said to have been navigable in the Minoan Age. We must assume that the whole island was more heavily forested in those bygone times, so that brooks and rivers would have flowed more evenly than they do today, when the precipitation of the winter season rapidly runs off the barren mountains and brooks are dry in summer, or have only a thin trickle flowing through their beds. In ancient times, it is said, a pier served the ships for unloading goods and passengers, who would come the 4 kilometers from the coast by water. Today we find it hard to believe this of a stream consisting of a few pools of almost stagnant water. The river bed is paved with broken stone and boulders, which would pose a danger to a vessel. But at high water the water gushes out of the ravine at such great speed that boatsmen could scarcely defy the current with sails or oars. If the river actually was navigable in antiquity, its drainage basin for a great way to the south must have consisted of dense woods. There must have been no agriculture, which causes the water to flow more rapidly, and no forest pasture, for grazing animals prevent the regrowth of young trees. In fact there must have been little settlement, which is always hostile to forest.

The hills along the upper course of the Kairatos, beginning with the margin of the fruitful coastal plain, are covered by stony, hard, shallow soil unsuitable for either the wooden plow or the stone or bronze hoe. These stony slopes were not opened up to agriculture until the iron plowshare and hoe were developed, and that was half a millennium after the ships presumably sailed up the Kairatos to the palace of Minos. At that time civilization was confined to the coastal plain. The palace was situated where the ecumene, the settled area of fertile bottomland that contained easily worked, deep, porous soil, bordered on the uninhabited, densely wooded hills and mountain ridges that made up central Crete.

If we leave the palace by the southern exit, passing through the south propylaeum and the covered staircase, we must cross the deep ravine through which runs the brook that flows from the west into the Kairatos. It, too, is virtually dry during the summer months. A series of massive fieldstone foundations is ascribed to a viaduct that made access to the palace from the south possible at high water times. Only a few steps further on is another Minoan complex of buildings which Evans dubbed the caravanserai. When Evans came to Crete before the turn of the century the Turks were still masters of the island and Turkish ways of life were quite widespread. Thus such a term sprang easily to his mind. He also borrowed from the language of the former Venetian masters of Crete when he spoke of the piano nobile in the west wing of the palace to denote the public rooms of the upper story. By now these names that Evans in-

vented have become so established in art and archaeological literature, in descriptions of Minoan sites and in the language of guides and travelers that people continue to use them without giving much thought to their original meanings.

By caravanserai Evans meant a resthouse with baths, of the kind that are found in areas of Turkish influence on the edges of cities and towns, by bridges and fords, and in ports. This is certainly a noble resthouse with its frescoed walls that portray aspects of nature. Thus the lifelike partridges, which are described in every account of Minoan art or history, are among the details in the caravanserai frescos. Water pipes and basins can also be identified. Nearby, a small chamber cut into the rock, lined with badly weathered alabaster slabs, musty and overgrown with moss, with a feebly flowing spring in the bottom, is called the "spring house."

If we follow the heavily overgrown path to the present-day highway that leads south, into the island's interior, we need go only a few hundred meters to reach the "Temple Tomb." A portico leads into a forecourt on the downward side of the slope. Cut into the mountain is a two-story structure with an upper and a lower hall, connected by a winding staircase. A so-called pillar crypt, resembling the one in the west wing of the palace, ushers us into the tomb proper, which is entirely hewn into the rock. The architectural style, the form and the use of the typical Minoan columns that taper toward the bottom, as well as the stylized bulls' horns, strongly remind us of the nearby palace. There, too, were found such massive bull symbols, like a two-pronged fork carved out of stone. These, together with the bull frescos and the many smaller votive images of bulls in terracotta or bronze, testify to the great importance of the bull in Minoan life. Does not this bear out the Greek legends of Zeus and Europa, of the Minotaur and the labyrinth? Or were these merely fantasies created by later generations to explain bull symbols whose meaning they did not comprehend?

FIG. 13 Temple Tomb, Knossos. View from the upper story of the sacred building, with its stylized bulls' horns above the lightwell and antechamber, to the barren limestone hills beyond the Kairatos Valley. The temple tomb, too, shows three fundamental components of ancient eastern Mediterranean funerary structures: several stories of cult buildings above the level of the burial chamber; bends in the approach; and enclosure within cyclopean masonry (without any original defensive function).

Our second day of viewing the Palace of Knossos has given us a plethora of new impressions, but has also suggested many questions and doubts. Even more pensively than on our first evening we board the overcrowded bus that takes us the few kilometers back to Herakleion.

4

Descent to the Queen's Apartment

❁

From the start of his excavation work Arthur Evans was sure he was uncovering the labyrinth of King Minos which legend reported. Were not the intricately winding foundation walls themselves proof of the mazelike nature of the structure? But the first rooms, which Minos Kalokairinos had already encountered during his tentative excavations twenty years earlier, apparently contained storage vessels. A large-scale storehouse for goods of all sorts could hardly have been a prison for the fabulous monster of Greek legend. Apparently the labyrinth served practical purposes pertaining to this world, not as the setting for the brutal sacrifice of Athenian youths and maidens.

If storehouses, religious and public reception rooms, a theater, cisterns and whole archives of inscribed clay tablets were found, the labyrinth must have been inhabited. But who in the second millennium B.C. could have afforded so lavish a structure if not the man whose name has been preserved in legend and after whom boy babies are named to this day on Crete. What was coming to light out of rubble and ruins simply must have been the palatial residence of King Minos.

But what a curious structure it proved to be, as it was reconstructed piece by piece! The western facade, which presented itself first to the visitor approaching from the Sacred Way, did

not contain the King's residential rooms or a throne room, but
magazines. Moreover, these were not only in the cellar, where
they would make sense in terms of reasonable use of space, unless the goods in question were highly perishable; the upper
story, which by all rights should have been reserved for reception rooms, was also used for storage. On the other hand the
Throne Room was in the lower story, and a singularly gloomy,
close and low-ceilinged room it is. This fact has had to be explained by reference to certain religious practices—that is, that
sacred snakes were kept in subterranean vaults and tended by
priestesses—or that it was an imitation of the cave sanctuaries
that presumably existed in the barren limestone cliffs of the
Cretan mountains. For the other rooms of the lower story in
the west wing—the endless corridors, ritual baths, temples, sanctuaries, pillar crypts, undefined substructures—a plausible function in a Cretan palace could just barely be conceived. The four
larger rooms supported on pillars in the upper story may have

Fig. 14   Temple Tomb, Knossos. Antechamber. The area is surrounded
by high walls. Access was by way of the left margin of the picture,
through a small entry into the antechamber, from there by way of the
lightwell (right center) to the two-story temple with rooms for worship
in the upper story and the anteroom to the tomb in the lower story.
The actual tomb, rectangular in layout and with a central rectangular
pillar, was cut into the steeply rising slope.

been used for festive gatherings. But one thing the rooms in both the lower and the upper story were definitely not suited for was to serve as the domestic quarters for the royal family. And if we are to believe the legend, there definitely was a royal family.

King Minos, the son of Zeus and Europa, had become successor to the throne by the marriage of his mother to King Asterios of Crete. Minos had married a daughter of the sun god, Helios; her name was Pasiphaë and she bore him seven children. Deukalion, the second-oldest son, later assumed power and became the father of the Trojan hero Idomeneus, who fought on the side of the victorious Achaeans against Troy. The third son, Glaukos, fell into one of the great honey pots that stood everywhere about the palace. Luckily the court had at its disposal a gifted physician named Polyeidos who brought the boy back to life by means of his therapeutic snakes, his staff (to this day the symbols of the medical profession) and a special curative herb. The fourth son, Androgeos, also caused trouble, in this case affecting foreign policy. During the Games on the Greek mainland Androgeos took part in international fencing matches and was so severely wounded by Aegeus, the King of Athens, that even Polycidos' medical talents proved inadequate. It is hard to tell whether this was an accident or whether Aegeus (after whom the Aegean Sea is named) wanted to kill the Cretan youth. In any case the incident caused King Minos to resort to arms and subjugate Athens, which henceforth had to deliver up a dread form of tribute. We will recall that Minos demanded neither gold nor goods nor gems, but seven youths and seven maidens every seven or nine years (some say every year).

These hostages never returned to Athens, so the assumption was that they all died in Cretan exile, sacrificed to sinister Cretan gods. But perhaps the fourteen were merely trained for those gay games with bulls that were regularly held either as part of the rhythm of the Cretan religious year or to celebrate the enthronement of Cretan kings. It does seem, though, that even as participants in the games their lives would have been forfeit. Evans asked experienced Spanish *toreros* whether it would be possible to seize an onrushing bull by the horns and perform a bold leap over his head, such as is pictured on Cretan frescos in the Palace of Knossos and on Minoan seals. The laconic answer he got was: Impossible—at least if you want to survive the leap.

Katreus, the oldest son of Minos, followed his father to the throne. Through his daughter Aerope he became the father-in-law of King Atreus of Mycenae, the father of Agamemnon and Menelaus, both well known from Homer's epics. Katreus was killed by his own son, Althaimenes.

In addition to his four sons Minos had two daughters. Ariadne has our full sympathy for her unfortunate love affair with Theseus, the Athenian prince. Theseus had come to Crete with a shipment of hostages. He won the love of Princess Ariadne, who helped him escape from the labyrinth after he had killed the Minotaur. It was she who gave him the thread that he fastened to the entrance of the perplexing structure so that later he could grope his way along it back to the light. On his flight from Crete Theseus took Ariadne with him, but on the homeward voyage he deserted her on Naxos, where she later consoled herself with the god Dionysus. But Theseus turned to her younger sister, Phaedra, whom he married after the death of his first wife.

Certainly Theseus never again enjoyed unclouded happiness after his dishonorable treatment of Ariadne. His homeward voyage to Athens was under an unlucky star, for he forgot to run up the white sails which would announce to his royal father that he was alive and victorious. At the sight of the black sails Aegeus, thinking his son had fallen victim to the Minotaur, took his own life. And later, when Theseus had taken Ariadne's sister Phaedra to wife, the young woman fell in love with his son by his first marriage, Hippolytus. When the handsome youth rejected her she went to Theseus and accused Hippolytus of improper advances. Theseus cursed his own son and called upon Poseidon to exact revenge. The god sent a tidal wave in the form of a great white bull, which caused Hippolytus' team to shy and dragged the chaste charioteer to his death on the rocks of the shore.

Four sons and two daugters makes a total of six children for King Minos. But Pasiphaë is said to have borne seven children. Who was the seventh?

He was no child of Minos, but a horrible creature, the offspring of Queen Pasiphaë's perverted love for a white bull.

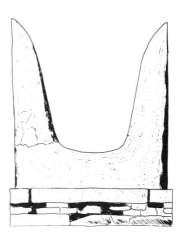

Fig. 15
Ritual
"horns of
consecration,"
Knossos.

Such was the origin of the Minotaur that Minos kept captive in the labyrinth and supposedly fed with Athenian youths and maidens. This labyrinth was said to have been built by Daedalus, and on an Egyptian model, moreover. This is the same Daedalus who first helped Pasiphaë to couple with the bull and who then made wings for himself and his son to flee from Crete. His flight succeeded. But Daedalus' son, forgetting his father's advice, flew too near the sun with his wings of feathers and wax. The wax melted under the heat of the sun's rays and reckless Icarus plunged to his death.

How strange is this world of Minoan myth, which has remained so vividly alive for more than three thousand years! Who does not feel its fascination, especially when he sees the labyrinth physically in Evans' reconstruction? Certainly there must have been "something to" these old stories—the evidence of the excavations supports the frequent references to bulls. But some of the stories have a libelous sound, as if the Athenians, in their resentment at their Cretan overlords, invented tales that made the monarchs of Knossos appear in rather nasty roles.

However that may be, we are acquainted with a labyrinth in Egypt. It was built at Medinet el Fayum around 1800 B.C. under Pharaoh Ammenemes (or Amenemhet) III of the Twelfth Dynasty of the Middle Kingdom. This is the one that could have served as the Cretans' model for their labyrinth at Knossos. It was erected as a temple of the dead alongside the pharaoh's pyramid tomb at Hawara. The bull cult was widespread in ancient Egypt also, as well as in Asia Minor and Crete; possibly

FIG. 16 Palace of Knossos: grand stairwell with Minoan columns and the shield fresco in the background. Reconstruction.

it was introduced there by Europa, King Minos' mother. The rites connected with it were evidently so alien to the later Greeks that they misinterpreted them. Scandalous versions of older cults by younger religions are not exactly unknown in later religious history.

Medical feats based on a sound knowledge of nature, especially of medicinal plants, easily lend themselves to mystical interpretations; this would account for the Glaukos legend. As for the Daedalus story, it was widely known that the Cretans were gifted

craftsmen. It is not improbable that they tried to use feathers
and wax, an ancient product of the island, to attain man's eternal
dream of flying.

There remains the problem of the close connection between
King Minos' family and the rulers of the Greek mainland. It
seems more likely that some sort of family quarrel set the houses
of Athens and Knossos at odds than a conflict arising out of
religious or racial antipathies. The mainland Greeks were quite
willing to take their royal wives from Crete, and their gods as

well; for they acknowledged that the birthplace of their supreme god, Zeus, was on Crete.

While we are thinking along these lines, trying to fathom the true meaning of these old stories, we are turning toward the east wing of the Palace of Knossos. In the west wing Evans had found no proper domestic quarters in either the upper or the lower story. Apparently there had been no third story, for no indications of stairways were found. The structures to the north and south of the central court also do not seem suitable for living quarters. They are ostentatious public access buildings with ramps and passages, with none of the relative privacy associated with domestic life. Hence there remains only the east wing. Here the living quarters of the royal family must have been situated. Would it not have been a good omen to live on the sunrise side, the lucky eastern side of the palace?

A grand stairwell restored by Evans receives us. The stairs, consisting of broad alabaster steps, run with right-angle turns around a light shaft down into the depths of the building. Very little of the upper stories has been preserved but the lower story permits certain deductions about the original condition and purpose of this section of the palace. There are actually two lower stories below the level of the central court. Massive russet-painted Cretan columns support the steps on the side toward the light shaft. At the level of the first lower floor the eye falls on an immense fresco composed of huge double shields, each in the form of a large eight, the pinch in the center presumably permitting the warrior to handle his weapons more easily. Evans reasons that behind this fresco lay the "guard room" for the king's bodyguard. Undoubtedly these shield frescos signify some sort of defensiveness. But would it have been sufficient to merely paint the shields on the wall as defensive symbols?

Suddenly I recall a find of Etruscan shields preserved in the Vatican's Gregorian Collection. In 1836 two amateur archaeologists, Father Alessandro Regolini and General Vicenzo Galassi, opened an undamaged Etruscan tomb in the Sorbo necropolis southwest of Cerveteri. They came upon a wall hung with eight large bronze ritual shields. Though the workmanship on these shields was very fine, they were so thin-walled that they could not possibly have been used in actual combat. The shields were not intended to guard the bodies of the living, but to protect the corpse of a royal lady named Larthi, warding off whatever evil influences might have disturbed her peaceful rest in the grave and her transformation during that rest. The Etruscans were well aware that the ritual shields on the wall were not stout enough for real defensive purposes, but they trusted in the effective power of their religion. In Etruria belief in the transformation of the dead in the grave under the protection of ritual shields had an ancient tradition. The graves of the so-called Villanova Culture (1000–600 B.C.) repeatedly contain shield stones, that is, shield motifs hewn out of stone. Again the intention was to fend off all dangerous influences.

On the time scale, Minoan civilization lies just before Italy's Villanova Culture and before the Etruscan period of the last millennium B.C. Of course, the two regions are separated geographically by the breadth of the Ionian Sea, but M. Porcius Cato and other ancient writers always maintained that the Etruscans originally came from Asia Minor. It seems at least conceivable that the Minoan shield motif in the stairwell of the Knossos labyrinth sprang from religious ideas similar to those behind the shield stones and ritual shields in distant Etruria. For the present, to be sure, we can compare the Minoan shield motifs with Etruscan ritual shields only on the basis of physical resemblance.

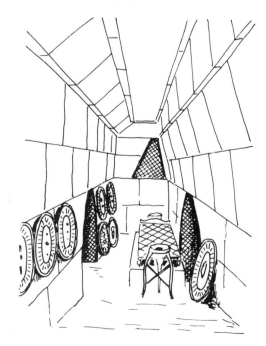

FIG. 17 Ritual shields in the Regolini-Galassi Tomb, Cerveteri, Etruria. View into the antechamber. From this chamber two dark entrances on either side lead into the tomb proper. In the background is a small niche for urns and other vessels.

Asia Minor, Egypt and Etruria are so far from Crete, it might
be argued, that parallels are out of the question; we must con-
fine our attention to the Cretan finds alone. But how, then, are
we to interpret those finds? Can we justifiably base our interpretations on the behavior and mode of life of twentieth-century
people? Conclusions by analogy that leap three and a half millennia and equate Minoans with people of the present day seem
to me far more questionable than comparison with cultures
much closer in time, even if geographically widely separated in
terms of the transportation of the period. Will we not learn more
about the thinking of people of the Late Bronze Age by studying their ways of life against the background of their contemporaries and their descendants in the vicinity? And surely we
may stretch "vicinity" to include the entire Mediterranean
region.

As we descend the grand staircase the shadows deepen around
us. Very little of the brilliant daylight of the central court level
penetrates to this depth. It is as if we were at the bottom of a
well. What can have prompted the Cretan royal couple to bury
themselves down here? The first lower story contained, in addition to the "guard room," the supposed bedroom of the queen,
the king's "treasure chamber," the "room with the stone bench"
and a small light shaft. In the second lower story we at last

Fig. 18   Shield fresco, Tiryns.

reach the royal "living rooms." Only here, in the depths, did. Evans find rooms that seemed to him in design and equipment proper living quarters for a Cretan royal couple.

After our long stay in the sun without any protecting enclosure, for the remains of walls reflect the sun's rays as shimmering heat waves, we at first feel this cool darkness as distinctly pleasant. But after we have remained in the close cellar rooms for some time we begin to wonder in amazement how these rooms could have served the royal family as permanent domestic quarters. It would be one thing in the hot Cretan summer, when the sirocco from Africa blows and the temperature rises into the nineties, so that all life seems numbed by the glare of the sun. But how comfortable would it be during the rest of the year? In October the winter rains begin without any real autumn, and the cold north wind blows gales from the Aegean almost every day. At present some warmth of the summer sun penetrates even to this depth. The tooth of time has gnawed off most of the two upper stories and caused the eastern facade to collapse down to the level of the first lower story. But when the building was intact it seems likely that in winter scarcely a ray of light would have found its way down here.

We can scarcely believe our eyes: A sign in Greek and French informs us: "The Queen's Megaron." This is the queen's hall? Could the consort of Minos have lived here? And we find ourselves wondering: As a free ruler, or as a prisoner atoning for her sins?

Our eyes are drawn to a large fresco of dolphins above the low door to the corridor that leads to the king's quarters. Is there anything gayer than disporting dolphins, those clever denizens of the sea who so frequently seek the presence of men, swim in the wake of boats, can be trained to do all kinds of tricks and sometimes have actually saved men from drowning? Ever since its discovery this dolphin fresco has been regarded as the symbol of Minoan *joie de vivre*, love of nature, attachment to the sea and appreciation of the sensuous pleasure in this world. In a loggia three floors higher this effect would be far more convincing. But down here, in the twilight of the second sublevel?

FIG. 19   Dolphin fresco, Knossos.

On the right, beside the door to the narrow cellar passage which the king is supposed to have taken when he wished to visit his spouse, a narrow winding staircase leads into the first sublevel above, with the queen's "bedroom." Why, we ask, did she not change her living room for her bedroom? It is certainly dusky enough in the first lower story, although not quite so close and oppressive.

Separated from the living quarters by a waist-high stone partition is the world-famous bathroom containing an earthenware bathtub. The walls and floors are sheathed with white alabaster with gray veinings. The upper part of the walls and ceilings are fresco paintings with, among other motifs, a spiral design that frequently recurs in other Minoan buildings.

The bathtub itself is strikingly small and short. Even if the queen was very petite, she would hardly have had room to stretch out in this clay vessel barely a meter long. Perhaps she only washed her feet in it, or perhaps she washed her body while standing. But what is even more puzzling is that the tub has a drainage hole but there is no provision for drainage in the floor. If the drain were opened, the apartment would have been flooded. Therefore the tub must either have been bailed out or carried out with its contents. But in either case what was the point of the drainage hole?

Thoroughly perplexed, we squeeze through the dark passage that connects the Queen's Megaron with her "toilet." On one side of the alcove there is a niche in the wall at the bottom of which a drainage channel disappears into the floor. At last we are standing before the proof of Minoan Crete's remarkably high state of civilization more than thirty-five hundred years before the present day.

While all the rest of Europe still dwelt in darkness, while our forefathers stepped behind any convenient tree in the woods that then covered most of the continent, the Queen of Knossos was using a flush toilet! The emperors of the Holy Roman Empire lacked such a facility. We look in vain for it in the castles and burgher houses of the Middle Ages and the Enlightenment. Even in the Sun King's palace at Versailles there was no such provision. But Knossos already was acquainted with this status symbol of modern civilization! The facilities that in Evans's day were slowly beginning to penetrate the rest of Europe—bathtub and water closet—had been available in Minoan Crete!

Our enthusiasm, however, is almost immediately dampened. We step out into a light shaft, at the foot of which spinning wheels were found. Here the queen sat with her ladies doing handicrafts. The area is about that of a small room in a present-day housing project for the poor. A narrow deep-blue rectangle above our heads promises sun, light and air far above. But down here we are surrounded by nothing but stale air and dampness. The walls around the shaft once rose four stories high; at its bottom the Queen of the Cretans and her court presumably led a shadow existence. A deep feeling of sympathy overcomes us. In return for somewhat fresher air to breathe, for a view of the hills and the sea, for a few bright rays of sunlight and the rustle of the stone pines around the palace, the queen would gladly have done without the comforts of the bath!

5

In the Sign of the
Double Axe

❁

We cannot help wondering whether it was any consolation to the queen to know that the king's apartment had little more air and light than the megaron that had been assigned to her. We enter the king's living quarters by way of the hall of the double axe, named after the Cretan religious symbols scratched into the wall at this point. Now at last we see before us the symbol of Minoan power and rule, the sign that (according to Evans) gave the palace its name. Apparently scholars had all been mistaken when they derived the word labyrinth, in accordance with ancient tradition, from the Egyptian *loperohunt,* meaning "palace (or temple) by the lake" (Lake Moeris). For it seemed that Evans had found visible proof of another etymology.

Evans believed that the labyrinth of Amenemhet III at Medinet el Fayum in Egypt, so vividly described by Herodotus and Strabo, could not have been the original source of the term "labyrinth." That term must have originated at the Palace of Knossos, he argued. For here double axes were found everywhere as religious symbols and in Greek the double axe is called *labrys.* Hence "labyrinth" means something like "palace of the double axes." It remains an oddity, however, that the Egyptian labyrinth was known by that name long before the rediscovery of the Palace of Knossos; it was in fact known by that name in classical antiquity, although no double axes were found on the Nile.

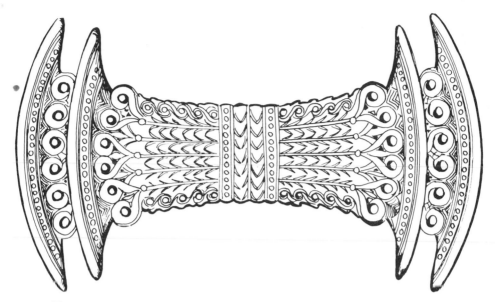

FIG. 20
Ritual
double axe,
Kato Zakro.

FIG. 21
Double axe
pithos,
Knossos.

On the north wall of the Sanctuary of the Double Axes there
stands a hewn block. Whether it was meant as a throne or an
altar cannot be unequivocally determined. It was formerly flanked
by two large symbolic double axes made of thin bronze and
attached to long poles, resembling military standards or halberds.
They can scarcely have had any practical purpose as weapons or
tools—the material is much too thin. In the Herakleion Museum
several such large double axes are lined up, some with filigree-
like drawings on their blades. Especially fine specimens are distinguished by incising, gilding, filigree patterns or duplication of
the cutting edges.

What were these double axes for? For the present let us continue our pensive tour of the labyrinth of Knossos; later we will
take up the many questions that arise in connection with the
excavation finds.

In front of the altar or throne in the Sanctuary of the Double
Axes curious clay idols were found. Today they are kept with the
other finds in the Herakleion Museum. Though this is a sensible
measure for conserving and safekeeping the finds, it no longer
accords with what we demand of a modern museum.

Unfortunately, many museums throughout the world are so
organized that lance head is placed neatly beside lance head,
flint beside flint, producing collections that are quantitatively
impressive but quite sterile of information. Even such splendid
collections as, for example, those in the Archaeological Museum

FIG. 22 Terracotta
idol from the Sanctuary
of the Double Axes, Knossos.

of Naples suffer from the sheer accumulation of specimens classified by material, form and size. Placing all silver or glass objects from Pompeii in one room may be very convenient for a specialist in Roman silver or glass, but it is instructive neither to the professional nor to the layman. Nowadays the progressive museum curator has changed his approach and the articles are presented as far as possible in the way they were once found, that is, in their original stratification and surroundings.

Today, after so many decades, it would surely be difficult to reconstruct the circumstances of the finds at Knossos before Evans undertook his restorations. A German archaeologist with experience in Near Eastern excavational practice, Dr. R. Hachmann of the Institute for Prehistory and the Archaeology of Asia Minor at the University of the Saar, comments on this question:

> Evans, who was knighted for his excavations in Knossos, was a man of genius and imagination and was constantly coming up with brilliant ideas. Often these ideas did not correspond to the results of the excavation, or not entirely. We have evidence that he often altered excavation reports in order to fit the data to his theories. The notes of his extremely competent and conscientious assistants, preserved in Oxford, expose many such falsifications. In fact, even the various plans published by Evans do not tally with each other. For some time a fierce debate has been going on in England between those who have "seen through" Evans and those who still believe in him.

The more often we visit the excavation site, the more uneasy we become about the meaning Evans put on his finds, though his interpretation, almost unchanged, remains the dominant theory. Our doubts concern the very basis of that interpretation, which all who have followed the great excavator in studies of the Palace of Knossos, of Minoan civilization and of the early history of the Mediterranean region have tacitly accepted. As yet, however, we cannot confirm this feeling. In Evans's reconstructions of the Knossos complex the modern additions and the original Minoan parts are so intermingled that it is scarcely possible to separate what was actually found from what was reconstructed by guesswork and deduction. There is no need to question Evans's good faith; he completely believed in his interpretations. But when we compare his versions with the actual relics of the Minoan period, we fall prey to deep uncertainty and feel obliged to look at everything with critical eyes.

The idols from the Sanctuary of the Double Axes are terracotta female figures of considerable size, up to half a meter in height, with a rounded lower part resembling a hoop skirt, slender waist, flattened torso, emphatic breasts, a somewhat blank expression, but oversized hands raised imploringly. The whole figure is a kind of plea incarnate. The rigid look recalls the small snake priestesses with exposed breasts from the Triple Shrine in the west wing of the palace. In fact, a similar terracotta figure was found at the shrine in the country house of Kannia near Gortyn in central Crete and has been assigned to the same Late Minoan period. The latter has snakes in both raised hands. What is variously called an idol, a goddess or a worshiper is at other times labeled a snake priestess or snake goddess, but the figures are clearly alike in nature. It would seem reasonable, therefore, to assume that the rooms in which such figures have been found should also be of like nature. The Sanctuary of the Double Axes is thus not a whit more likely to have been a royal residential chamber than the so-called Triple Shrine with its snake priestess.

Full of curiosity, we turn to the next room, the last, with the exception of a narrow colonnaded hall and the small court for light, in the king's apartment. It is empty except for the copy of a wooden throne, very much like the one in the Throne Room in the west wing, and a stone bench for sitting. Apparently the king also liked to have a throne in his living room.

Evans insisted that this was the King's Megaron. How easily it might have been considered the throne room. Just like the Throne Room it has a throne and stone benches; as with the Throne Room there is a shrine adjacent to it—this one a shrine of the double axes and not the Triple Shrine of the west wing, but likewise containing female terracotta idols with the same prayerful air. Had there been other rooms in the palace that might have been taken for living quarters, Evans undoubtedly would have preferred to regard the room now called the King's Megaron as one of the public rooms. But the royal couple had to be lodged somewhere. So why not here, where several fairly suitable rooms were available?

Today the King's Megaron seems fairly bright and sunny. From the court outside, by way of the colonnade which surrounds the living room on two sides—south and east—an occasional ray of sunlight finds its way into the room when the sun is low in the sky. In the booklet that is serving us as a guide through the intricacies of the ground plan we find a sketch of the megaron with a view of the fruitful Kairatos Valley and the range of hills opposite. We try to obtain this view on the spot by going through the columns into the open air. Now the view to the east ought to open out. But how odd. The builders could have taken advantage of the favorable slope which here, falling toward the valley, would allow the living quarters to emerge from the side of the hill. There was room outside the megaron for a loggia or garden terrace with a view of valley and hills. But instead of providing that view, the builders permitted a high, windowless cyclopean wall to close in the narrow court from the east. This is the solid, archaic-looking eastern facade of the palace whose forbidding aspect we had felt earlier when we left the small eastern gate and gazed with astonishment at the staircase winding down to the Kairatos River, accompanied by a drain.

The king's light shaft, then, is hardly bigger than the one provided for the queen and her ladies. Here, too, the enclosing walls once towered up several floors, admitting only glimpses of daylight to the cellar story.

In the King's Megaron we again notice the double shields which undoubtedly were once found here—there are only copies of them now. Was the king suddenly inclined to defend himself with arms in his apartment, after he had so grandly dispensed with any military precautions outside the palace? Or were these shields merely decoration for the room, mementos to remind the otherwise peaceloving sovereign of exploits on the battlefield or the tournament ground?

Between the Sanctuary of the Double Axes and the Queen's Megaron a narrow corridor with a double bend is the connecting link. Here again we encounter the fundamental principle of the labyrinth: no access routes run in straight lines.

The "living quarters" of the royal family illustrate another fundamental principle of the labyrinthine structure: the multiplicity of stairways side by side in the same wing. Of course to

this day it is customary to have servants' stairs in addition to the grand staircase in elegant residential or public buildings. But here there are no less than three separate stairways in a distance of little more than 10 meters, and the "back stairs" connect the queen's living room with her bedroom! Evidently rooms that belonged together functionally were here distributed through several stories one above the other—or rather, one below the other. The rooms clustered around the grand staircase form a unit through at least three stories, down to the subcellar or second lower story. Immediately adjacent on the north side are again

FIG. 23 Palace of Knossos: view of the east wing from the southeast. The antechamber with the court was completely enclosed on the outside by a wall higher than a man. The stairway in the center of the picture did not lead to the court and the king's so-called apartments, but past these into the upper story with the shrines.

totally undomestic-looking magazines with vessels for stores. Thus not only the west wing provides such magazines filled with pithoi; the living quarters are also so equipped, although it is certainly hard to understand why the storerooms should have been scattered over so many different parts (as well as floors) of the palace. This is surely not in the interests of good economic organization and simple access. But perhaps the royal couple did not want to let the more valuable goods out of their sight—especially since pithoi of considerable size were found even in the queen's living room. It is rather odd for a queen to have barrel-sized vessels of olive oil, grain or honey placed in her living room.

The northern part of the east wing again contains, besides long corridors with many bends, endless "magazines" of various sizes, without window openings, accessible through narrow doors only and built of coarse fieldstone. Amid the familiar windings of walls and foundations only a few points attract our attention. One is the site of the giant pithoi, tremendous clay vessels twice as high as a man. These enormous pithoi astound everyone who sees them. In form they resemble the usual type that we have seen in the western magazines, in the sarcophagus room of the Herakleion Museum and in the queen's "living room." Even the more normal-sized storage vessels make one wonder how they could have been emptied and cleaned, since even with long dippers one could scarcely reach the bottom, and then only by standing on a stool. But the giant pithoi present an insoluble problem. They could not even be tipped, which would have been possible with the others (though it would have taken considerable effort) wherever there was room enough in the narrow storage rooms.

Storage vessels the size of the giant pithoi must have been installed before the enclosing walls were erected. They must have been set up and then walled in, so that later there would be no way to replace them by other vessels. They could have been filled and emptied only by means of tools, using the principle of the siphon. But how impracticable to build such vessels in places so difficult of access! We turn away from them with some irritation, after first admiring the artistry with which they were made, the massive, needle's-eye handles and the three rows of stylized rosettes separated by patterns of circles.

The other remarkable feature of this area is the so-called workmen's quarter. It consists of pottery studios and a stonemason's workshop, and ends—we can only wonder at the sense of such planning—on the north, right up against the royal family's residential wing. No more than 10 meters by direct line separate the king's apartments from the stonemason's workshop. Evidently they were not sensitive to noise at the court of ancient Crete. Nowadays we find only sparse indications of what these rooms might have been used for; there are only a few built-ins, whose purpose is hard to determine, and a few blocks of unworked hard stone. This is supposed to have been the "raw material" from which the king's masons made artistic figures and utensils. The blocks are of Labrador porphyrite, a basal igneous rock that must have been procured from far away, since it is not to be found anywhere in the immediate vicinity of the palace. But this type of stone hardly lends itself to carving. Nor did I discover anywhere in the palace or in the museum a single sculpture made of this raw material. Perhaps the workmen realized too late that the stone was not right for them, and left it unworked. But it seems much more probable that these blocks are the remains of an originally far more massive block used as a sacrificial stone and later smashed into several pieces. Unfortunately it is no longer possible to reconstruct the original arrangement and sites of the other finds that led Evans to identify this as a Minoan artisans' workshop.

Disappointed, we turn to the southern part of the east wing, having first paced off the massive exterior wall that encloses the northeastern part of the palace. From the columned hall of the northern entrance to the vicinity of the stairs beneath the small eastern gate run huge foundations, with several sections serrated in the manner we have also seen in Troy VI of the Middle and Late Bronze Age. This part of the Palace of King Minos belongs to somewhat the same era, and from this side it gives a distinctly citadellike impression, although the walls here had neither the gigantic height nor the breadth of those on the hill of Hissarlik in Asia Minor.

The southeast wing is not protected by an enclosing wall as is the northeast wing. In this direction the labyrinth breaks up into a loose group of isolated structures which have been given interesting names: House with the Sacred Tribune; Southeast House; House of the Fallen Blocks; House of the Sacrificial Bull. These buildings, of several stories, look like small copies of the royal living quarters. There are stairways, rooms for religious ceremonies, winding corridors with magazines, colonnaded porches with narrow light shafts. As with the House of the High Priest outside the South Propylaeum, Evans assumed that these were the residences of the higher palace officials. In the southeast wing also, but part of the palace proper, are two "bathrooms" similar to the queen's, and close by lies the Shrine of the Dove Goddess of Late Minoan times, with an altar, cult vases and a large number of votive offerings.

On the other hand, nowhere in the whole palace is there a

usable kitchen for the court, officials and servants. There are no armament rooms and stables—to mention only a few practical matters. Or were all these once tucked into the upper story of the east wing, in exchange, as it were, for the royal living quarters' being in the cellar? We also cannot identify anything that might have been an adequate dining room. Evidently each of the numerous inhabitants of the palace must have boiled up his pot of soup on his own and consumed it in solitary splendor. But then there are scarcely any signs of proper hearths such as would be expected in a normal household of the period. To make up for this lack, there are a great number of cult rooms, altars and "lustral basins," votive offerings, ritual baths. Was the Minoan world actually so disdainful of worldly things? Is it conceivable that a resplendent palace would have innumerable separate bathrooms but no kitchen?

6

The Rise and Fall
of Minoan Hegemony

To understand Arthur Evans we must think ourselves
back to the period just before the beginning of the twentieth
century. When Evans began digging in Knossos the Minoan Age
was unnamed and, except for the highly imaginative accounts of
Greek myth, unknown. Thus he was entering entirely unexplored
country, and he carried out pioneering work of incontestable
value. That must be fully acknowledged even today. But must we,
for that reason, accept his interpretations as they stand, rather
than examining the data on our own and drawing our own conclusions?

According to Homer, Idomeneus, grandson of the ruler of
Knossos, fought side by side with the Achaeans against the Trojans. In the famous catalogue of ships in *The Iliad* the Cretans
are listed along with the rest of the Achaeans, not at all as foreign auxiliaries:

> Idomeneus the spear-famed was leader of the Kretans,
> those who held Knosos and Gortyns of the great walls,
> Lyktos and Miletos and silver-shining Lykastos,
> and Phaistos and Rhytion, all towns well established,
> and others who dwelt beside them in Krete of the
> hundred cities.

Of all these Idomeneus the spear-famed was leader,
with Meriones, a match for the murderous Lord of Battles.
Following along with these were eighty black ships.°

So the passage runs in the second book of *The Iliad*, lines
645–652. A little earlier in this grandiloquent survey of the
Achaean fleet Odysseus is mentioned as heading the Cephal-
lenians and Thoas as leader of the Aetolians. After the Cretans
come the Rhodians and the inhabitants of the islands of the Greek
archipelago. There is no indication that the Cretans are anything
other than "Danaeans," that is, Achaeans or Greeks. Because of
the hegemony of the densely populated mainland provinces,
these are listed before the islands. But the Cretans, with their
sizable contingent of eighty ships, head the list of Aegean participants in the war.

We also learn from Homer that several dialects were spoken
on Crete, among them that of the Eteocretans around Sitia in the
eastern part of the island—the "true Cretans," as they called
themselves. Even in the Greek classical age the people here spoke
an old-fashioned idiom which was not written in Greek letters,
but presumably in the Cypriot syllabary. But before the discoveries of Arthur Evans there were no indications that the Cretans
had not been Greeks.

From the very beginning of the excavation, however, the finds
at Knossos differed fundamentally from the art and artefacts that
were regarded, around the turn of the century, as typical of classical Greece. Evans found no temples, no large sculpture, no
Greek amphitheaters with seats carved out of the rock of a rising
slope, no inscriptions that bespoke the deeds of gods and men,
nor even the familiar characters of the Greek pantheon.

Instead Evans came upon strange-looking columns tapering
toward the bottom, and an architecture like no other in its shapes
and arrangement of space. He found magazines of pithoi and
deposits of clay tablets inscribed apparently with endless statistical notations devoid of any historical or mythological references.
He found curious clay idols, strange male and female dress, unfamiliar religious customs and deities.

° *The Iliad of Homer,* translated by Richmond Lattimore. (Chicago and
London: The University of Chicago Press Phoenix Books, 1970), p. 93;
lines 645–652.

There were indeed certain resemblances to finds at Mycenae and Tiryns in the Peloponnesus, where Evans had previously visited the excavations of Schliemann and Dörpfeld. But the finds there were regarded as rather exceptional. Perhaps the similarities could be attributed to Cretan influence, as Schliemann had already suggested. Possibly the lords of the citadels of Mycenae and Tiryns had paid a visit to Crete on one of their piratical expeditions and had carried off objects of art or even kidnapped the artists themselves. The frescos of women in Tiryns, with long black hair, exposed bosoms and slender waists; the dolphins, lotus blossoms and spiral motifs; and especially the characteristic Cretan double shields on a fresco in the citadel of Tiryns, plainly showed the hand of Cretan artists. Weapons, ceramics, gold and silver could be obtained by trade or robbery. But frescos have to be painted on the spot; they cannot be imported without importing the painters.

Yet the newly discovered civilization of Knossos presented no clear parallels to the other known cultures of the eastern Mediterranean and adjacent lands. At this time, the turn of the century, Cyprus had scarcely been explored archaeologically. In Asia Minor Schliemann's sensational excavation at Troy had attracted the world's attention, especially because of the phenomenal finds of gold that the excavator had promptly named Priam's Treasure, without suspecting that it was about a thousand years older than the lord of the Trojan citadel who figures in Homer's epic. Schliemann's rapid excavation work on the hill of Hissarlik had prematurely and completely removed the very strata that might have been compared with Knossos. The Palace of Mari on the Upper Euphrates was not uncovered by French archaeologists until several decades later. Thus at the turn of the century the only possible comparison aside from the Greek mainland was Egypt, whose past was relatively well known archaeologically. But what a difference there too! Knossos offered no pyramids, no mummies, no sphinxes or obelisks, no monumental statues of gods or pharaohs, no walls filled with hieroglyphs glorifying rulers and their deeds. Comparisons of artistic styles or architectural principles likewise revealed little evidence of close ties between Crete and Egypt.

From the beginning, therefore, Knossos appeared in so singular a light, without parallel to any of the then known neighboring civilizations, that Arthur Evans felt perfectly justified in introducing a new name to archaeology and art history for this culture he had rediscovered. As we have seen, he chose the name of the king whom myth described as the ruler of Knossos and the labyrinth. It is only since Evans that we speak of Minoan culture.

Then, as from year to year new and hitherto unsuspected artistic and practical achievements of the Minoans were unearthed, Evans came to believe that the inhabitants of Knossos had attained a height of civilization unique for the Middle to Late Bronze Age, with technical devices at their disposal that seemed strikingly modern. The great mystery was why this highly-developed civilization had not lasted. True, the grandson of King Minos had taken part in the Trojan War; and Homer's epic had become thereafter part and parcel of the culture of all the Greek tribes. But some obstacles must have prevented a complete cultural and civilizational exchange; otherwise the decline into the Greek Dark Ages (between Minoan and Hellenic or "classical" Greek culture) would be incomprehensible. The Cretans, therefore, must have been of another origin and race than the Achaeans and later Hellenes, and except for marginal remnants they must all have been destroyed.

Was not the russet skin color of the Minoan men on the frescos in the Palace of Knossos also a distinct sign of their alien nature? Not fair-haired Achaeans but brown-skinned, dark-haired tribes had been the civilized people of Crete. The tall, light-skinned Hellenes, led by the Dorians who, according to the accounts of classical writers, advanced southward around 1200 B.C., had presumably expelled the old Cretan tribes, destroyed the culture of the people they had conquered and become masters of the island in their stead. Compared to those dark-skinned ancient Cretans the actual Greek immigrants seem like barbarians, devastating and destroying the art and culture that the Minoan artists had created in peaceful rivalry.

Oswald Spengler, incidentally, *before* the outbreak of the First World War had already eloquently expressed the mood of universal doom that was to be felt by the postwar "lost generation" and had introduced the idea of catastrophe as the decisive principle in the history of civilizations. Spengler's idea seemed brilliantly confirmed by the example of the Minoans. Evidently they had once been great and powerful rulers of the seas, lovers of peace and art, engaged in commercial exchanges, open to all new things. Then along came the young, still vital conquerors who put an abrupt end to the Bronze Age paradise in the eastern Mediterranean. The island was subjugated; the palaces went up in flames; art and culture were crushed. History took a breathing spell of several centuries before civilization rose again, more radiant than ever before, in the Hellenic culture of "classical" Greece.

What a plausible picture that was of the rise and fall of the city of Minos, and how well it accorded with the views of the period. Between the two World Wars and afterward catastrophe was more or less "in the air." It was somehow reassuring to know that our fate was not unique; we were merely joining all the other now-submerged civilizations of world history. Under the aegis of such a philosophy each individual could consider himself only a tiny cog in the universal works, governed by laws he could not possibly resist. How pleasant to let things take their course, to have historical reasons for one's passivity and to find corroboration of one's fatalism in archaeological research.

The Europe between the two World Wars could view its own future in the past, could study the "decline of the West" through the downfall of Minoan civilization. Perhaps out of that mood the poor Minoans were made the victims of a veritable orgy of annihilation during the next several decades.

The first of these theories concerned earthquakes which were, after all, fairly common in that part of the world. Scientists had established that there had been a tremendous explosion of the volcano on the island of Santorin around 1450 B.C., and this was now cited as the event that had shaken the power of the Minoans. Had not, in 1883, the "phreatic" (subterranean) explosion of Krakatoa in Sunda Strait between Sumatra and Java shown what enormous powers of destruction slumbered in volcanos? Seawater had penetrated the vent. The sudden evolution of steam led to the most violent volcanic disaster in recorded history. The wave of air pressure went several times around the entire globe. The report of the explosion was distinctly heard within a zone of 3400 kilometers' radius—one-fifteenth of the surface of the earth. The greater part of the volcanic island flew into the air; the volcano disgorged some 18 cubic kilometers of pumice which fell over an area of 750,000 square kilometers. The resultant dust clouds that rose high into the atmosphere produced abnormal twilight conditions and falls of dust for days afterward over great portions of the earth. In addition to these apocalyptic events the enormous explosion so churned up the waters of the ocean that a destructive seismic wave, a tsunami 30 meters in height, swept over the coasts of Indonesia, taking a toll of forty thousand human lives.

The Minoan empire had been founded on dominion of the seas. It seemed a fair assumption that ships in that widely scattered world of Aegean islands would be particularly susceptible to similar disasters. If the Minoan fleet had been annihilated by a tsunami, would that not explain the sudden disappearance of the Minoans from the concert of Mediterranean powers at the end of the Bronze Age?

Presumably barbarian invaders would have had an easy time conquering the wretched remnant of survivors who had escaped the earthquake and volcanic eruption, the seismic wave and the epidemics which would have surely followed these disasters. Those who survived this last of the "Egyptian plagues" probably took refuge in the mountains, where they forever lost all desire to install water lines, bathtubs and flush toilets—so that these achievements of civilization fell into oblivion and had to be painfully reinvented thousands of years later. Apparently the scattered groups of displaced Minoans vegetated for a while in the western and eastern mountains of Crete; these were the Eteocretans who continued to cultivate their strange Minoan idiom, the unknown language spoken by King Minos and written down in the Linear A or Linear B scripts, which the Greek conquerors of the island could not read. Ultimately these Eteocretans "died out" or "merged" with the population of the intruders.

"An unknown language written in an unknown script cannot be deciphered, either with or without a bilingual text," the American scholar Alice Kober had decided in 1948 in reference to the Minoan language and script. Thus she exonerated, as it were, Arthur Evans for his failure to decipher the texts, although Knossos had yielded more than four thousand tablets. Yet what really prevented Arthur Evans from finding the key to the riddle was, as we shall see, the nature of his preconceptions, his arbitrary premise about the special position of the Minoans in descent and civilization, and his concept of their catastrophic end. His picture of the Minoans' mode of life, his conviction that they were unique among ancient peoples, were so firmly entrenched in his mind that he was incapable of an unbiased examination of obvious possibilities.

Ultimately Michael Ventris, a British architect and cryptographer, hit on the idea that was to bring the more recent of the Minoan scripts, Linear B, closer to decipherment. His hypothesis was that Greek had been spoken in the labyrinth. Not an utterly strange, unknown and forgotten tongue for which there were no clues because all who had spoken it had fallen victim to the ravages of nature and the violence of barbarian conquerors, but an archaic Greek dialect had been the official language of the palace and could be read on the masses of clay tablets.

For all the adherents of Evans's interpretation this premise was so staggering that they have not come to terms with it yet. In order to preserve their notion of an alien Minoan populace some have tried to cast doubt on Ventris's translations. Others have tried to assign the Linear B texts to the late "decline phase" of the palaces under the alien rule of the Greeks, when the glorious Minoan Age had already been ended by military or geological disasters.

The "universal doom" image of the end of the Minoan empire continues to be seductive. Serious attempts have been made to link that downfall with the legend of Atlantis.* The Atlantis story originates with Plato. In the dialogues *Timaeus* and *Critias* he told of the submergence of a great island in the ocean west of Spain. "There came terrible earthquakes and floods, and in the course of a day and a night full of horrors the entire island of Atlantis vanished beneath the waves." Plato was even specific about the size of the island—2 million square kilometers—and the time of the disasters—nine thousand years before the Greek philosopher's own period (427–347 B.C.). To be sure, these data should have disproved the later theory: neither the size of the island nor the date of the catastrophe remotely coincided with

---

* See J. V. Luce, *Atlantis—Legende und Wirklichkeit* (Bergisch Gladbach, 1969).

the Minoan world. Moreover, the Greeks of Plato's time knew
perfectly well where Crete lay. Yet the catastrophe Plato described fitted Evans's concept so neatly that Atlantis has been repeatedly associated in one way or another with Minoan Crete.
For almost all historians and archaeologists it seems to have
become an article of faith that the ancient Minoans must have
been exterminated by some means or other to have been so
utterly forgotten by world history. In the face of that conviction
what does it signify that to this day in Herakleion you can encounter human types who seems to have stepped straight out of
the Minoan frescos?

Evans seems to have leaned heavily on twentieth-century sen-
sibility for his picture of the ancient Minoans. We have already
noted what emphasis he gave to the presence of plumbing in the

Fig. 24   Bull-leaper fresco, Knossos.

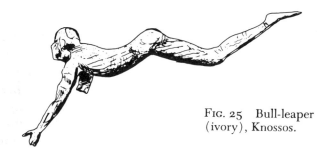

Fig. 25   Bull-leaper
(ivory), Knossos.

Palace of Knossos. Similarly, he decided that the art of the Minoans shared certain essential characteristics with the artistic trends of the turn of the century, especially the style of art nouveau that had recently come into fashion. It seems a curious coincidence that frescos in the Palace of Minos painted thirty-five hundred years ago should have anticipated neither the baroque nor classicism nor romanticism nor impressionism, but the very style so recently born in Europe.

Evans's excavations seemed to dispose of the grim notions the ancient Greeks had had about the legendary labyrinth. After all, would there have been any need for warehouses, oil magazines, throne rooms, ritual rooms and clay tablet archives in a gloomy prison built for a monster like the bull-headed Minotaur? At last the archaeologist's spade was introducing light into the darkness of that ancient tradition. The horror tales of human sacrifices at the court of Minos had probably been atrocity stories concocted for propagandistic reasons by the then defeated Hellenes. For what Evans was finding testified to an entirely different world, and a happy one at that.

The frescos of Knossos seemed to speak in a clear language, drawing a distinct picture of the daily life of the palace's inhabitants. We see the Minoans passing in a long procession, holding themselves proudly as they bring artistically wrought vases, bowls and funnels to their beloved sovereign. There is no question that this was a people of outstanding artistic gifts. The figure of a noble leader, gesturing eloquently and impressively —the "Lily Prince" or "Priest-King"—leads them into the palace. Within, King Minos receives them in the midst of his advisers in a handsome throne room; but before receiving the delegation he has performed the prescribed ritual washings and queried the sacred snakes. The king's subjects have brought the entire annual harvest to his vast storage rooms. Careful notation is made on clay tablets recording who has delivered or received what. Now the people can turn without a care to the beautiful things of life, the entertainments which have been prepared and will be staged in the central court of the palace or outside in the open, under the shady trees of the western court, or in the theater.

Already a tremendous crowd is assembled in the court. The athletic bodies of the Minoan men, steeled in sports and tanned to a russet brown by the glaring sun, eagerly await the contest in which they will test their strength. The graceful ladies, their faces and breasts aristocratically pale from their habit of living in the dim underground parts of the palace, have donned their finest robes for the occasion, arranged their curly dark hair in artful coiffures and emphasized their charms by no less artful use of rouge, powder and eye paint. Their precious gay-colored dresses modestly fall to the ground, covering slender bodies down to delicate ankles—all are lovely young women. But their bodices are so cut as to expose their breasts. A refinement of eroticism? Sexual emancipation? In a moment the snake priestess will step forth from the palace chapel, the Triple Shrine, and with the sacred snakes in her raised hands give the signal for the beginning of the Games. Assistants with libation vessels, intricately ornamented vases in the form of sacred animals—rhytons, as they are called—will bless the earth, the plants and animals, and the inhabitants of the palace.

For months seven young men and seven girls, especially invited for the Festival Games from distant Athens, have been practicing the death-defying leap over the bull. The first of the Athenian youths has just seized the horns of the onrushing beast and with a bold *volte* let himself be hurled aloft to land in the white arms of his girl partner. The foreign acrobat is as deeply tanned as the native Minoan men. But the daring young girls, who in their turn prepare for the deadly leap over the bull, strangely display the elegantly pale complexion that fashion dictates for women at the Cretan court.

After the bull dancers have displayed their art the fête moves out into the world of nature. There, in woods and fields, blue monkeys and brown partridges are on view. The people stroll about, amusing themselves picking flowers or going down to the beach to watch the merry dolphins disporting, until everyone assembles again for the evening performance. This takes place in the theater, where a cluster of lovely Minoan maidens perform charming dances in the open air, until the happy day comes to its end.

Such was the first excavator's vision of the life of the ancient Minoans. Was that how it had been?

7

The Concrete Crete and Its Doubters

Was this vision of the Minoan paradise that Evans discerned in his finds the authentic world of ancient Crete? The world of Minos, of which Homer speaks when he has Odysseus, pretending to be a brother of King Idomeneus of Crete, say to Penelope:

> One of the great islands of the world
> in midsea, in the winedark sea, is Krete:
> spacious and rich and populous, with ninety
> cities and a mingling of tongues.
> Akhaians there are found, along with Kretan
> hillmen of the old stock, and Kydonians,
> Dorians in three blood-lines, Pelasgians—
> and one among their ninety towns is Knossos.
> Here lived King Minos whom great Zeus received
> every ninth year in private council—Minos,
> the father of my father, Deukálion.
> Two sons Deukálion had: Idómeneus,
> who went to join the Atreidai before Troy
> in the beaked ships of war; and then myself,
> Aithon by name—a stripling next my brother.*

---

* *The Odyssey of Homer*, translated by Robert Fitzgerald (New York: Doubleday Anchor Books, 1963), p. 359.

The poet seems to have forgotten, between *The Iliad* and *The Odyssey*, that in the Catalogue of Ships he had given the number of Cretan cities as one hundred. The Dorians seem to have already entered the country, only two generations after the reign of King Minos, but apparently without effecting much change in political conditions. For the dynasty of the Asterides is still in power. This dynasty took its name from Asterios, the adoptive father of Minos and husband of Europa. Minos had had a reign of peace, we may assume; and the reign of his son Deukalion also seems to have passed in games and dancing, in power and glory. The bellicose grandson Idomeneus set out for Troy to prove on the field of battle that Minoan princes no more feared the fury of war than they shrank from raging bulls. The Atreids mentioned in this speech are Agamemnon, King of Mycenae and leader of the Achaeans in the Trojan War, and Menelaus, King of Sparta and husband of beautiful Helen, whose abduction by the Trojan Prince Paris was supposed to have caused the war. The two Greek leaders were the sons of King Atreus of Mycenae.

Homer says not a word about conflicts among the various peoples inhabiting Crete. On the contrary, in his report the different tribes live harmoniously side by side and equally harmoniously take part in the Trojan War along with the mainland Achaeans. The Eteocretans are not defined as a small remnant of authentic Minoans who have retreated to the inaccessible mountains of the interior. The fact that different languages—or rather, it would seem, dialects—were spoken on the island seems to have bothered no one, or at any rate not to have hampered communication. Moreover, Knossos has not yet been destroyed, although the Achaeans and Dorians have already landed there.

There is some question about the meaning of the line concerning Minos, whom great Zeus "received every ninth years in private council." Some suggest that every nine years, that is, after the elapse of a Greek Great Year, Minos approached the supreme god of the Greeks in his sanctuary. On this occasion subject Athens had to provide a tribute of seven youths and seven maidens for his companions. Robert Graves suggests in his *The Greek Myths* that the king himself may originally have been sacrificed at the end of a Great Year to the Triple Goddess, though later rulers were able to escape death by offering surrogate victims.

"Aithon" (Odysseus) continues his account of Crete:

> But I saw with my own eyes at Knossos once
> Odysseus.
>   Gales had caught him off Cape Malea,
> driven him southward on the coast of Krete
> when he was bound for Troy. At Amnisos
> hard by the holy cave of Eileithyia,
> he lay to, and dropped anchor in that open
> and rough roadstead riding out the blow.
> Meanwhile he came ashore, came inland, asking
> after Idómeneus: dear friends he said they were;
> but now ten mornings had already passed,
> ten or eleven, since my brother sailed . . .
>   Twelve days
> they stayed with us, the Akhaians, while that wind
> out of the north shut everyone inside—
> even on land you could not keep your feet,
> such fury was abroad. On the thirteenth
> when the gale dropped, they put to sea.[*]

In the time of Homer, it is here apparent, Crete was no unknown land in the endless sea. Its character and location were quite well known. Homer mentions Mallia, where the French have excavated a palace of the Minoan period that is little inferior to Knossos in size and importance. On his voyage to Troy Odysseus wishes to land on the long and safe beach at Mallia. But the wind drives him westward to the narrow bay of Amnissos, in the vicinity of the grotto of Eileithyia, which can still be seen. From ancient times it had been dedicated to a goddess of fertility. Friedrich Matz has suggested that the stalactites in the cave, some of them huge, may have prompted the religious rites. Because of the gales Odysseus landed with difficulty at Amnissos. He proceeded straight to the city of Knossos. The distance between Amnissos and present-day Herakleion is only about 4 kilometers. Odysseus intends to visit King Idomeneus, whom he knows well from earlier occasions. But the king had left for Troy with the Cretan contingent; and Odysseus is held up while a

[*] *Ibid.*, pp. 359f.

storm from the north rages for twelve days, preventing the ships from sailing.

Anyone who could tell his listeners so much about Crete in a few lines must have been well acquainted with both the Mediterranean and the island. He had been on the spot himself, had tried in vain to leave against the blast of cold Boreas, the north wind, which often smites the northern coast of Crete for days on end. Nor could he have confused this island with any other, with, say, the legendary Atlantis. We must not imagine that the ancient peoples around the shores of the Mediterranean had no accurate geographical knowledge, even though they lacked the cartographic resources of later ages. They had the position of the stars, the direction of the winds, the currents and the soundings in their heads as they sailed the same routes year after year. They did not need marine charts; and in the autumn when the sun and stars hid behind dense clouds they drew their ships up on land to await better weather in the spring.

They managed well enough without charts, magnetic compasses or sextants, since they seldom sailed out of sight of the coast. Thus Odysseus proceeded to Troy by sailing south along the west coast of the Peloponnesus, past Cythera and Anticythera to Crete, where he meant to join Idomeneus's eighty ships. He kept to the north of Kasos and Karpathos, turning northward some distance west of Rhodes, passing through the archipelago of the Sporades along the west coast of Asia Minor until he reached the coast of the Troad, north of Lesbos. The direct route across the Gulf and Isthmus of Corinth and through the Gulf of Aegina would have involved a long overland portage of the ships. Any effort to locate an island the size of legendary Atlantis in this crowded archipelago, and what is more to set it there only a few generations before the outbreak of the Trojan War, can hardly be taken seriously. The ancient Greeks knew their geography too well.

We learn that Idomeneus is an old friend of Odysseus. This is mentioned as casually as if the two did not live on different islands more than 500 kilometers apart. This would imply that there was intensive traffic from island to island; otherwise the Lord of Ithaca (and of the surrounding islands, including the adjacent mainland coast) would not have been on such friendly terms with the King of Crete (and grandson of great Minos). There is no mention of hostility between the old inhabitants, the repressed, brown-skinned Minoans, and the cunning commander of the light-skinned Achaeans. None of Homer's listeners would have credited the story of the crushing of the Cretans by the Achaeans. Achaeans and Dorians lived on Crete side by side with other tribes that had settled there earlier; no group had felt the need to exterminate another. Undoubtedly perfect peace had not always reigned from residence to residence; but there seem to have been no difficulties of understanding due to different dialects. And where something sacred to the Hellenes was concerned, such as beautiful Helen, all joined forces to punish the audacity of the thievish enemy.

To judge from Homer, then, the apocalyptic myth of a sudden, violent end to the joyous, sunlit Minoan kingdom was entirely unknown to his contemporaries, although the poet was well acquainted with the people supposedly involved in that doom. Was that one of Homer's mistakes—after all, he was known to have taken many poetic liberties and as a historical source he had long been regarded as dubious. Moreover, the visionary sketch of Arthur Evans had an archaeological foundation. The specialists accepted the new thesis almost without demur. Homer must have been mistaken. The facts of science proved him wrong.

But initial acceptance was followed by fresh doubts and in some cases disagreement. Objections were raised not so much to the historical thesis and the problem of the downfall of Minoan civilization as to Arthur Evans's restoration work in Knossos. C. W. Ceram comments:

> People at the beginning of our century saw the Cretans as Evans saw them. But had he seen correctly? . . . More and more archaeologists today are sharply questioning Evans's restorations.

The Austrian archaeologist Camillo Praschniker was the first to express criticism of the "movie city," as he called Evans's reconstruction of Knossos in 1930:

> Recently I had the opportunity to visit the palace once more, after a long interval, and unfortunately was compelled to recognize that my worst expectations had been far surpassed.

There is so much new construction that it is scarcely possible to see old stones any longer; we walk through hypotheses of reinforced concrete which are not thereby rendered any the less shaky.

And C. W. Ceram again:

There was no doubt that Evans had permitted his imagination a freer range than he finds justified (or should we not pay tribute to the great discoverer and say vision rather than imagination?). For his reconstructions he put together elements of ancient buildings that were completely unknown to the Cretans. Many archaeologists nowadays say that he erected a "concrete Crete."

In *The March of Archaeology* Ceram then compares what actually was left of the "Prince in the field of Lilies" (or "Priest-King") when it was found and what the creative imagination of the painter, Edouard Gillérion, made of it as a "restoration" under Evans's direction. Suddenly it becomes clear why the art nouveau of the turn of the century seemed to have been "anticipated" in the distant past.

The original consisted of parts of the torso, the bent right arm and remnants of the rest of the painting, such as a necklace and a few strands of hair. Only a fragment of the left arm remained, only part of the thigh and the calf of the left leg. In the restored painting we see a scantily dressed young Minoan, his body superbly muscled, his arm outflung in a bold gesture, a lyrical expression on his face, his head decked by a remarkable bit of millinery which would surely have created a stir on the boulevards of Paris before the outbreak of the First World War: a "crown of feathers" with three sweeping peacock feathers. Modern as is the headdress, the loincloth and codpiece seem quite alien. The prince (for so Evans identified him, we may wonder why) is walking through a field of chaste lilies, among which butterflies flutter.

Such a portrayal of youthful manliness, charmingly delineated and beautifully colored, was bound to make a strong impression at the turn of the century—far more than the few original fragments covered with dust in a glass case would have. And now we see what drew disciples and admirers to Evans and why his

FIG. 26 The "Lily Prince" or Priest-King, Knossos.

reconstructions exercised such sway. Visitors to Knossos felt that they were really entering an ancient world; at the same time they could feel at home amidst the handsome decor and identify with the idealized figures of the Minoan past. Inadvertently Evans had supplied his contemporaries with a congenial realm of fantasy into which they could escape from the realities and evils of the present, a utopia situated in a faraway age. In evoking the "wholesome world" of the Minoans, and bringing it to life in a kind of archaeological Disneyland of reinforced concrete, Evans released a variety of emotions in his adherents. So powerful were these emotions, and so important was the legendary realm of Knossos, that no one wanted to consider the raw data on which Evans's vision had been based.

There can be no question of denying Arthur Evans's great achievement as a discoverer, and he was accorded ample recognition during his life and after. But however much we respect a great master we cannot cling to his theories once serious doubts have been cast on their validity. Scientific method and responsibility require the constant testing of the foundations on which a hypothesis has been built. Inevitably oversights and errors will be discovered and corrected. Such correction is not nit-picking but basic work essential to the furtherance of scientific knowledge. Nor does this in any way impugn the dedication and the labors of the great men of the past. New knowledge—and this is true for all the branches of science—is possible only when thought is liberated from the grip of traditional tenets. "He thanks his teacher ill who always remains only his pupil."

We have already mentioned that Minos Kalokairinos and Heinrich Schliemann had been interested in Knossos before Evans, and that French archaeologists had meant to buy the site for extensive excavation when Arthur Evans forestalled them. In fact French excavation of the Palace of Mallia and the Italian work at Phaistos began only a little later. In neither place did the archaeologists attempt any such extensive reconstruction in concrete and embellishment in oil paint as were done at Knossos. Consequently, pictures of Minoan excavation sites almost always show Knossos. Knossos offers such fascinating and photogenic material that the modest foundation walls of the other palaces shrink to nothingness in comparison. Neither Mallia nor Phaistos stir the soul. And there again is the reason why the enthusiasts are concerned only with Knossos, why Evans alone has a devoted band of followers.

The richly illustrated volumes of *The Palace of Minos* with their gilt edges (London 1921–1935), generously printed and generously distributed, made Evans a celebrity. Who, on the other hand, knew the names of the excavators of Mallia: E. Chapouthie, P. Demargne, H. Gallet de Santerre, J. Deshayes, A. Dessenne, H. and M. van Effenterre; or of Phaistos: L. Pernier, L. Banti and D. Levi? Through no less intensive work than Evans they all contributed to increasing our knowledge of the Minoans, but their quiet, responsible spadework and restoration work conducted over the decades was quite aloof from the publicity surrounding Evans. They carefully avoided letting restoration effects not supported by firm evidence stir emotions that could interfere with scientific observation. For that reason there is no school of enthusiastic followers of Pernier or Demargue.

In addition to the elements of art nouveau, the philosophical slant of *The Decline of the West* and the appurtenances of modern hygiene, Arthur Evans carried over from his own present to the Minoan past of the Late Bronze Age the particular structure of privilege characteristic of his native land. Thus King Minos and his spouse live in the big palace. Only a few steps separate it from the Little Palace, the residence of the crown prince. In neat hierarchic arrangement there follow the mansions of the other princes down to the country estates of the nobility. Thus even the social order of the Victorian era could be found anticipated and corroborated in Knossos.

But now let us hear from a few of the skeptics.

C. W. Ceram writes:

> The snake goddess with the large, expressive eyes, rich garment, and exposed breasts, has been, perhaps even more than the "Prince in the field of Lilies" [also known as the Priest-King and the young prince] a key figure in our conception of ancient Crete—as evoked by Evans. . . . It is amazing that a very few specimens of this kind have been able to form our whole concept of the culture. This picture, in particular, was very widely published, especially in histories of costume, where it was used to represent women's fashions in Crete. . . . Of the thing the painted figurine holds in its right hand, only the upper part existed; it might have been anything other than a snake. The small fragment found apart from the figurine might be anything other than a seated lion worn as a hat ornament. The entire face, the two fore-arms, and the greater part of the body, are hypothetical. . . . The worn round seal . . . with the two dancing princesses, formed one of the few "proofs" of the style of exposed breasts. But are these princesses? Perhaps they are temple prostitutes. To attempt to deduce a Cretan fashion from these proofs is more than daring.

Ceram then quotes Ernst Buschor (*Handbuch der Archäologie*, 1939): "The falsification of monuments by deceptive restoration or reconstruction verges on the deliberate production of fake monuments, on forgery."

In a considerably milder vein Professor R. Hachmann has expressed his own severe strictures in a letter:

At present I see all too many contradictions between Evans's own data on different occasions, and in addition contradictions between his evaluation of the data and the documentation of his associates. Since this documentation has not been published, it is not possible to examine the whole situation.

"Contradiction" is the right word. Evans left the deposits of tablets in a state of chaos. His excavation reports likewise were not sifted and objectively put into order. He did not work up and work out his finds in any systematic way. He arrived at his picture of the Minoan world largely on the basis of intuition, rather than scientific data.

Spengler, who should have seized upon Evans's idea of the downfall of Minoan civilization since it so well agreed with his own theories, accepted Evans's version with great reserve. He saw inconsistencies and contradictions in Evans's picture of the Minoans; he sensed echoes of the religious customs of other contemporary cultures and ancient views of the hereafter. He was struck by the lack of a defensive wall around the so-called palaces. Evans's interpretation of the images of bulls seemed to him dubious. He considered the Minoan "royal throne" more likely to have been the seat for a religious image or a priest's mummy.

Skepticism concerning Evans's theory of the labyrinth as the residence of enlightened monarchs was also expressed by Karl Kerenyi. In his *Mythologie der Griechen* ("Mythology of the Greeks") he speaks of Theseus:

> An ancient vase painting shows him in the initial position of his duel with the bull-headed creature, who here bears the name Taurominion. With one hand each clutches the enemy; in his other hand the hero holds a sword, the half-animal creature a stone. It is also said that Theseus had no weapon in his possession, but strangled his opponent with his bare hands in the course of a boxing and wrestling match. However, he is often depicted carrying a club or a stick. Thus he is shown victorious at the gate of the *underworld* building, unless he is dragging the dead bull-man after him.*

Kerenyi is reminding us of the ancient Greek tradition: the labyrinth's reputation was not as a palace open to all who came,

* *Mythologie der Griechen* (2 vols. Zürich, 1958).

home of a wise sovereign who fostered sports and the arts, but as a sinister place belonging entirely to the underworld.

As a sensitive literary man and thoughtful admirer of the Cretan scene, Thomas Münster in his account of travels in Crete (*Kreta hat andere Sterne*), admits he is puzzled:

> What about the palace's access to light, air and sun? Where, for example, are the big windows without which we can scarcely imagine elegant living? When you look closer you see, to be sure, that the royal palace has open loggias, colonnaded halls, roofed-over courts, but that there are scarcely any windows. A good many rooms are so completely boxed in within the complex structure that they do not even border on an outside wall. There is something very odd about the idea of constructing a luxurious building in whose interior people would necessarily feel as if they were inside a cave. Yet they had the means to build in totally modern windows, perhaps even glazed windows.[*]

He then refers to the light shafts and to the "lovely quality" of the colored light that would have been reflected from the painted walls, also to the possible presence of blinds for keeping out excessive sun.

Münster pays tribute to the livability of the palace and the graciousness of its occupants. He remarks that the diagram of the passages and magazines is actually quite logical, once we see it laid out before us, so that Ariadne's thread would hardly be necessary. "In a state of devastation the place must have looked like a tangle of artificial caves in which nobody could find his way about . . . and the impression of mystery, vastness and confusion must have been complete." Some quality of strangeness seems to have clung to the place long afterward. "No materials were carried away from Knossos to be used for peasant villages. . . . The place was avoided with superstitious fear." "What exactly happened, why Knossos was avoided like the site of a gallows or a witches' dancing floor, remains to be clarified."

Once again we are faced with the conundrum of why a structure so much of this world, as is the Palace of Knossos in Arthur Evans's reconstruction, should be represented in myth as "under-

---

[*] Kreta hat andere Sterne (Munich, 1960).

worldly" and should have been shunned as a place of settlement by the later inhabitants of the island. So strong has this dread been among the people of the island down to the present century that Evans, leaving behind an ordinarily courageous man to act as night watchman of the excavation, found the man distraught the next morning. He had had troubled dreams, the watchman declared, and had wakened hearing—as Evans wrote in his diary —"lowing and neighing. Something about, but of ghostly kind. . . ."

8

On Pourers of Bathwater and Nine-Footed Tables

◎

Both those who embraced and those who resisted Evans's interpretations hoped that all the questions and doubts would be clarified once the many thousands of clay tablets found in the course of the years in Knossos and elsewhere were deciphered. It does not appear, however, that Evans himself regarded this task as of crucial importance, for otherwise he would surely have seen to the expeditious ordering and publication of the clay tablet finds.

Only a dozen years after Evans's death a sensational report reached professionals and the lay public alike: Linear B, the latest of the Minoan scripts and the one of which there were the most examples, had been deciphered by a young man who was not himself a trained archaeologist but an architect, Michael Ventris, with the collaboration of a philologist, John Chadwick. The result of the decipherment was even more sensational: the Linear B texts had not been written in an alien, unknown language but in Greek, the very same language that is still spoken on Crete. It was, to be sure, an archaic Greek and difficult to understand, but it was incontestably the language of Homer.

How revolutionary this fact was in 1953, the year of the decipherment, can be seen from the international questionnaire Ventris had sent out only three years earlier to all specialists concerned with the subject of Linear B. Of the ten foremost scholars

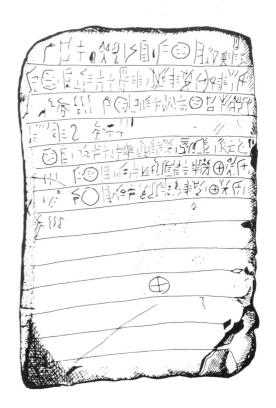

FIG. 27   Linear B. Tablet
Py An 607 (*pate matede*).
Female barley reapers,
female cloth workers
or female prison wardresses?

then working on a decipherment of the Cretan texts, or at least concerned with the problems involved, not one had hit on the idea that the language spoken in the Palace of King Minos might have been Greek.

Present-day Crete belongs without question to the Greek cultural sphere. The island contributed a rather significant share to the ancient Greek pantheon, has been amalgamated politically with Greece since 1912, and the people, despite centuries of Venetian and Turkish occupation, still speak Greek. What, then, was so surprising about Ventris's observation that Greek had been spoken in Crete at the time of the Palace of Knossos? Anyone unprejudiced by Evans's interpretations might almost have taken this for granted. But professional archaeologists were so captivated by Evans's theories that they regarded the obvious as impossible. Evans, who had wanted above all to decipher the clay tablets he had found, himself was a victim of his preconceptions.

The Minoans had built a vast complex embracing anywhere from twelve hundred to fourteen hundred rooms, with magazines, clay tablet archives, water pipes and drainage systems. With such features as these, the complex could only have served as a dwelling. Given the scale, it could not have been the home of an ordinary Cretan. Consequently it must have been the residence of great King Minos. The objects that looked like bathtubs and drainage shafts therefore must be construed as bathroom fixtures and flush toilets. Hence the Minoans had a civilization unique for the period. For such amenities were absent even in the great period of the Greek classical age. It followed that Minoan civilization must have been destroyed without leaving traces upon its immediate posterity. The art, modes of living, dress and architecture likewise had no parallels in the world of the period. Therefore the destruction must have been sudden and complete. The Cretan palaces were not enclosed within walls and bastions. Therefore the Minoans lived at peace on their fortunate island, devoting themselves to their art and culture, protected by the thalassocracy of their navy, just like Merry England at the time of Shakespeare, "this precious stone set in the silver sea." But Minoan Crete had been destroyed. Consequently foreign powers must have conquered the island and subjugated its inhabitants, as happened so often later in history. These barbarian conquerors could hardly have been any other than the Achaean or Dorian Greeks. Therefore the Minoans themselves were not Greeks. That was also evident from the fact that the Minoans pictured themselves as black-haired and dark-skinned, whereas the Greeks had been light-skinned and many of them fair-haired.

Therefore a harsh struggle between Minoans and Greeks had ensued, a struggle for possession of the prosperous island. The overcivilized Minoans, no match for the rugged invaders, eventually went under. Those who did not die in the fighting were forced to retreat into the mountains where, according to Homer, they were able to hold out a while longer as the "true Cretans," the Eteocretans. There they lived speaking their own language and writing in their own script—both obviously incomprehensible to the Greeks—until they merged into the Cretan melting pot of peoples and races.

They themselves were partly to blame for their downfall in spite of their legendary sea power. They succumbed to the assault of young, fresh "nordic" races who were out to wrest for themselves the "living space" they deserved. The Minoans had been too relaxed, too peaceable, too light-hearted to survive in the grim struggle. They had also been victims of natural forces, having been so weakened by earthquakes, volcanic eruptions, rains of ashes, seismic waves and other disasters that they were incapable of offering effective resistance to the invaders. To Evans and his contemporaries they were one more example of the certain end that awaited every overrefined high civilization.

Even before the Palace of Knossos fell into ruins the Greeks had obviously been at home there. They seem to have arrived peaceably, for there is no separation between the pre-Greek and the later phase of palace building under Greek influence. The language of the Linear B clay tablets is Greek. Does this mean that the Greeks had been in Knossos from the beginning? In that case the destruction of the palace could not be ascribed to them. But . . .

Perhaps Michael Ventris and John Chadwick were wrong in asserting that the Linear B tablets are written in archaic Greek. That would save the older view. And in fact the validity of Ventris's decipherment of Linear B is still contested by a few scholars. We shall have occasion to discuss this later.

Clay tablets with Linear B inscriptions were found not only in Knossos. They also turned up in the Peloponnesus. As early as 1939 some had been found in Pylos (a total of 534 tablets, published by Emmett L. Bennett, Jr., in 1951) and in Mycenae (33 tablets found by Alan Wace). Whatever the content of these tablets and whatever the language, the clay tablets of Knossos, Pylos and Mycenae were so alike in script and in the general arrangement of that script that it was clear the same language and script had been in use on Crete and in the Peloponnesus before Knossos, Pylos and Mycenae were destroyed.

As Knossos had been the seat of King Minos, Pylos, according to legend and Homer, had been the residence of aged Nestor, the oldest of the Achaean leaders at the siege of Troy and the confidant and adviser of Agamemnon, the leader of the Greek host and King of Mycenae. If, therefore, the Knossan Linear B tablets had not been written in archaic Greek, those of Pylos and

Mycenae could not very well be in Greek either. That meant casting doubt on the entire Achaean tradition as depicted by Homer. If Pylos, Mycenae and Tiryns (where frescos of the Cretan type were found) were not Achaean, but remnants of a submerged pre-Greek settlement, a "Cretan-Mycenaean" civilization that was overwhelmed by the Achaeans, then there were practically no archaeological finds from the epoch of Homer's heroes.

Fortunately, the translations by Michael Ventris and his successors have proved good enough to confirm Ventris's premise: that Linear B, whether from Pylos, Mycenae or Knossos, is archaic Greek. At the time those tablets were inscribed, therefore, the lords of Knossos felt like Achaeans and were using the same language as their cousins on the mainland. At least in this era the people who represented Minoan civilization were Greeks!

If that is so, there must be a flaw in the seemingly integral and logical chain of reasoning that had led to Evans's conclusions. But where was the broken link? That is the controversial question which has remained unsettled to this day. And as always when fundamental questions are at issue, two groups have formed, each totally committed to its partisan views.

On the one hand the followers of the Evans theory—let us call them the traditionalists—have tried to protect the discoverer's work against all efforts to change or reinterpret it. They argue: If the Linear B tablets actually were written in Greek, then the Achaean conquerors must have subjugated the native Minoan population at precisely the time the tablets were written, and settled down comfortably as the new lords of the palace. Very likely, then, the tablets dated from the late phase of the building of the labyrinth. And artistically speaking, this late phase shows distinct signs of decadence. But whether the decipherment of Linear B can be regarded as valid enough to draw such far-reaching conclusions from it remains to be proved. For as yet there are too many inconsistencies in the attempts at translation.

On the other hand the adherents of Ventris's Linear B decipherment have not had an easy position to maintain. In spite of splendid initial successes new problems repeatedly crop up. All sorts of special assumptions have to be made in order to cope with these strange texts. There are baffling forms and turns of phrase; there is mention of female barley reapers or barley cooks, of headband makers or bath assistants, of pourers of bath water, or chair-makers, room sweepers, fire kindlers and musicians; there are four-legged animals and nine-footed tables. Leonard R. Palmer, who himself participated actively in this translation work, speaks intriguingly of "ghost-forms" and "ghost-occupations."

Almost more baffling is the problem of what really happened to Minoan civilization if the Greeks, in combination with the forces of nature, did not destroy it. It seemed beyond doubt, after Arthur Evans's discoveries in Knossos, that the level of civilization of the post-Mycenaean Greeks was markedly lower than that of the Minoans. Since the Greeks of the so-called Geometric Period display no comparable high civilization, they cannot very well have had one previously, during the Minoan Age. This cultural deterioration seemed strikingly borne out by the modern-looking architecture and art of the Minoans, whereas during the following centuries of the early Greeks virtually the only cultural product known is the series of funeral urns with geometric patterns. There are no palaces with thousands of rooms, no delightful frescos, no drainage systems and flush toilets.

There seemed no escape from the conclusion that Minoan civilization had undergone final destruction and that the Minoan people—pre-Greek and of unknown race—had been annihilated by geological disturbances and the power of Greek arms. Thus the age of Minoan civilization had been followed by the bleak Greek Dark Ages, a relapse to a lower cultural stage during the Late Bronze and Early Iron ages.

A few selected quotations will suggest the bitterness with which the scholarly dispute has been waged. Thus Werner Ekschmitt examines the translation of clay tablet Kn Ch 896—a tablet found at Knossos and translated by Chadwick as follows: "Tazaros (has) a pair of young draft oxen, (namely) Aiwolos and Kelainos." Ekschmitt concludes:

> That something of this sort is offered as scholarship by professors with international reputations, with the aid of the Oxford, Cambridge and University of California Presses, is a curiosity that is destined ultimately to become an embarrass-

ment to our enlightened century. The Ventrisians have ridiculed Sundwall because he decided that one of the commonest ideograms in Linear A represented poppyseed, and suddenly found himself confronted with enormous quantities [of poppyseeds in the lists of the texts]. They themselves with their "Foal FOAL"—"Cheese CHEESE" [that is, with simultaneous reproduction of the textual content in syllabic and ideogrammatic scripts] with their four-legged animals and their nine-foot tables, with their 51 kilograms of mobilization bronze and their 840 kilograms of unguent essense [a reference to controversial texts], are in exactly the same situation. Only the familiar displacement of mote and beam prevents them from seeing that.[*]

What has engendered such a sharply polemical tone?

In 1936, on the fiftieth anniversary of the foundation of the British School of Archaeology at Athens, the elder statesman of this association, Sir Arthur Evans, gave a much discussed lecture. Once again he spoke on his favorite subject, the Palace of Knossos. He spoke of its beauties and of the clay tablets found there, whose texts had not yet been deciphered. Among the listeners to the portentous words of the eighty-five-year-old master of British archaeology was a gifted fourteen year old boy, the son of a well-to-do family. The boy was fascinated by the exotic world of the Minoans presented to him. Evans had a faculty for stirring the enthusiasm of his listeners. After all, he was discussing his life's work. Then and there the boy became cognizant of the unique task that awaited him. He decided that he would decipher the unknown texts, would unravel the secrets now lost in the darkness of the past.

Michael Ventris did not become an archaeologist, but an architect. Nor was his employment incidental; he threw himself ardently into this profession and won recognition. But Minoan script remained his hobby. He did not forget the resolve he had taken in his boyhood. Whenever his occupation left him a free hour he devoted it to the study of Minoan texts. Only four years after Sir Arthur's memorable lecture, in fact, he published an independent scientific paper in which he tried to

---

[*] *Die Kontroverse um Linear B* (Munich, 1969).

demonstrate that the Minoan language was related to the likewise uninterpreted Etruscan language.[*]

Ten years later the work of decipherment had not yet made much progress. The war and the demands of his profession had held up Ventris. At this point he sent out a questionnaire to determine the status of international research on Linear B. Ten well-known scholars replied, giving their opinions on the problem of the Minoan language and script. Ventris translated their answers into English, added detailed comments of his own, and sent this collection of "state-of-the-art" comments back to the respondents as a working paper which has since become known as the "Mid-Century Report." For the time being the project seemed to have reached an impasse. Then suddenly things began to happen.

In 1950 Emmett L. Bennett succeeded in demonstrating that Linear A and Linear B tablets employed different number systems, which also seemed to suggest that they were written in different languages.[†] The very next year the same scholar published 534 Linear B tablets that had been found in Pylos twelve years before. The amount of material at hand for decipherment multiplied manyfold. In 1952 Sir John Myres published the Linear B documents accumulated between 1900 and 1905 by Evans and left unpublished after his death in 1941. Moreover, the excavations at Pylos were resumed; and again in 1952 Sir Alan Wace turned up the first thirty-three Linear B tablets to be found at Mycenae. There was at last enough material available to encourage a serious effort at decipherment.

Ventris went at the task with modern methods and with a frankness unusual in scholars. He issued a series of twenty Work Notes, mimeographed reports to keep interested specialists informed on how his current investigations were going. The twentieth of these Work Notes, dated June 2, 1952, announced his surprising conclusion that the Minoan language had been an ancient Greek dialect. A month later the BBC broadcast a

[*] "Introducing the Minoan Language," *American Journal of Archaeology*, 1940, pp. 494–520.
[†] Fractional Quantities in Minoan Bookkeeping." *American Journal of Archaeology*, 1950, pp. 204–222.

talk by Ventris on the subject. His theory aroused the interest of the Cambridge philologist John Chadwick, who henceforth became his knowledgable collaborator. In 1953 Ventris published his "Evidence for Greek Dialect in the Mycenaean Archives" in the *Journal of Hellenic Studies*. But before the great follow-up by Ventris and Chadwick was published (*Documents in Mycenaean Greek*), Ventris, only thirty-four, died in an automobile accident.

Ventris's Work Notes indicate that he tried different methods in the course of his decipherment. One attempt was based on the already know Cypriot syllabary which, however, came into use centuries after the Minoan clay tablets. A second effort was more or less on a trial-and-error basis; Ventris tried to find correspondences for words or word groups. He proceeded on the assumption that clay tablets from the Palace of Knossos were bound to contain geographical names from the vicinity. For example, in the passage from Homer's nineteenth book of *The Odyssey*, previously quoted, such place names as Cape Malea (Mallia) Amnissos and the cave of Eileithyia are mentioned in conjunction with the coast of Crete. The port of Amnissos, near Knossos, was the kind of name that might be expected to appear on the clay tablets. Kristopoulos, who had devoted much study to Minoan texts, believed he had already identified the most common initial sign, the double axe, as the symbol for the letter A. With the aid of the Cypriot syllabary it proved possible to identify the N series (na, ne, ni, no, nu) among the ninety different signs. Given these two known signs, the next step was to search until a word was found in which these two were separated by another sign (mi) and followed by a fourth (so). After the decipherment of Amnissos (Minoan: A-mi-ni-so) new syllables were available which could be applied to the name Knossos itself (-no-so). Other names that played an important part in the decipherment of Linear B were the spice coriander and the tripod, the latter article frequently mentioned in *The Iliad* and clearly recognizable on the clay tablets by the ideogram, a stylized tripod, standing next to the signs for ti-ri-po-de.

Along with this approach Ventris employed the cryptographic techniques used for the decipherment of codes during the Second World War, among them the statistical method and the method of combination. The statistical method compares the frequency of signs with the frequency of sounds in the language, equating sounds of high frequency with signs of high frequency. This is fine for a known language, but how can it be applied where the language is not known? The Tubingen philologist Ernst Sittig first tried applying this method to the Minoan writings. He saw possibilities of comparison with the language of the original inhabitants of Cyprus, the Eteocypriots—whose script, however, had likewise not yet been deciphered. A prerequisite for statistical work is a given underlying language, for the frequencies of sounds differ from language to language. Consequently, these attempts could not have led anywhere without Ventris's hypothesis that the language of the Cretan Linear B script was ancient Greek. None of the scholars had even considered this possibility.

The combinational method analyzes the unknown texts for the occurrence of substantives with distinct endings which correspond to different cases, and of other recurrent verbal forms, stems and prefixes. The American scholar Alice Kober had used this method to make important contributions to the decipherment of Linear B before her death at the age of only forty-three —the same year in which she had curtly replied to Ventris's questionnaire that the whole thing was a sheer waste of time. Yet Ventris persisted along this path, and with the far larger amount of published material now available to him he was able to perfect his "grid," a tabular key to the signs of Linear B.

A simple example will clarify for us the principal difficulty in the translation of the texts. The tablet in question is one from Pylos, Py Ta 711. It forms the beginning of a series of thirteen tablets containing a lengthy list of utensils and furnishings. The first line of the tablet deals with an inspection, in the course of which the objects subsequently named were declared to be present. Someone named Pukequiri carried out the inspection. The point at issue is the reason for this inspection, which is mentioned in the second part of the first line.

Here are three different readings for the document. According to Ventris and Chadwick, it reads: "Thus Pukequiri made inspection on the occasion when the king appointed Sigewas to be a *damo-koros* [official]."

According to Doria, *Damokoros* is a proper name: "Thus Pukequiri made inspection when the king appointed Damoclos *?kewa* [name of an unknown occupation]."

Palmer gives the translation a wholly new meaning by interpreting the Greek verb for "set, place, lay" not in the sense of "appoint" but in the sense of "lay away" or "bury": "What Pu-ke-quiri saw when the Wanat [King] buried 85-*ke-wa* the *Da-ma-ko-ro*."

In the first two cases we are required to imagine an administrative act upon the installation of a high official of the court. Before the new man assumes office an inspection must determine that his predecessor has not embezzled any of the inventory. Palmer's translation, on the other hand, minor though the change in wording is, implies that the entire inventory consists of grave goods. When we read the following list of jars decorated with goddesses, bulls' heads, shell patterns, charioteers, spiral patterns, portraits of women and battle scenes, we are reminded of Schliemann's shaft grave finds at Mycenae. As part of an official's belongings such objects would seem very strange, especially when their listing extends over thirteen tablets and they seem quite unfit for practical purposes. Among the treasures of the Greek National Museum in Athens, however, they would look quite in place among the gold and silver utensils from Mycenae.

What difficulty a scholar who did not know our language, but had to translate it word for word, might well have with such newspaper phrases as "services held for . . ." or references to "the departed." The reports might easily be taken as ceremonies for the installation of a priest or regret at the departure of a relative on a long journey. In fact, everyday language in such cases makes a point of not using the straightforward "he is dead." Circumlocutions are deliberately employed, euphemisms that are intended to cloak the harsh fact in ambiguity and somehow make it more bearable. The briefer the text, the more ambiguous it will seem unless the circumstances and the context are at least approximately known. Since the Linear B tablets contain mostly lists of contributions it seemed obvious to interpret them as tax rolls or something similar. The names of rulers or other data from which we might derive historical information so far appear to be extraordinarily scanty in these tablets. Consequently, the decipherment of Linear B, great though the achievement of all the participating linguists has been, has not been so informative, nor perhaps so convincing, as many people expected it to be. But that is no reason to dismiss the whole of the painstaking translation work as unsatisfactory, or for calling the decipherment unsuccessful. Moreover, in the twenty years since Ventris and Chadwick published their first translations no alternative decipherment has been offered on the basis of any other language.

It is regrettable that the present controversy between the traditionalists and the Ventrisians at times threatens to degenerate into an unscientific bicker. Differences of opinion in science ought not to lead to personal antagonisms, but should instead promote a closer study of the questions. That alone makes such disputes meaningful and useful.

9

The Stumbling Block

❁

The fronts continued to harden. Traditionalists and Ventrislans defined their contradictory opinions so forcefully that there seemed no room for compromise. Again and again the arguments and counterarguments were presented. Some fresh light was required, and it had to come from a quarter that as far as possible was unbiased—not from the one camp or the other, but from outside. New observations in the field were sorely needed.

It seemed at first that the Linear B decipherment was a dispute among specialists and one which could be settled only by the archaeologists themselves. The separation of academic specialties has already gone so far that interdisciplinary studies in many countries are not encouraged, to say the least, and often held in abhorrence by the representatives of the traditional subjects. Every professional group tries to cultivate its own carefully fenced-in research area and to protect that area from invasion by outsiders. We may best imagine the field of learning as a neatly divided allotment garden parceled out in equal sections. In the center of every parcel there rises a tallish plant of the accepted doctrines in the specialty, surrounded by straight rows of carefully tested smaller plants whose effect is of a rather boring and sterile monoculture. It has long been known that powerful new impulses can rarely be expected to arise within the centers of each discipline. Specialists hesitate to venture out on the margins of their fields, where the ground tends to be slippery and they can easily muddy their scientific reputations.

But is it precisely in those regions, near the "fences" between the parcels, where the footing is uncertain, that the young shoots of new knowledge flourish. To investigate them one must have the courage to oppose prevailing doctrine, to leave the well-ordered beds and seek new ways into pathless regions. These offer a unique opportunity. In the wild strips interspersed among the disciplines, where stimuli from various professional fields meet, where, as it were, the superphosphate put on by one gardening neighbor mixes with the peat moss contributed by another, there is still hope of discovering new and hitherto unknown species. Almost always the seedlings of new insights spring up in the uncultivated interfaces between neighboring sciences.

One such interface where there has been no significant contact has long existed between the two sciences engaged in research in and on the ground, archaeology and geology, both strictly separated in the traditional university system, especially in Germany. The course of study for the would-be archaeologist familiarizes him with the humanities, with ancient languages, ancient history and art. He acquires practical experience in excavation on the site, either by working under his teacher or in one of the archaeological institutes. Neither during his university years nor later is he likely to see the inside of an institute of geology, or to take even a short course in petrology. The aspiring geologist, on the other hand, is happy not to have to learn the classical languages. And for him human history dwindles to the duration of a second against the background of millions of years of the earth's history. The practical work of discovering new sources of raw materials or collaborating with engineers beckons him. Usually he has no time for archaeological hobbies.

The modes of thinking and working could not be more different in these two disciplines. Faced with a sphinx of greenish-black stone, the archaeologist will be interested in the aesthetic form and in the hieroglyphic inscription on the base, chest and sides which identify the work of art, as, say, a product of the period of Pharaoh Amenemhet III of the Twelfth Dynasty of the Middle Kingdom, 1839–1791 B.C. The history of the discovery and unearthing of the find will also concern him, insofar as these circumstances allow him to draw conclusions about the thinking and the life-style of the period. The geologist, of course, will not be entirely immune to the fascination of the figure with its compact shape and impressive bearing. But the ancient Egyptians' concepts of the hereafter, their social order and their religious rites, lie outside his professional sphere of interest. He observes that the block is one of dense amphibolite, a metamorphic rock made up mainly of hornblende and distinctly difficult to work. He will want to know how the masons of the period obtained the block and worked it, how it could have been transported to its site, and how it was possible with Bronze Age or perhaps even Stone Age tools to create the tracery of the lion's mane or the carefully polished surface of the torso.

Each of those modes of observation has its rationale. I am not describing them here in order to widen gulfs, but on the contrary to lay a basis for mutual understanding. For adjacent sciences can only profit from each other if they are able to summon up understanding of differing viewpoints and a readiness to receive new suggestions from the outside.

My first visit to Crete was not prompted by any desire to poach on the archaeologists' preserve. It is true that in the course of much traveling as a geologist to various parts of the Mediterranean basin I had repeatedly been attracted to archaeological excavation sites, all the more so since they were often in the immediate vicinity of geologically interesting items. In several cases, moreover, there was a direct connection between archaeological sites and geologic events. But for the eruption of Vesuvius in A.D. 79 there would be no Roman Pompei or Herculaneum whose relics make such an impression on countless visitors at the sites or in the National Archaeological Museum in Naples. For the geologist these buried cities provide a first-class object lesson from which he can reconstruct the course of events during such a disastrous volcanic eruption.

It had long been assumed that the Minoan civilization of ancient Crete had been destroyed by geological catastrophes. Arthur Evans himself experienced several severe earthquakes during his long residence on the island, and had feared for the survival of his reconstructions. Would Knossos, painfully won from the ground and resurrected, once again fall victim to seismic shocks? It seemed quite logical to assume that the end of the Minoan world had been brought about by such a severe earthquake, that the palaces had collapsed to the ground under the force of the shocks, burying beneath the ruins finely-wrought objects of art and remarkable achievements of civilization.

Shortly before the Second World War Spyridon Marinatos, the Greek historian and archaeologist, associated the destruction of the Cretan palaces with the volcanic eruptions on the Aegean island of Santorin or Thera (see p. 69). The examples of Pompeii and Herculaneum showed what devastating effects could be produced by volcanic forces. And, in fact, after the war, when excavations began on Santorin, the remains of Minoan buildings were found buried under masses of volcanic ejecta. Akrotheri had ceramic vessels such as we are familiar with from Knossos: beaked jars with barley-ear decoration, fragments of Minoan frescos on which dark-haired, russet-skinned male figures bowed before palms. The magazine and cult rooms unearthed by Marinatos in the course of many years of work undoubtedly belong to the Minoan cultural sphere. The magazines of pithoi within squares of fieldstone walls might have come from any of the great Cretan palaces; so also might the rooms identified as shrines. Radioactive carbon-14 dating indicates that Akrotheri was destroyed in the early fifteenth century B.C. by the eruption of the nearby volcano and was not rebuilt. Volcanic ash from this eruption could be traced, by means of probes of the sea bottom, up to 800 kilometers to the southeast. But the island of Crete, the center of Minoan culture, lies only a little more than 100 kilometers from Santorin.

These findings provided a new and highly plausible basis for Evans's theory about the catastrophic downfall of the Minoans. An eruption like that of Krakatoa, but six or seven times more powerful, would presumably have wiped out the flourishing Minoan civilization at one blow. Those Minoan dwellings that were not directly shattered by the force of the explosions, the earthquakes and the masses of volcanic material falling from the sky would have been annihilated by equally effective remoter effects: the rains of ashes and the seismic waves. Amnissos, the port of Knossos, and Mallia, some 35 kilometers east of Knossos, would have been vulnerable to tidal waves surging in from the north. Above all, the Minoan fleet was helplessly exposed to the elements—the fleet on which the wealth and sea power of the Minoans depended.

Like southern Italy with its famous archaeological excavation sites, the Aegean and the arc of islands extending to Crete lies in one of the belts of recent uplift mountains in which the geological forces of the earth's interior have remained active to this day. There are clear indications that mountain formation, with all its concomitants, is still in process in the southern part of Europe. Here we can hope to be the direct witnesses of events that took place in northern Europe long before the "present," geologically speaking.

If on Crete and the islands of the Aegean there are archaeologically datable sites that were destroyed by geological events of this sort it should be extremely interesting to a geologist to track down the traces of such events. Here archaeology touches upon actuotectonics—that branch of geology that deals with mountain processes in the present and in historical times. When we study archaeological sites from that point of view, we are interested not so much in questions of architecture and art as in practical considerations of the durability and utility of the materials employed. A fire inspector trying to determine the cause of arson cares less about the style and period of an object rescued from the fire than about what material it is made of and what clues it provides.

Every traveler to Crete is bound to take a general interest in the ruins of one of mankind's early civilizations. My own interest, at the time I first visited the excavation sites, centered chiefly on a search for the traces of geological influences upon the past. I wondered what material the Minoans had used to build their works, how these were constructed and how enduring the building material had proved to be. And it was in this respect that my very first visit to the Knossos area brought a surprise. The guidebook had extolled the natural beauty of the alabaster slabs with which a great many rooms in the palace were finished. The point was made that the close-grained crystals of the whitish stone reflected the indirect light from the light wells like marble, bringing a subtle radiance to the shady rooms of the lower story.

Even the slabs of the floors, the thresholds and the steps of the stairways had been made of precious alabaster, proof of the lavishness of the palace's inhabitants. Indeed, does not the word "alabaster" connote a noble, valuable material?

But when I looked about me I saw that the floors, thresholds, steps of the stairways and orthostats that gleamed softly with the reflected glow of the bright sunlight—somewhat ameliorating the shade of the tall porticos and the twilight of dusky cellar rooms—these famous alabaster slabs were in fact nothing but *gypsum*. They were made from natural gypsum slabs and blocks, some of which had been obtained from quarries in Minoan times and employed in the building of the palace, others of which had been brought in in recent times by the restorers to replace destroyed portions.

At first sight natural gypsum cannot easily be distinguished from marble by the layman. Both stones have a similar crystalline appearance and, frequently, fine gray veinings. But marble is made up of calcite crystals, whereas the alabaster slabs of the Palace of Knossos consist of gypsum crystals. In spite of their deceptively similar appearance there is a significant difference. Marble is relatively hard and resistant to abrasion. Gypsum, on the other hand, is distinctly soft and has little resistance to scratching or rubbing. No special knowledge or equipment is needed to distinguish the two stones. A fingernail is sufficient. Gypsum can be scratched with the fingernail, marble cannot. That is the difference.

What could have prompted the Minoans to use such soft material in their most important royal palace? Were they really as wealthy and powerful as Evans and his followers assumed? For if so they surely could have obtained genuine marble. After all, it is known that they undertook sea voyages as far as Egypt, across a thousand kilometers of open sea. The Aegean marble island of Paros was practically at their doorstep, only 150 kilometers away and within the immediate sphere of Minoan influence. And even if not marble, there was plenty of white marblelike limestone on the island—in fact, plenty of it close to Amnissos, halfway between Knossos and Mallia.

But if the Minoans had used gypsum instead of marble or limestone because they were ignorant of the qualities of the material, that fact did not speak well for their technical abilities, which had been assumed to be highly developed because of their water lines, drains and sanitary facilities.

Here was a dilemma that the archaeologists, busy taking sides in the dispute between the traditionalists and the Ventrisians, had completely overlooked, although every beginner in geology found it staring him in the face wherever he looked at the excavation site. What could be the explanation for all those many gypsum slabs and orthostats that had been in place since Minoan times?

During his stay in Knossos Arthur Evans had noted from the rapidity with which the steps wore down that this alabaster was not very durable. In his concern he wrote to an American geologist of his acquaintance. The geologist pointed out that alabaster had been commonly used for sculpture and that certain types of alabaster were quite hard, especially those from Egypt. Evidently there were different hardnesses among alabasters, and if some of the slabs were of softer stone, what did that matter in a structure of such vast proportions as the palace of Knossos!

The trouble is that the "different types of alabaster" mentioned in older books on petrology do not belong in the same mineralogical category. So-called calcareous alabaster is a sinter limestone of crystalline calcite; it often builds up at the point of efflux of unusually hard spring water, taking the forms of crusts and sinter barriers. The stone referred to as alabaster in Egyptian archaeology, and used for sculptures, is evidently this calcareous alabaster—at least that was the case for all those I have had the opportunity to see in the original. But applying the term "alabaster" to crystalline sinter limestone is no longer customary or permissible in modern geological nomenclature. *In contemporary mineralogical terminology alabaster means a fine-grained, pure-white gypsum.* Any handbook or reference work will bear me out on this.

It is not difficult for the layman to convince himself, by fingernail tests, that all the alabaster used throughout the Knossos excavation site is not calcareous alabaster but soft gypsum. As might be expected, the steps of the staircases are already badly worn from the feet of hordes of tourists. But in parts of the palace that are not so heavily visited, and in the Little Palace,

there are many floor slabs, thresholds and steps that show remarkably little wear, even when it can be proved that they are
the original stone.

This observation permits only one conclusion: wherever such
scarcely worn gypsum slabs of the Minoan period are present
there cannot have been any significant amount of traffic. The
rooms in question were little used, or not used at all!

But perhaps, it might be argued, the Minoans covered the
floors of their dwellings with rugs, so that the soft stone underneath was protected. The stairs, too, could have been covered
with runners. But let us recall the great western magazines of
the Palace of Knossos, the first part of the palace to be excavated. Here, too, walls and floors are sheathed with gypsum
slabs which extend under the large pithoi. Even some of the
thresholds of the rooms are made of gypsum. Who would have
covered a cellar for storing olive oil, honey or barley (or whatever it was that may have been stored in those big jars) with
rugs just to keep the soft alabaster of the floor from being
scratched? And as a matter of fact, even in the domestic rooms
the use of rugs over alabaster slabs is not entirely logical. If the
alabaster was selected for its beauty, it would be illogical to
cover it with rugs so that it could no longer be seen. If rugs were
going to be used, the slabs could have been dispensed with and
some harder, less ornamental material used, such as limestone or
slate.

Of course it is possible that some slabs were replaced after
they became heavily abraded. But to suggest that considerable
parts of the palace must have been renewed just before the
final catastrophe seems rather farfetched. The far more likely explanation is that easily worked stone was deliberately chosen, in
spite of its softness, to create an impression of wealth and dignity
in a place where little traffic over the floors, thresholds and stairs
was expected. After all, the Minoans had had several centuries
to try out various materials and learn their characteristics. It
would be simply unhistorical to assume that they had insufficient
knowledge of their native stone although they were millennia
closer to the Stone Age than we are.

Gypsum has another quality that restricts its utility as a building material: it is not resistant to flowing water. The parts of the

excavation site exposed to rain already show, after at most seventy years of exposure, channels several centimeters deep in the direction of rainwater drainage. One can easily foresee that by the end of the century many of these blocks will be ruined unless they are quickly roofed over.

FIG. 28   Limestone gutters, Hagia Triada. The Minoans must have known that gypsum was soluble in water. When they wanted to make genuine gutters for drainage they made them of limestone.

In addition to these channels innumerable hairline cracks are forming, and these will widen in the course of time until the entire block falls apart. Originally all the parts of the palace where gypsum was used were roofed over and therefore not exposed to weathering. Wherever gypsum was used for the huge wall blocks in the western or northeastern facades, it must have been coated with a waterproof layer of stucco. If the northeast wall was once built of such material only to the height of the central court, it would later have dissolved once the protecting roof had collapsed; but while it stood, more than 6 meters in height, it must have presented an appearance no less imposing than the famous walls of Ilion.

Had there been any intention to enclose Knossos in walls? Were fortifications not yet completed when the place was destroyed? Testimony against this is the unprotected western entrance, which should have been the first to be protected by wall, moat or bastions since the terrain offered no natural protection on that side. Evidently, then, the walls were not primarily intended to fend off some external enemy who might attempt to conquer the palace by force of arms.

But another surprise awaits us: even the so-called bathrooms and "lustral basins" for ritual washings are faced with gypsum! But gypsum and running water are mutually exclusive. The function Evans ascribed to these rooms is at variance with the mineralogical facts. Those rooms cannot have been bathrooms; those objects cannot have been basins for water. The Minoans must have discovered in their very quarries that gypsum is not resistant to running water. That they used it here implies that the purpose of these rooms was different from what Evans imagined.

These observations astonished me on the very first day of my visit to the excavation. But on that day I was not sure whether I should be more astonished by the ancient Minoans' foolish use of inappropriate building material, or by the inadequate knowledge of materials on the part of archaeologists who fashioned elaborate hypotheses about the functions of palace rooms without considering the suitability of the building materials.

There is still a third quality of Minoan alabaster that requires mention. We have repeatedly heard of the disastrous fire that presumably reduced the palace to rubble and ashes so that it could never again be rebuilt. And traces indicative of fire have actually been found in many places in the ancient Cretan palaces. Soft clay tablets were hardened by fire, tiles and walls blacked, and wood charred. Apparently, in addition to the earthquake and the eruption of Santorin, in addition to the tidal wave and rain of ashes, a great fire had broken out in the palace (misfortunes seldom come singly). Earthquakes do start conflagrations, as the disasters in San Francisco in 1906 and in Tokyo in 1923 have shown.

But strangely enough, many of the gypsum slabs and blocks still show their original gray veining, which is the special beauty of this otherwise impractical building material. Now this veining consists of a fine mixture of bitumen, a natural organic substance, in narrow strata. This organic substance comes from the remains of animal and vegetable organisms that were embedded when the gypsum was deposited and that in the course of millions of years have undergone extensive chemical changes.

If gypsum containing its original bitumen content is heated, the bitumen escapes from the stone and burns. What remains is a pure white stone without the gray streaks of organic content. The discoloration begins at only 60° C. at which point fine cracks form in the stone. At the boiling point of water, 100° C. to 120° C., the process is finished. The previously gray-tinged natural gypsum stone has become snow-white. No gypsum can stand a higher temperature than 120° C. without losing its original bitumen.

Two of several samples of material taken from the Palace of Kato Zakro were covered by layers of gypsum *plaster* 7 to 8 millimeters in thickness, which was probably intended as a base for fresco painting; however, no traces of the painting were left. This gypsum plaster was free of bitumen; it had undoubtedly been burned, ground and, before working, diluted with some powdered brick in order to reduce shrinkage during the drying process and thus keep hairline cracks from forming. Obviously the Minoans were thoroughly familiar with the technique of manufacturing plaster out of gypsum; they knew that the burning process had to be stopped at the right moment so that with the addition of water the semihydrate would harden into gypsum again, whereas gypsum burned until it is "dead" (the anhydrite) is no longer able to incorporate water into its crystalline structure—or rather, can do so only very slowly, within "geological" spans of time, which of course the plasterer cannot wait for! The shrinkage and dilution of gypsum plaster was also known, as well as the speed of its setting time. Delicate air bubbles in the samples show that the workmen must have gone at their task very briskly in applying the plaster. Morsels of information on the technological knowledge of the Minoans may possibly be more important and illuminating (especially since they can be confirmed) than the highly imaginative vignettes of Minoan life with which the literature is replete.

The presence of gray bituminous gypsum, then, enables us to determine the maximum temperature attained at a given spot. Everywhere that the gypsum used in the Palace of Knossos still retains its original bitumen content—in other words, shows grayish veining—the temperatures during the fire in the palace could not have risen higher than 100° to 120° C.

Now we know that for an uncontrolled fire to break out the temperature must be greater than the kindling temperature of flammable objects. Fire specialists put the temperature for common flammable objects at 140° C. In serious fires, however, temperatures rise far above this minimum, reaching several hundred and even a thousand degrees centigrade. But given the nature of the gypsum in the Palace of Knossos, and the method used for preparing gypsum plaster, such temperatures must be excluded. The samples taken from central positions in the palace, and the specimens of gray-veined gypsums in their original positions, prove that the kindling temperature could not have been reached or surpassed.

This, to be sure, does not mean that all kinds of fire are excluded. "Burning" may very well have occurred at some places in the palace. But the temperatures then remained so low, or the fires so small, that these fires could never have escaped from human control. In other words, they were deliberately lit and maintained, either for illumination, warmth, burnt offerings or ritual purposes.

FIG. 29. Section of a sample of alabaster from the Palace of Knossos. The black spots and streaks consist of an organic substance (bitumen) which melts out of the stone when heated above 60°C. Consequently, this sample of Minoan alabaster cannot have been exposed to a higher temperature, since the bitumen content of the stone is still present. (Magnification app. 200 x.)

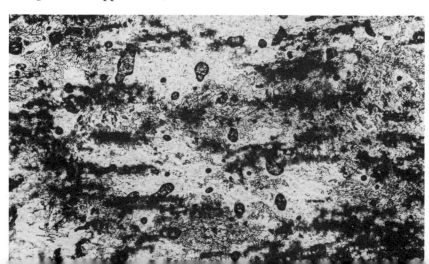

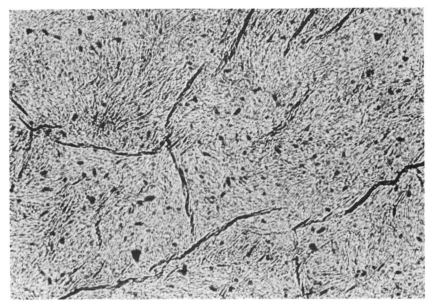

Fig. 30. Section of a sample of alabaster from the Palace of Knossos. The sample contained bitumen before being heated to 120° C. From 60°C. up, this bitumen escaped through the shrinkage cracks which formed in the stone due to the evaporation of the water content. (These cracks show up as black in the photograph.) The originally bituminous gray alabaster was thus transformed into pure white burnt gypsum (plaster). Wherever in Minoan buildings bituminous original stone is present, the stone could never have been heated to the kindling temperature of 140°C., which marks the beginning of uncontrolled fires.

Without being aware of it, consequently, and without intending anything of the sort, the ancient Minoans built into their structures mineralogical thermometers that permit us today to read off the maximum temperature reached in the vicinity of the stone. Again, no elaborate investigation or apparatus is needed; you have only to keep your eyes open. In doubtful cases it may be necessary to heat a small sample to observe whether there is discoloration. This method can be applied to all archaeological excavation sites where gypsum with primary bitumen content has been used as a building material. What this method does prevent, however, is the free play of imagination that theorizes about great conflagrations before the finds on the site have been examined and there is proof that temperatures of at least 120° C. have been surpassed.

BOOK TWO

The Living Dead

10

From Phaistos
to Mallia

✿

Visitors to the excavations, both scientists and the curious, have been most interested in the artistic achievements of the Minoans. And these were unquestionably of a high level. Arthur Evans came to archaeological digging by way of ethnology and the study of scripts. He cannot be blamed for having been insufficiently informed in the natural sciences. The great majority of his followers, too, did not come to archaeology by way of these sciences.

On the other hand I am a geologist who acquired some experience in the planning and construction of buildings during twenty years as a building site consultant. I have added to that experience by supervising the construction of two residential buildings. It is only natural, therefore, that I should not accept unexamined everything that is propounded about the technical abilities of the ancient Minoans by archaeologists whose orientation is chiefly historical and aesthetic. The geologist sees the Minoan buildings from a "disenchanted" point of view, with all the sober objectivity of the technical man. Was the layout sensible for construction and execution? Was the material appropriate to the demands that would be placed on it? Had experienced artisans been at work and had they observed the rules of building? That is the question the law asks when responsibility for the collapse of a building must be decided in a court. Would a building inspector have cited defects of omission or commission?

The use of soft gypsum, not resistant to water, could certainly be regarded as "a violation of the building code" even three and a half thousand years ago. Either the Minoan builders had no inkling of the properties of their material or—and this we would prefer to assume out of respect for them—the building could be built of soft material because no serious abrasion was expected. But in that case it could not have been a normal dwelling!

The west wing of the palace once upon a time rose two stories high. Because of the descending slope there were actually four stories in the east wing. The wall construction was certainly adequate. But what about the pillars? Down to the second lower story the weight of the structure is borne on pillars. And these famous Minoan pillars were made—of wood! There is also a web of wooden beams between horizontal layers of fieldstone that make up the walls of the lower stories. Now wood is certainly an excellent building material and can last for centuries, provided it is protected from moisture or can quickly dry out again after temporary wetting. It has even been suggested that the wooden beams in Minoan walls were built for security against earthquakes, a clever form of protection which was forgotten by the later inhabitants of the Aegean region (not that the beams would have helped very much during serious quakes).

But if wood is used for beams in masonry and for pillars in basements without being carefully isolated from rising ground moisture, the building will not last long. Even though the wood is not infected by the dreaded dry rot, it will disintegrate in a relatively short time. This is why in Europe the "uncultured" population of the Middle Ages avoided the use of wood in masonry or as props in basements, as we still do. The half-timbering technique with wooden beams inserted into the masonry structure began above the splash apron of natural stone. Such structures have survived earthquakes no worse than the Minoan buildings. In Knossos, on the other hand, the second lower story, containing the royal couple's "domestic quarters," was also built with wooden beams, even where these should not have been used because of rising ground moisture. The wooden columns are planted right on top of the stone bases, and consequently could not help "drawing water." Such construction, without any moisture barrier, is not viable in the long run. In such cases nowadays the two materials would be separated by a barrier layer, or else the foot of the pillar would be sheathed in metal.

It is possible that in spite of these risks the mighty cedar beams and columns would have acted as supports for a considerable time. But the method of covering the wood with a layer of plaster, so that it was no longer able to breathe, raises questions. I know of houses in the Old Town of Göttingen that survived without damage for almost four hundred years. But during the present century their half-timbering was covered with stucco, and the wooden beams crumbled like tinder within a few decades.

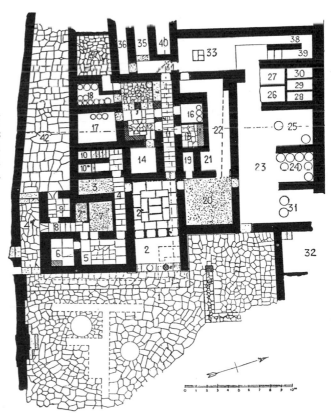

FIG. 31   Minoan "villa" of Niru Chani, 12 kilometers east of Herakleion. Ground plan from Marinatos and Hirmer, 1959.

Arthur Evans divided the Minoan Age into three periods, Early, Middle and Late Minoan, each of which is in turn divided into segments (Early and Late into I, II, III; the Middle Minoan period into I, IIa, IIb and III). The Middle Minoan period, extending from about 2000 to 1700 B.C., corresponds to the "oldest Palace period" or "Protopalatial" in the sense used by Nicolas Platon, the contemporary Greek authority on Minoan matters. Evans's Late Minoan is comparable to Platon's Neopalatial, from 1700 to 1400 B.C. Platon, the discoverer of the fourth Cretan palace (Kato Zakro in eastern Crete), believes that each of the six divisions of the Protopalatial and Neopalatial was separated by devastating earthquakes which repeatedly forced the inhabitants of the palace to rebuild. Finally, after the last catastrophic quake between 1450 and 1400 B.C., no one was left to rebuild and inhabit the palace. Such is Platon's view. In others words, Platon has constructed a kind of earthquake chronology, with terrible upheavals succeeding one another at intervals of about a century.

Anyone who has even a casual acquaintance with Crete knows that it is situated in a seismically active part of the Mediterranean region. From that point of view there can be no objection to Platon's version. Given the above-mentioned defects in construction it would take only relatively mild quakes to cause the collapse of the wooden parts, which would have badly rotted in the course of a century, thereby bringing down the entire building. It is not even necessary to postulate earthquakes. The plastered pillars, unprotected from the rising ground moisture, probably could not have survived all the many centuries of the Minoan Age.

The Palace of Knossos has been so rebuilt by Evans that the characteristic features of its construction are not so apparent. Other Minoan sites provide a better example. The small Minoan structure of Niru Chani, 12 kilometers east of Herakleion, is highly instructive. Here, too, the wooden pillars were plumped directly on top of the stone bases and supported a pergolalike entrance hall. The slabs of the floor, obviously subject to heavier traffic and exposed to rainwater, were not of gypsum but of limestone or slate. This suggests that the Minoan builders were aware of the properties of gypsum. A carefully chiseled gutter in Niru Chani, with elbows and joints, was not made of the easily worked gypsum but carved out of the far harder limestone at the cost of much more labor. The chisel marks can still be plainly discerned. This is more evidence that the Minoans did not employ gypsum out of ignorance.

A few rooms in Niru Chani, on the other hand, are faced and floored with gypsum slabs. Among these are, of all places, the elegant main entrance. It has been posited that the building was inhabited by a Minoan priest who incidentally carried on a trade in devotional objects. This assumption is made because along with storage vessels of the pithos type, "stores" of cult objects have been found. But busy traffic of "customers" at the entrance to the house is incompatible with gypsum slabs used as flooring. One stairway of gypsum steps in the upper story has also been preserved. The lower steps are badly worn and furrowed by the runoff of rainwater. But the upper step, where the stairway now ends blindly in the open air and is therefore no longer stepped on, shows strikingly little wear.

All the door openings show broad, deep notches. Wooden trapdoors, it is said, were once moved up and down in these. This sounds like a highly utilitarian, indeed brilliant, device for saving space. But the Minoans apparently did not consider one factor. A sliding trapdoor can be got out of the way by letting it disappear into a slit in the floor. In that case it will soon cease to function properly because this slit will also catch a great deal of sand and dirt. The other possibility is to raise the trapdoor.

FIG. 32 Corner bench of gypsum slabs, Niru Chani. Note the notches in the doorjambs.

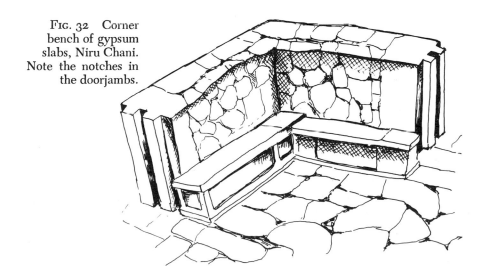

FIG. 33 Corner bench (*kline*), Etruscan rock tomb cut into volcanic tufa. Compare the corner bench from Niru Chani.

But then it is a nuisance in the upper story, unless the door is made so low that everyone who enters bumps his head. The solution is to build the rooms twice the height of the door—but many rooms are not that high. The archaeologist who assumes trapdoors has a responsibility to explain how they could have functioned.

The notches in the Minoan doorjambs have just the right thickness for gypsum slabs, fragments of which have been found in many rooms. Could the trapdoors once have been of gypsum? Or is it possible that these doors were normally not opened at all, but firmly closed with stone slabs? The latter theory would explain at once the reason for the minimal wear apparent in so many of the rooms, while it would also justify the use of soft gypsum by the Minoan artisans. If the rooms were closed up by stone slabs immediately after being built, and therefore not exposed to constant traffic, the use of hard stone, which was difficult to work with Bronze Age tools, would be altogether superfluous. There is only one hitch: in that case the rooms were not intended as living quarters.

One room in Niru Chani has a stone corner bench, covered with the usual gypsum slabs. It instantly reminded me of rooms similarly equipped with objects of daily use shaped out of soft stone. That room and those objects were not intended for the use of the living, but as provision for the dead: in tombs in distant Etruria, where the *klines* (biers) for the dead had been cut out of the soft tufa of the hills around Cerveteri in the shape of corner benches. The tomb was also filled with models of household utensils and even with domestic animals carved out of gypsum. It is true that the Minoans and Etruscans were separated

FIG. 34   Palace of Phaistos. Ground plan from Marinatos and Hirmer, 1959.

in time by a thousand years. But the coincidence is remarkable. And according to ancient tradition the ancestors of the Etruscans came from the East, emigrating to Italy from Asia Minor by way of the Aegean and Ionian seas. Even without assuming a direct connection, the resemblance in arrangement, form and material might well suggest a similarity of function.

Fortunately, we are not restricted in our investigations on Crete to a single palace or dwelling. Besides Knossos, Niru Chani, Amnissos and Kato Zakro there are available the two larger palaces of Phaistos and Mallia.

All three of the great palaces show certain correspondences in ground plan. In particular, all have a central court around which the buildings are grouped. Even the length-to-breadth proportions of the three central courts are in striking agreement, almost exactly two to one. In Phaistos, however, the southwestern part of the court and the surrounding group of buildings have vanished because of an avalanche. In all three cases we find the same rectangular pattern and similar orientation by the points of the compass, though there are considerable differences in the size and distribution of the rooms. Knossos is the biggest of the three labyrinthine structures; moreover, nowhere else on Crete is there evidence of a comparable number of stories built one atop the other. All three palaces are distinguished by the typical sharp turns in the course of the corridors, by the magazines in the west wing, by a forecourt in the west and by a larger number of subsidiary rooms in that wing. Phaistos rises on a plateau sloping shallowly toward the south, high above the Messara Plain, a fruitful depression in the southern part of Crete. The situation of Knossos, on the slope and hill above the fruitful Kairatos Valley and the equally fertile coastal plain of the north coast, has already been described in detail. Mallia, on the other hand, lies close to the coast on flatter terrain that rises only a little above the coastal plain. Nevertheless, in all three cases the physical proximity to fertile lowlands, largely covered with rich, friable soil, is quite remarkable. These parts of the island are easily worked and have probably been used for agriculture since the Stone Age. They offered no difficulties to the relatively primitive agricultural implements of the Stone and Bronze ages.

In all three cases, on the other hand, the soil in the immediate vicinity of the palaces is hard and stony and would have to be toilsomely worked and lightened in order to grow anything at all. Before the introduction of iron hoes and plowshares such land was prohibitively difficult to cultivate. Probably, in fact, all three palaces were situated outside the limits of what was at the time regarded as tillable soil, especially Phaistos on its high, arid plateau.

A drive of about two hours over well-paved roads (which are still far from common on this mountainous island) brought us from Herakleion by way of Dafnes and Hagia Varvara to the Messara Plain and Phaistos. The central part of Crete between Herakleion and Phaistos is also hilly, almost mountainous, but not so steep, harsh and bare as it is further to the east and west. Rich villages line our way. Good wine grapes grow here. Everywhere along the road mounds of the grapes lie on huge canvases, freshly cut and ready for shipment. The moment you stop to look at the picturesque harvest you find yourself showered with gifts of bunches of grapes. They are a delight in the dry heat of a Cretan afternoon.

A detour is taken to Gortyn, the ancient Roman capital of Crete and for a while also of Cyrenaica. The Minoans also had lived there. But the town's boom began during the Dorian period, when the Greek acropolis with magazines, a theater and the famous wall with the inscription of Gortyn's legal code was erected. It is the oldest preserved Greek inscription, written around 450 B.C. and incorporated into the Roman Odeon that dates from the time of Emperor Trajan (A.D. 98–117).

Extensive Roman temple structures have been excavated along the southern part of the highway, among them a temple of Apollo, of Isis and Serapis, a nymphaeum and the praetorium. When I was there, Italian archaeologists were busy unearthing tremendous cracked monolithic columns. But the goal of our journey is not Roman, Byzantine or Hellenic Gortyn.

Only 10 kilometers further to the west the mountain ridge of Phaistos towers over the lowland. The road descends by several serpentine curves to the plateau. The view from this height is overwhelming. At our feet stretch the green farmlands of the

Messara, framed on almost all sides by rough mountains shimmering in the grayish-blue haze. From the parking area a gently rising path leads to the cafeteria with its inevitable souvenir stand. Large numbers of tourists have taken refuge in the shade of its roof. From this vantage point you have a view of the entire palace, and of the glorious panorama surrounding it.

But we do not linger long. In spite of the noonday heat the excavation site, which lies like a ground plan before us, exerts a strong pull.

The path is paved with stone slabs and descends gently downhill. Alongside it are two oblong stone cist tombs made of limestone slabs placed on edge. Possibly these are not from the Minoan Age, but are more recent and were intended for horizontal burial without any significant grave goods.

The northern side of the west court is flanked by an impressive grand staircase. It is not in front of an entrance, but placed against a simple high supporting wall. Consequently, it was probably intended mainly to provide a large crowd of spectators a good view of the palace forecourt when festive events were in progress there.

On the east side the forecourt is terraced up to the palace, the west portal of which rises above a broad staircase. Here, too, are massive walls made of huge blocks of stone, but no signs of any defensive installations. There are no fortifications on the palace itself or in the vicinity. In that respect Phaistos presents the same appearance as all the other preserved Minoan sites.

At Phaistos the succession of at least two major palaces can be recognized with particular clarity. The more recent building has been shifted from 5 to 10 meters further to the east; the foundations of the older building form the terrace that marks the eastern boundary of the west court.

In Phaistos, too, the principal entrance is from the west, the sunset side of evil omens and of death. The western magazines are less extensive than those at Knossos; they consist of comparatively small, dark, windowless rooms with snake-ornamented pithoi, as in Knossos, and were also originally faced with gypsum slabs. Alongside one of the big storage jars is a low, drumlike "hassock" with two indentations on the sides to serve as

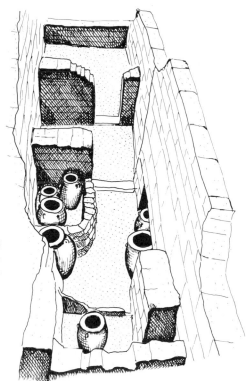

FIG. 35
Pithos magazine,
Phaistos.

handles. With the aid of such footstools the palace populace
supposedly removed their daily requirements of foodstuffs from
the upright jars that are tall as a man. But even with a footstool
and long-handled dippers it is hardly possible to reach to the
bottom of the huge pithoi.

"Lustral basins" for ritual washings were, apparently, also in
use in Phaistos and likewise faced with gypsum. Three gypsum
steps lead down into the room, which is about 2 meters by 3.
Remains of the original gypsum facing are still there; archaeologists have attempted to protect these from disintegration due
to weathering by setting them in concrete.

In the west excavations are in progress on the level of the
older palace. Corridors and magazines not yet opened to the
public can be seen from above when the canvases over the metal
frames of the excavation tent are thrown back. Here there are
especially interesting magazines in which the storage vessels do
not stand freely in the room, as they do elsewhere. At the end
of a long corridor with pithoi on both sides a single jar stands

in a narrow niche. Obviously it contained some exceptionally precious contents; indeed these contents must have been so valuable that special protective measures against unbidden visitors became necessary. The jar was therefore *walled up* inside its niche with stone slabs set on end! What a problem filling and emptying, cleaning or replacing this pithos must have been. When the maid was sent down to the cellar to fetch supplies she must have been accompanied by a couple of masons; otherwise how could she get at the preserves?

In the Palace of Knossos, too, we had noticed such pithoi walled up in narrow rooms, jars much too large to be moved in through the narrow doors, or to be tipped or replaced by others if ever one should be cracked or broken. What in the world did the ancient Minoans put into these storage jars that prompted them to enclose them so carefully in narrow cubes, corners or niches as though for eternity? And at other places the roof above the pithoi is so low that the vessels, which stand close together side by side, could neither be filled nor emptied!

The rooms with porticos at the north and east ends of the central court have been identified as domestic rooms. Not far from them is the remains of a forge. So the "workmen's quarters" were again only 10 or 20 meters from the living quarters— was there no other place on the broad plateau for the workshops with their noise, dirt and smoke?

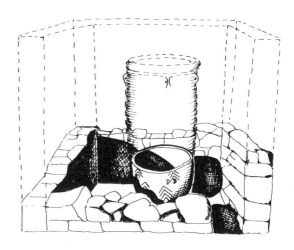

FIG. 36 Knossos: single pithos set in a walled square. The small entrance at right is too narrow to let the jar pass through.

FIG. 37 Phaistos: pithos magazine in the western part of the palace. The squat jars, about 1 meter high, are buried so tightly under the floor that access to them was practically impossible.

High temperatures must have been attained at the forge; the sinter encrustations are proof of that. But this was no uncontrolled fire; there was a well-defined hearth within an open area of from 300 to 400 square meters. Normally furnaces for potters, glassblowers, smiths or enamel workers are attached to the workshop. But here the fireplace was out in the open. Why?

And yet the craftsmen had to fetch water from one of the distant cisterns that supposedly supplied the palace with water on the otherwise arid plateau. A number of such cisterns are to be found on the margin of the west court, the same side of the palace as in Knossos. A particularly well preserved one, dug deep into the rock, lies at the southwest corner of the central court. At the top of the shaft the opening is three-quarters of a meter wide; as it descends to a depth of about 10 meters it widens out in the shape of a pear. At ground level a channel lined with clay tiles enters it. Presumably this gutter brought the rainwater collected from the roofs to the shaft. The capacious shaft is bone-dry. Perhaps the porous rock at these few places, or at one or two of them, did not let the stored water trickle away underground immediately. But unquestionably the water supply on this exposed, rocky plateau must have been a matter of daily concern. It is true that the inhabitants of a good many North Sea islands also have to get along on rainwater alone, when the ship bringing their drinking water fails to arrive or when supplies from the mainland become too expensive. But in the North Sea it rains regularly even in summer, often as frequently as once a day, at

Fig. 38 Phaistos: walled round shafts from the vicinity of the west forecourt. These structures, hitherto considered cisterns, are probably shaft graves of the Late Minoan–Mycenaean period.

least for a short time. On Mediterranean islands, however, there is often no rain for months; and on such an isolated, rocky hill the soil retains no water. In spite of the splendid view, therefore, the site is poorly chosen for a sizable settlement, at least in terms of the water supply. To be sure, European feudal castles often had the same problem of scanty water. But then the castle dwellers did not have the Minoans' advanced notions about bathing, and people will do without a great deal when the times are uncertain and life is perilous. The Minoan Age, however, is said to have been peaceful. And the palaces were unfortified.

But were these cisterns actually intended to store water?

Where had we seen such curious shafts before, about a meter wide at the top and widening like a bottle toward the bottom? The memory returned: the Etruscan *pozzi* of Tuscany, of Poggio Renzo near Chiusi, or Poggio alla Guardia near Vetulonia. Some were built of masonry, some were cut into the rock, in all sizes, doorless and hollow, the deepest extending down as far as 23 meters, but at one time filled to the brim with bits of broken tufa, animal bones, *cippi* (gravestones), votive offerings of all sorts. These were once votive shafts, *mundi subterranei*, which received the offerings from the world of the living to those in the hereafter. At the Minoan Palace of Kato Zakro Nicolas Platon actually found a bowl of olives in a supposed well. Which is more likely: that this bowl accidentally slipped from a maid's hand while she was washing the olives and fell to the bottom, or that it was deliberately lowered into the shaft as a gift for the dead in the world below?

In the southwestern part of the Palace of Phaistos a temple to Rhea has been discovered. This is evidence that the plateau still served as a place of worship for the mother of Zeus in Hellenic times. But at that time, apparently, no one lived there any longer. From the time the famous Phaistos Disc was made (an Early Minoan clay disc 16.5 centimeters in diameter with 241 inscribed hieroglyphs, which was found in the northeastern part of the palace) down to Hellenic times, the hill of Phaistos was a place dedicated to gods and men.

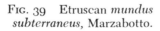

FIG. 39   Etruscan *mundus subterraneus*, Marzabotto.

Mallia is situated on the northern coast, where seismic waves from the Aegean can easily reach it. From Amnissos to Niru Chani there are several places along the Cretan north coast where Minoan foundations lie underwater; J. V. Luce has concluded that a tsunami once surged over the buildings represented by these foundations, wiping out all life.

At first glance these drowned Minoan walls are an impressive argument for the tsunami thesis. But the geologist recognizes another, and important, aspect of the matter. Whatever the purpose of these Minoan structures close to the coast may have been, originally they were not built in water but on land, since they are too small to serve as ships' basins and too irregular to have been used for aquaria in which to raise murex or other molluscs or fish. If the buildings did once stand on land and are today in the water, the land must have subsided or the water level risen. No tsunami is needed to destroy structures that are in the water anyhow. A seismic wave, after all, does not bring about any lasting elevation in the water level. Once the wave subsides, the water is no higher than it was before.

What we have here is an obvious flaw in reasoning. Instead of proof of the effects of seismic waves, we see signs of a slow coastal subsidence on the northern coast of Crete, which since Minoan times has robbed the island of valuable cultivated land. A good many of the ninety to one hundred Cretan cities Homer speaks of may have been doomed by this subsidence, since many of them were probably situated between the sea, teeming with fish, and the tillable land near the coast. Here, unquestionably, is a promising field of investigation for underwater archaeologists. I hope that professionally trained young people also interested in the sport of skin diving will take up this challenge.

At the excavation site of Mallia itself there are no patent signs of any such sea flooding. Mallia does not look basically different from the other Minoan sites. The main access route is in the north, while again the entrance gate opens to the west. A small Late Minoan sanctuary seems to have been added on at an angle, occupying the front end of the west court. On the edge of the inevitable central court, alongside the grand staircase, there is a circular limestone slab, presumably for offerings; in addition to the concave center of the carefully worked and polished stone

FIG. 40 Minoan foundations with the waves washing over them, coast of Niru Chani, 12 kilometers east of Herakleion. Since the foundations are now at about the level of the sea, no seismic wave is needed to account for their destruction. The normal action of the surf would be quite sufficient. The coastline has probably subsided; a considerable rise in the sea level is hardly likely in the Mediterranean, which belongs to a relatively dry climatic zone.

there are thirty-three small hollows and one large hollow around the outer rim.

In the deep magazines of the subsidiary building to the northwest we are shown an astonishingly rational arrangement devised by the practical and thrifty Mallian palace administration, an idea far more ingenious than anything thought up by the stewards at Knossos and Phaistos. After all, the pithoi were subject to considerable pressures, and one might burst, wasting the precious olive oil, or else a servant removing the oil might carelessly spill some. In order to forestall such unwelcome losses an oil-collecting groove terminating in a basin was cut into the tramped earthen floor. How clever and practical! But let us consider the matter realistically for a moment. If one of those barrel-sized jars were to break, there would be such a flood that

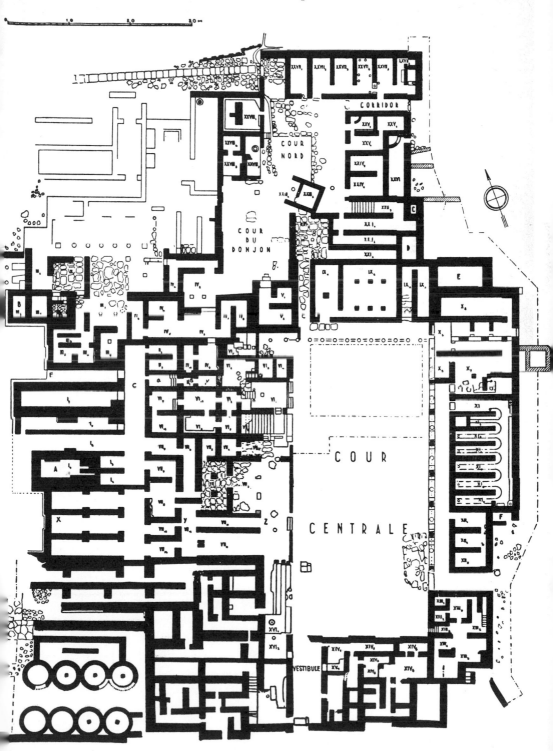

FIG. 42 Limestone slab with hollows for offerings, Palace of Mallia.

the tiny half-gallon basin at the end of the groove would hardly make any difference. And if some oil were in fact spilled on the dusty outer rim of the jar, or even on the floor, is it likely that those wealthy and prodigal Minoan lords would not grant the few drops to the gods, while all around them they had a store of thousands upon thousands of liters of the best oil! Had they behaved that way they would have been curiously unpractical in their thinking. Surely there must be some other reason for the "groove for collecting oil."

The problem of water supply was seemingly solved in an equally impractical manner. Here on the coastal plain there was no lack of water. A well a few meters in depth would have sufficed to yield any desired quantity of ground water. But—cisterns were built (high up on the hill, as at Knossos and Phaistos). Moreover, there were eight of them side by side in two rows on the southern edge of the west court. A good many of these cisterns, made of round fieldstone masonry, have a pillar in the middle in order to support the corbeled roof. Thus instead of digging a well in the vicinity of the so-called kitchens in the northeastern part of the palace, eight superfluous cisterns were built at great labor at precisely the opposite end of the palace! But, again, similar structures are known from elsewhere—the Etruscan pillar tombs of Casal Maritima or of the Pietrera at Vetulonia. The mighty square pillar was not needed for support of the roof, but served as a symbolic prop of the vault of heaven in a tomb equipped as a *templum sub terris*, an underground temple. Is this pure coincidence?

Fig. 43   Pillar tomb, Casal Marittima, Etruria. The pillar has no function; the "false" arch (corbeled roof) supports itself. This type of pillar crypt can only be explained in religious terms.

11

When the Earth Shakes

○

I had visited the Minoan sites to explore the traces of early geological catastrophes but what I found were curious contradictions. Were the excavated labyrinthine complexes really the palatial residences of glorious kings, of the legendary Minos and his brothers Sarpedon and Rhadamanthys? In fact, could these places be regarded as residences at all? My geological observations argued against any such assumption. Places of worship, shrines, sanctified earth, yes, but not places for human settlement. Comparison with other Mediterranean cultures suggested a cult of the dead. And in fact most of the inconsistencies I discovered could be aptly explained as a consequence of funerary rites, a natural outcome of the lavish ancient Mediterranean methods of preserving corpses and preparing for the afterlife. Given that interpretation, the hitherto largely isolated Minoan civilization would fit easily into the framework of the other Mediterranean cultures. That would mean, however, that Minoan culture, to the extent that we now know it, was almost entirely a funerary cult. We see the real life of the Minoan world only in the mirror of rites for the dead. What the excavators have unearthed are not the homes of the living but the dwellings of the dead.

Since, however, the Minoans pictured the "life" of the dead as largely parallel to that of the living, the testimony of these sites may well be more rewarding than anything we could learn from excavating a few strata of authentic settlements with not much more than postholes and kitchen middens. But if the palaces were tombs, where did the Minoans live? Naturally, where the Cretans are still living today, in the fertile lowlands, near springs and coasts, not on the barren *karst* of the plateaus where the view is splendid but water scarce.

And what about the ultimate annihilation of the Minoans as the result of geological catastrophes? Of course we have repeatedly witnessed the terrible effects the earth can produce within a few seconds by quakes, volcanic eruptions and seismic waves. Let us recall the chronicle of destruction for this century alone: The earthquake of San Francisco on April 18, 1906, took 1000 lives and led to the terrible fire that reduced the whole city to ashes. Only two years later, on December 28, 1908, 84,000 people were killed in Messina and Calabria, many of them by a seismic wave. Then for a number of years during the First World War nature seemed to cede the field to man. But in 1920 nearly 200,000 people died in the Ping-Liang earthquake of December 16 in the Chinese province of Kansu. Three years later, on September 1, 1923, nearly a quarter of a million fell victim to the Sagami Bay earthquake in Japan and the subsequent burning of Tokyo and Yokohama. A whole series of severe earthquakes afflicted Turkey in 1939, 1944, 1945, 1967 and 1970. The many quakes in Alaska during this century did relatively little damage because the density of population is so small. And in the Second World War man once again surpassed in destructive fury all the records set by nature. But who can forget the great earthquakes of the sixties: Agadir (March 1, 1960); Chile that same year (May 21, 1960—the severest earthquake since the start of instrumental recording); Iran (September 1, 1962); Skopje (July 26, 1963); Sicily (two quakes in January 1968). And so it goes, year in, year out, with far more than a million earthquake victims in a single century. How, in the face of such figures on casualties, can there be any doubt that the Minoans were destroyed by geological catastrophes!

Moreover, the calamity is always so sudden that there is no time to save any possessions. After one major earthquake at night nothing is left of modern dwellings but a rubble heap.

In addition, people who live far from the epicenter of the earthquake can fall victim to the dread tsunamis. The "tidal wave" after the Chilean earthquake of 1960 surged over the entire Pacific Ocean in less than thirty hours, causing great damage and loss of lives in Asiatic coastal regions more than 15,000 kilometers distant. One such seismic wave reached the almost incredible height of 65 meters at Cape Lopatka on the peninsula of Kamchatka.

As if ordinary earthquakes are not enough, the eruptions of volcanos add to the sum of horrors. We have already spoken of the effects of the Krakatoa eruption. On May 8, 1902, on the small French island of Martinique in the West Indies, a fiery-hot cloud raced down the slopes of the Mount Pelée volcano into the valley at a speed of 150 meters per second. The volcanic vapors, at a temperature of about 800° C., laden with glowing volcanic dust, in a fraction of a minute destroyed the small town of St. Pierre at the foot of the mountain, killing all 26,000 inhabitants. The impact of the shock wave that preceded the hot cloud pushed entire buildings right off their foundations.

If examples from the present still fall short of justifying the catastrophe theory, why can we not assume that geological disasters many times more dreadful took place in the past?

Naturally a geologist does not ignore these phenomena. But he also knows how difficult it is, only a few years after a city has been almost totally destroyed, to find enough clear traces of the destruction to take movies that will be informative to students. If you go around San Francisco, Messina, Tokyo, Skopje or Agadir with a camera, searching for earthquake damage, you will be disappointed. Even the bomb damage of the Second World War has mostly vanished. What remains has usually been left deliberately as a memorial and undergone that peculiar transformation that is the fate of monuments. We might even presume that ruins such as the cathedral of Coventry or the Kaiser Wilhelm Gedächtniskirche have been preserved as "mementos" because these structures no longer have any more important function in present-day society. If they did, they would have been replaced by suitable new buildings.

None of the cities that suffered wartime damage or geological disasters were actually "destroyed." All of them have gone on merrily living, usually larger and grander than they were before. After all 26,000 inhabitants of St. Pierre were killed, others come to settle on the same soil. Even Pompeii and Herculaneum did not disappear for good from the surface of the earth. The towns still exist as they did in antiquity (to the grief of archaeologists, who must first remove the houses of the living in order to get at the traces of the past).

It is only when a site no longer seems suitable that it is gradually abandoned. Then, if a natural disaster strikes, rebuilding is not done on the site itself, but in a more favorable place. In fact, however, I know of only one small town that was not rebuilt after its destruction and has been preserved as a ghost town and tourist attraction in its state of ruin. That is Bussana Vecchia near San Remo. Driven from the coast into the mountains by the Saracens and the Normans, the Bussanese stuck it out for centuries in their hidden rocky refuge high in the mountains overlooking the coast. Then came a severe earthquake, on Sunday morning at mass hour. It killed almost the entire population and made the houses unlivable. The remaining inhabitants moved back to the coast, where with government help Bussana Nuova was built. But in fact the people had only returned to their starting point, from which their forefathers had once retreated into the mountains under the pressure of foreign invaders.

As a rule, even war and expulsion do not result in the "destruction" of cities or entire peoples. In most cases the conquerors settle down in place of the exiles. It scarcely matters whether the new arrivals are "racially" or culturally similar or different. What often develops is a symbiosis between the native population and the "conquerors," and after a few generations they can no longer be told apart. Most functions and many modes of behavior are simply continued. Even such severe catastrophes as the Second World War have hardly left a mark on the practical ways of life of Europe's populations. People take up where they had to leave off at the outbreak of the war. Homes of 1950 can scarcely be distinguished from those of before 1939. East German cities such as Breslau have been rebuilt by their new inhabitants with such fidelity to prewar construction that no archaeologist of later millennia could deduce what sort of blow that city received or that 400,000 persons had been expelled from it.

Of course disasters have happened and continue to happen.

But they hardly mean the end of a city's life, let alone that of a whole nation. Styles of art, conceptions of the hereafter and rites for the dead undergo gradual changes even without the intervention of catastrophes. Later it will seem as if the ancient tradition was annihilated, when in fact it was merely superseded. Usually considerable portions of the traditional forms and modes of behavior are incorporated into the new system. On the other hand even without catastrophes those things that are no longer needed in a changing world will decay. Thus many citadels and castles have been destroyed not so much by the effects of war as by neglect; they have gradually collapsed because maintaining the structures was an expensive matter, bearable only so long as people thought they could not possibly do without the protection of stout walls.

The Palatine in Rome was not destroyed by the Teutonic conquerors of the Roman Empire. Long after Romulus Augustulus was expelled by Odoacer in A.D. 476 Roman popes lived there. But eventually the vast pile, having lost most of its original function as the spiritual center of the Roman Empire, gradually decayed because no one was interested in preserving the buildings. It was then used as a quarry.

In this respect the twentieth century (we may well call it the century of catastrophes) has provided an excellent object lesson. As we have mentioned, it produced the philosophical concept of the "decline of the West." But it also showed that various political and natural catastrophes by no means mean cultural doom. On the contrary, Western culture conquered other continents as never before, and is at present in the process of expanding into a universal, unitary civilization.

Thus though the concept of the decline of the West appears highly logical, though it stirs the imagination and arouses the emotions, it is simply false. The decisive societal transformations are not those produced by catastrophe but those produced in the minds of people. Thus the Thirty Years' War, for all the suffering and disruption it caused, proved to be fairly unimportant to the cultural evolution of Europe. But the thoughts of Luther a hundred years earlier, and the discovery of America—without concomitant catastrophes—changed the face and fate of humanity for all time to come.

There have been more than a million earthquake victims in this century alone, and far more than ten times that number of war dead. The total is surely more than the combined populations of all the Minoan towns. But despite such tolls of lives and property none of these catastrophes extinguished an existing culture or even a single city. That is true even for such catastrophes as the atomic blasting of Hiroshima and Nagasaki. Some people are always spared, or come in from outside, to rebuild what has been destroyed. For the individual, for whole families, such events are disastrous—but not for whole nations and civilizations. On the contrary. After catastrophes the restorative factor, the persistence of ideas and memories of "the good old days," is often especially marked. We have had ample chance to observe that after two world wars. Revolutions, intellectual upheavals, on the contrary, as a rule take place in times of seeming calm, not in times wracked by natural disasters.

It is therefore a mistake to ascribe the end of institutions and the destruction of a civilization's buildings to the total annihilation of the people concerned. Institutions and buildings are allowed to go to ruin only when they no longer have a living function. The *inner change in function* is far more telling as a factor leading to the death of a civilization than any number of outward catastrophes. The disaster is only assigned as a cause because no one has taken the trouble to recognize the underlying change in function.

Curiously enough, the opposition between the theory of catastrophe and the theory of evolution crops up in practically all branches of science that take a historical approach. In biology the catastrophe theory of Cuvier (1769–1832), a contemporary of the French Revolution, was replaced by the evolutionary theory of Darwin (1809–1882). In geology the influence of K. E. A. von Hoff (1771–1837) and Lyell (1797–1875) produced a bias toward the idea of evolution and away from certain of the catastrophic notions put forward by Niels Stensen (Nicholas Steno, 1638–1686). Catastrophism has survived down to this century only in tectonics, due to the work of E. Suess (1831–1914) and H. Stille (1876–1966). But it is becoming more and more apparent that even such decisive upheavals of the earth's crust as those involved in mountain formation do not take the form of one or more tremendous catastrophes, but happen almost continuously. They are the summation of an infinitude of comparatively trivial movements. It is quite possible to live on an upfolding mountain chain without being aware of these developments. In tectonics, too, the trend to evolutionary thinking is inescapable.

In historical thinking the catastrophe theory became established in this century largely due to Spengler (1880–1936), and replaced the nineteenth century's evolutionary belief in progress. As we have seen, Spengler's *Decline of the West* was actually written before the outbreak of the First World War. The analogous intellectual development (rising uncertainty and overall loss of confidence in a positivistic view of the human situation) had already taken place, almost imperceptibly, long before 1914. The First World War was not the cause but possibly a consequence; people were waiting for the catastrophe to come, and it did. One wonders whether the peoples of Europe, had they not had this basically pessimistic attitude and the accompanying will to self-destruction, would have plunged into the adventure of two world wars.

But then, when in spite of two vast military cataclysms and a good many others caused by nature, the expected doom did not descend, the catastrophe theory in historical philosophy should have been put aside. Instead it was only moderated by adducing inevitable cultural crosscurrents. That was the burden of Arnold Toynbee's *A Study of History* (1934–1949) and *Civilization on Trial* (1949). Persuasive though they seem in many passages, such intellectual systems do not say very much more than that change is the only constant in history, with or without catastrophes. The notions so common in archaeology of peoples as the carriers of certain characteristic cultures, of the migration and downfall as well as the strengthening and blossoming of new cultures in place of the old—these notions are outmoded ideas dating back to the end of the nineteenth and the beginning of the twentieth century.

When we visit archaeological sites we cannot fail to be struck by the fact that the transitions in time and space between civilizations and their "carriers" are completely fluid and as a rule do not coincide with national boundaries. On the one hand there are often marked cultural differences from locality to locality within a single people; on the other hand persons of widely differing descent often live together in close cultural and civilizational harmony. The exaggerated importance given to an artificially whipped-up nationalism in the last century, with its unfortunate consequences for the generations of the present century, is just as false—not to say criminal—as the stress on religious antagonisms at the beginning of the modern age, or as the deliberate intensification of ideological differences. By comparison the frankly predatory campaigns of absolutist rulers seem almost honest. The intention here was simple aggrandizement; the rulers did not try to hide their purpose behind ideological masks.

When we consider the problem of the end of the Minoan world we have to ask whether, in the light of the foregoing material, it would have been possible for all the representatives of Minoan civilization to have been so weakened by geological or military disasters that they could no longer rebuild their palaces. Does it not seem more likely that we may be dealing with a change in function, with an abandonment of traditional ideas and modes of behavior?

The very fact that every imaginable type of catastrophe and secondary effect has been fetched up as an explanation for the destruction of the Minoans indicates the theoretical difficulty involved in trying to account for the nearly complete extinction of a great, wealthy, culturally advanced population. The argument becomes even more knotty if we examine it in terms of practical knowledge of geology.

Let us first take up the question of earthquakes. The energies released in a major quake can amount to several billion kilowatt hours (10^{11} KWH), several hundred thousand times as much as the bomb that fell on Hiroshima. Every year the earth has approximately 8 full-scale quakes yielding energies of more than 108 KWH. There are also some 130 quakes that can be registered on instruments at distances of up to 10,000 kilometers, and many thousands of smaller earth tremors.

The energy released in an earthquake depends on the depth, the cause and the shape of the epicenter. In tectonic quakes resulting from major horizontal displacements of the earth's crust, as in California or northern Anatolia, a comparatively extensive reservoir of energy is available when the crustal movement, delayed by friction, passes a boundary value for internal tension and suddenly is transformed into a jerky motion. Two extensive areas of fracture, long prevented from sliding, abruptly let go. The energy stored up in the rock in the form of elastic tensions is discharged in the form of a violent shift and a seismic impulse that spreads out in waves from the epicenter. The greater the friction along the fault, the more extensive the line of disturbance will be; and the longer the interval between successive tremors, the more energy will be released in the earthquake.

Thus the energy of the San Francisco quake of 1906 approximated that of a mass of 26 billion metric tons falling upon the earth from a height of 280 kilometers. Destruction corresponding to shocks of strength 10 (on the twelve-division Mercalli-Sieberg scale) extended along a coastal strip almost 500 kilometers long but only a few kilometers wide. Shocks of strength 8–9, with accelerations between 25 and 100 cm/sec^2, causing severe damage to houses from cracks and partial collapse, and some deaths, were experienced for about 15 kilometers to either side of the San Andreas Fault. At a distance of some 70 kilometers crumbling of plaster was observed, as well as lighter external damage to houses and the collapse of chimneys. At distances of up to 200 kilometers small movable objects quivered as a consequence of more moderate shocks. Beyond that range the earthquake was observed only by a few persons who happened to be favorably situated. On instruments, however, it was possible to detect the quake all over the globe.

Thus even such powerful earthquakes are concentrated in a comparatively narrow coastal strip. The depth of the epicenter is also slight, no more than 10 to 20 kilometers. The impulse spreads rapidly in all directions, the amplitude of the vibrations of course diminishing as the frequency increases. But even when the epicenter is at a greater depth, no increase in effect is achieved. On the contrary, experience shows that with increasing depth of epicenter the energy released diminishes.

The heaviest casualties are not due to the immediate shock, or even to the collapse of houses during earthquakes of strengths 10–12—which occur within the restricted area near the epicenter.

The major causes of casualties are the secondary effects—fires, landslides and seismic waves. Thus in San Francisco only about a thousand persons were killed in 1906, whereas in Tokyo and Yokohama in 1923 the toll was nearly a quarter of a million.

An explosion of the volcano on Santorin similar to the Krakatoa eruption would necessarily have had a shallow epicenter and a small, concentrated focus of destruction. Even if we assume for the epicenter a strength of 12 on the Mercalli-Sieberg scale (maximum acceleration up to 1000 cm/sec^2 with catastrophic destruction of all buildings down to their foundations), the effects on Crete, 120 kilometers away, would be similar to those at a distance of 15 kilometers from the epicenter of the San Francisco quake: that is, damage to dwellings and a few scattered deaths. For the complete extermination of the inhabitants, the shock of an earthquake alone would simply not suffice.

For that reason Denis Page had to have recourse to the secondary effects of an earthquake to explain the destruction of Minoan civilization.[*] But on the basis of geological observations in the Palace of Knossos, a conflagration such as devastated San Francisco, Tokyo or Yokohama seems improbable. In any case it would have affected only the major complexes, not the scattered villas and country estates. There remain two possibilities: rains of ashes and seismic waves. Pompeii is only 10 kilometers from the center of the eruption, not 120 kilometers distant, like Crete. Moreover, if people and animals had suffocated under a layer of volcanic ash and larger debris (lapilli up to several centimeters in diameter and "bombs" of even several meters in diameter), layers of ashes meters thick would remain. All signs of massive blankets of ashes on Crete are lacking. Crete certainly provides the necessary conditions for landslides, but such phenomena are always limited to specific localities and would never affect an entire island.

Although the thesis that Minoan civilization was destroyed by an eruption of the Santorin volcano was proposed by the Greek archaeologist Spyridon Marinatos more than thirty years ago, it has not won general acceptance to this day. The reason is quite simple. Whereas Pompeii and Herculaneum lay (and to a great

[*] *The Santorini Volcano and the Desolation of Minoan Crete* (1970).

extent still lie) buried under volcanic deposits many meters in thickness, so that there can be no doubt about the cause of their destruction, comparable volcanic deposits are not to be found on Crete. A prolonged search turns up a little pumice at the excavation sites, but this proves nothing; even today pumice is washed up on many coasts in the Mediterranean. According to J. D. Evans * it also occurs in the neolithic excavation levels at Knossos and is still esteemed as a light building material, so it can scarcely be taken as a proof of volcanic disasters. The lava described by Nicolas Platon (1968) as found at the Palace of Kato Zakro has been examined by the geologist G. J. Boekschoten and judged to be "not of volcanic origin." I myself have undertaken microscopic studies of samples from the upper layers of soil in northern and northeastern Crete and have found materials of volcanic origin of the kind found on Santorin only to a depth of a few centimeters. These consisted of oblong green pyroxene, colorless, idiomorphic feldspar crystals, black, glistening magnetite octohedrons and colorless to brownish volcanic glass. This means that the fall of ashes was only centimeters in thickness, and particles larger than .07 millimeters were limited to the north of the Psiloritis and the Dikte range. Evidently the low-lying clouds of ashes were caught by the mountains of central Crete, so that the south as well as the entire western part of the island were largely spared. Thus volcanic minerals up to the size of a grain of sand are found in Knossos, but not in Phaistos, although it is Knossos that seems to have functioned longer.

The controversy over whether a volcanic eruption of Santorin could have influenced Bronze Age Crete was the subject of a scientific congress held in September 1969 on the volcanic island itself. But archaeologists continue to differ widely. Marinatos, basing his opinions on investigations of deep-sea deposits around Crete by Ninkovich and Heezen, has clung to his original views. M. I. Finley, however, has recently expressed great skepticism on this score.† He considers military conflicts much more likely

---

* "Summary and Conclusions" in "Knossos Neolithic," *Annals of the British School of Archaeology at Athens* 63 (1968).

† *Early Greece: The Bronze and Archaic Ages.* (London, 1970)

as the cause of Bronze Age destruction of the Minoan palaces. From the geologist's point of view, even an unusually powerful eruption of the Thera volcano would scarcely explain the end of Minoan civilization. The advocates of the Santorin thesis repeatedly urge parallels with the Krakatoa eruption, emphasizing the effects of tsunamis. But tidal waves of even 80 to 100 meters in height, such as the Greek seismologist Angelos Galanopoulos assumes for the explosion of Thera, could have reached only part of the Minoan palace complexes. And severe earthquakes, such as supposedly accompanied the eruption of Santorin, were not observed in connection with the Krakatoa eruption. Boekschoten emphasizes this point.

One theory adduces so rare a phenomenon as the poisoning of vegetation, and thus of pasturing animals, by a volcanic rain of ashes. S. Thorarinsson has in fact reported in 1970 on the fluorine poisoning of sheep by the volcanic eruption of Hekla in Iceland. But as we have seen, the mountains of central Crete apparently served to shield the rest of the island from the low-lying clouds of ash, so that considerable portions of the island were unaffected. Total destruction of the livestock of Crete by fluorine poisoning is therefore highly improbable. At any rate, no effect on the vegetation can be demonstrated. And partial destruction would have permitted regrowth from the less stricken or unaffected areas.

James W. Mavor, Jr., in all seriousness has sought to identify the Atlantis described by Plato as situated between Crete and Santorin. He would have the "enormous central square" of the sunken island located on Minoan Crete, so that in effect he is claiming Crete is virtually equivalent to Atlantis.*

It would take another book as large as the present one to examine this hypothesis in detail. But we need only look at a map of the eastern Mediterranean area and study the geographical relationships among Crete, Egypt, Syria, Sicily and the Greek mainland to convince ourselves that the Bronze Age peoples of this area must have had perfectly clear ideas about their geographical position. Otherwise, finds evidencing constant trade among them would not occur in such great numbers in Bronze Age sites. The finds indicate not accidental occurrences of foreign

* *Voyage to Atlantis* (1969).

goods, but regular exchange of all types of objects over distances of many hundreds of kilometers, by land and by sea. It is quite untenable to assume that Egyptian priests did not know where Crete was—or that they might have confounded legendary sunken Atlantis with familiar Crete. When, moreover, Plato has an Egyptian priest tell the Greek lawgiver Solon that the kingdom of the "Antlantides" in "the remote west" sank beneath the waves nine thousand years ago, he is writing with the knowledge that the Egyptians had had a fairly precise calendar for thousands of years. Consequently, such a tradition cannot be juggled about and shifted from the distant past to the period of the well-known Eighteenth Dynasty. Solon himself, moreover, is said to have visited Crete and studied the Gortyn tables of the law (the forerunners of the inscription still preserved at Gortyn). The Egyptian priest, therefore, would have been able to say precisely: "In the time of the son of Re, Thutmosis III, peace and health to him!—between the land of the Keftiu and the northern mainland, whence you yourself come, O stranger . . ."

As we have said, there is no reason to disparage the geographical knowledge of the ancients just because they left no charts behind. They did not need charts. Sailing instructions were learned by heart and passed on orally to sons and grandsons. From the viewpoint of the then known world, which included Egypt and the entire Greek-speaking area, Atlantis was to be sought "far in the west," and Plato explicitly states that it was in the Atlantic beyond the Pillars of Heracles—that is, the Straits of Gibraltar. Whether it was one of the many volcanic islands in the Atlantic or a sunken part of the continental shelf on both sides of the Straits must remain an open question for the present.

Nor would the population have succumbed to the scourge of pestilence, which usually follows in the train of a disastrous earthquake. The landscape of Crete is so varied and broken up, and so much of the water supply comes from natural springs, that the spread of an epidemic throughout the entire island, even to the remotest and most hidden bays and mountain valleys, is virtually out of the question.

There remains only one element that could have caused destruction on a large scale: seismic waves. Since such waves are capable of reaching several dozen meters in height it is conceivable that the coastal cities were destroyed, and above all that the Minoan fleet was wiped out. In that case the battered Minoans would have been unable to defend themselves when the Greek invaders attacked. But when we consider where these attackers might have come from, we are immediately faced with certain contradictions. If it is supposed that the conquerors were Greeks, that is, inhabitants of the same Aegean region, then their ships would likewise have been overwhelmed by the tsunami (unless all their vessels, by remarkable chance, happened to have been drawn very far up on land). It would make more sense to theorize that Egyptians or other, more distant coastal residents of the Mediterranean were the invaders, because their fleets would have gone untouched. But to suggest that the Achaeans, having just finished toilsomely repairing their own damage and building new ships, should have set out immediately to raid Crete before the Cretans could renew their own fleet this is sheer fantasizing.

In any case the tsunami could not have been dangerous to the inhabitants of Phaistos, situated at a high elevation and on the southern side of the island, away from the Aegean. The same is true for the inhabitants of the mountain valleys.

Tsunamis have another characteristic that the layman is usually unaware of. The Japanese name means "great wave in port." A seismic wave is not effective in the open sea, but only along the coasts. The same is true for regular tides as well, which rise only a few feet in Hawaii or the other small islands of the Pacific. It is only where the depth of water lessens over a continental shelf that tides and tidal waves can reach imposing heights. Only continental shelf coasts and large islands are prone to dangerous tsunamis, which dash up against them to enormous heights. Small islands, such as the innumerable rocky islands of the Aegean, for example, are relatively safe from seismic waves.

Since the Minoans were at home not only on Crete but also on the islands of the Aegean (for example, Melos, noted for its obsidian quarries), a tsunami cannot have wiped out their entire fleet. What is more, there is evidence that there were also Minoan settlements even in distant Phoenicia and Egypt.

To reiterate: I am contesting neither the possibility of geological catastrophes nor the probability of military conflicts. Such events always have and unfortunately probably always will take place. My doubts are directed against the notion that natural disasters or wars can account for the disappearance of certain cultures, and especially the Minoan. Cultures vanish by adjustment to more advanced neighboring cultures, by inner change, more rarely by abandoning areas on the fringes of the habitable world—a result, usually of having abused the environment. But that a highly developed, technically gifted people in a fertile area within a region the size of the Aegean world should be destroyed at one blow is a fiction which seems to be required only because Evans viewed the Minoans as an altogether extraordinary element who did not fit into the culture and civilization of the age. To sustain this view an imaginary Minoan world had to be created, which then had to be made to vanish. We shall see, on the contrary, that the Minoans were authentic members of the ancient Mediterranean world, in such close contact with the other peoples of the area, their manners and institutions displaying such a wealth of parallels to those others, that there is no reason to assign them any special position and exceptional character. Only inadequate knowledge of the other peoples could allow the impression to arise that the Minoans were unique and must have been wiped out in a body, leaving nothing of their secret to posterity.

It should not surprise us, therefore, that when Herodotus speaks of the twofold depopulation of Crete he mentions neither earthquakes nor volcanic eruptions nor tidal waves, but only the all too familiar disasters of war, famine and plague. In Book 7 of *The Histories* (sec. 170f) we read:

> The story goes that Minos went to Sicania—or Sicily as it is now called—in search of Daedalus, and there met a violent death. In course of time all the Cretans except the people of Polichna and Praesus, in obedience to some sort of warning from heaven, undertook a mass expedition to Sicania. Unable to take the place . . . they finally gave up and went away. In the course of their voyage they were caught by a violent storm off Iapygia and driven ashore, and, as their vessels were smashed up and they had no apparent means of getting back to Crete, they built for themselves the town of Hyria Oria between

Tarento and Brindisi. Here they stayed, thus losing their name and status of Cretan islanders and becoming known as Iapygians of Messapia. . . . According to the tradition in Praesus, men of various nationality, but especially Greeks, came to settle in Crete after it was depopulated by the expedition to Sicily.

From this passage it has generally been concluded that previously no Hellenes lived in Crete. But the sentence can also be read as indicating that the new immigration, consisting predominantly of Greeks but of other nationalities as well, merely added to an existing population of Greeks and others. In any case the new Hellenes did not come as hostile conquerors but as settlers to repopulate the partially deserted island. Nor is there any suggestion of a sudden natural catastrophe. An unsuccessful overseas military expedition reduced the able male population of the island so that the rest, consisting largely of old men, invalids, women and children, could no longer adequately cultivate the soil. But let us listen to Herodotus as he continues his tale:

> In the third generation after the death of Minos came the Trojan war, in which the Cretans proved themselves by no means the most despicable champions of Menelaus; their reward for this service on their return home was famine and plague for both men and cattle, so that for the second time Crete was denuded of its population. Thus it happens that the present Cretans, together with the remnant of the former population, are the third people to live in the island.*

Once again there is no question of total annihilation, but of fresh immigration after famine, probably due to prolonged drought and crop failures. And once again there is no mention of enemy attack, but of peaceful resettlement alongside the older population. On these points, at least, we have no reason to doubt Herodotus' words.

---

* Herodotus, *The Histories,* translated by Aubrey de Sélincourt (Penguin Classics, 1971), p. 474 f.

12

The Secret of the
Minoan Palaces

After my observations at the excavation sites had
reached this point I was faced with alternatives. I could content
myself with noting that a geological field investigation of the supposed catastrophes could not be carried out, and I could then leave
it to the Minoan archaeologists to devise new hypotheses and pro-
pose new solutions. Or else I could frankly state that I found
the previous interpretations unsatisfactory on geological grounds.
If I took this line, I would be casting myself as an interfering
outsider. Moreover, I would be defacing the lovingly painted
picture of the life of the ancient Minoans. But was it right for
me to remain silent concerning such faulty evaluation of the
observed facts and such glaring misinterpretations?

Since I did not know any German archaeologists who had participated directly in excavations on Crete (I think there are none
at present; in any case none has spoken up so far), I could only
turn to the press. The facts were so patent that at any moment
some other geologist or someone with training in geology would
arrive at the same conclusion I had. I had had a number of bad
experiences with the time-lag in publications by scientific jour-
nals. So it seemed to me that I must take my findings to a non-
professional organ that would then publish rapidly, so I could
stake out priority, at least for the time being.

At the same time I regarded such publication as a test. I had no doubt about the correctness of my geological findings. But I did not know how Minoan archaeologists would react. Would they be willing to consider the new concept? Or should I expect savage attacks of the kind the Linear B controversy had stirred up?

While still in Crete I had found time after my geological excursions—they ended early because of the autumnal shortness of the days—to record some of my thoughts on the problem of the Minoan buildings. Over an evening glass of red wine a good many phrases may have come out somewhat more challenging than is usual in scientific articles. But I was after all not writing for a professional journal, and not as an archaeologist I was taking on a problem for the pleasure of solving it. Some people thought I was maligning Sir Arthur Evans or the whole of Minoan archaeology, which of course I had not the slightest intention of doing.

After my return to Germany for the winter semester of 1970–1971 I delivered my inaugural lecture at my new university, Stuttgart. Shortly thereafter I received a request from a periodical intended chiefly for physicians, *n+m* (*Naturwissenschaft und Medizin*—"Science and Medicine"). The magazine wanted to publish the text of my first public lecture in Stuttgart. Since I prefer to speak extempore, I had only some notes, and now with the semester beginning, I had no time to work up the text into printable form. I therefore offered my Crete manuscript instead. It was accepted and printed.

The article outlined my doubts about the cogency of previous interpretations of Minoan buildings and attitudes on the basis of my geological observations. It lacked an extensive scholarly apparatus, for that had not been available to me in Crete. Later on, as I looked further into the subject, and partly as the result of letters and discussions, I began to see a good many additional elements which I had not considered earlier. Here and there my views changed somewhat, as will become apparent in the following pages—though not in regard to the geological observations about Knossan gypsum and my general tendency to see the Cretan palaces not as the homes of living kings, but as abodes of the dead. Since at the time I was unfamiliar with what Spengler had written in 1935, I made no reference to his suggestion that Knossos and the other Minoan "labyrinths" might have been temples to the dead. Basically, I agree with this view, although I would regard the term "palaces for the dead" as more accurate.

After setting forth my geological observations, as I have done here, I went on to say:

"Even before the actual era of palace building (in the Neolithic, Prepalatial period) the ancient Cretans were already proving their artistry in simulating wood, basketry and even metallic surfaces on pottery. During the period of the first palaces (*ca.* 2000 B.C.) they produced a type of ceramic whose dark-green grain with a subdued metallic gleam can at first glance scarcely be distinguished from bronze itself. (This type of pottery was first discovered in a cave of the Ithi Mountains near Kamares and has since been known as Kamares ware.) Heavy vase saucers of clay in this pseudometallic manner completed the illusion. Wonderfully thin cups of bronze-colored painted clay, known as "eggshell" ceramic, seem to be clever imitations of thin-walled bronze vessels. Such ware is hardly suited for practical everyday use. When the discoverers hailed these eggshell cups as signs of the overrefined luxury of the Minoan Age, they were probably thinking of fine Chinese porcelain—which, however, has much greater hardness and durability.

"The Cretans showed a similar faculty for simulation in their gold utensils: cult vases of considerable size were carved out of the very soft silicate mineral steatite, then coated with gold leaf to give the appearance of heavy embossed gold work of solid noble metal. This gold overlay was later removed, except for small bits, from the steatite core (which was valuable only from the artistic point of view). This sort of thing almost forces us to think of robbery of the palace sites, of a kind common to Egyptian and Etruscan tombs ever since antiquity. Nor did they scruple to imitate even the religious symbols of the Minoan realm, the famous double axe (*labrys*). Many of the specimens found are so thin that a vigorous blow on a hard object would have bent them.

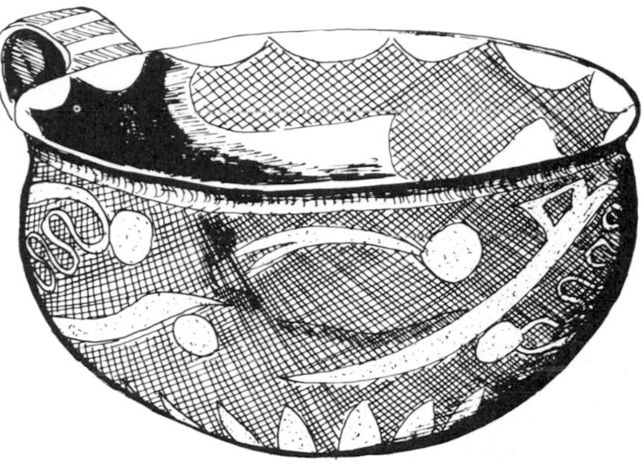

FIG. 44 Eggshell cup (Kamares ware), Old Palace of Knossos.

"It is a curious sham world we encounter in the Cretan palaces, full of imitations, although some of them are extraordinarily well made. The desire seems to have been an impressive appearance rather than solid workmanship for practical use. Any simple sandstone slab for a pathway or threshold, any ordinary stone column, even if rough-cut, any ordinary piece of rustic clay pottery, any primitive flint axe, would be more suitable for practical uses than this sham art. The impression remains, after repeated intensive visits to the archaeological museum of Herakleion, where most of the Minoan finds in Crete are collected, that only a few of the pieces served the practical ends of life. When we do think we have come upon real objects of daily use, the site of the find makes it clear that they were grave goods. . . .

"But what purpose could be served by a palace complex such as those of Knossos, Phaistos, Mallia or Kato Zakro when many of their rooms were rarely entered, scarcely any of the found objects ever had any practical use (except for ritual purposes) and the arrangement of the rooms with those innumerable zigzag corridors and stairs was as inconvenient as it could possibly be? Certainly the complexes could not have served the ordinary domestic purposes of a Priest-King, his family and servants, for in the course of the excavation the archaeologists had the greatest trouble finding even a few halfway "livable" rooms among all those big and small magazines that resemble honeycombs in some gigantic beehive. And then such rooms were finally found in the deepest core of the complex, two floors below the level of the central court of Knossos, without a direct view of the landscape below the palace hill, walled in by adjacent stories, with

air shafts which are more reminiscent of big-city courtyards than
of palaces. . . .

"In the 'king's domestic quarters' in the Palace of Knossos were
found two double axes which had originally stood, it would seem,
at the front of the room on a broken sandstone object that was
alternately interpreted as a throne and an altar. But since the
king already had a throne in the "official" part of the palace, and
had still another right next door in the living room adjacent to
the Sanctuary of the Double Axes, the altar interpretation seemed
the more probable. This was supported by comparison with paintings on the splendidly preserved sarcophagus from the Palace
of Hagia Triada in the southern part of the island. This sarcophagus is the pride of the Herakleion archaeological museum and
offers a graphic picture of the rites of the Minoan cult of the
dead. We see what are plainly two young Cretan women in the
company of a lyre-playing 'priest' in female dress. The women
are pouring the contents of large conical vessels with handles on
both sides into a kettle standing on a raised altarlike platform.
This kettle is flanked on both sides by upright double axes. In
the right portion of the picture the dead person can be recognized; he is shown in upright posture, though somewhat smaller

FIG. 45   Hagia Triada sarcophagus: offering to the dead.

than the other figures, and wrapped in shrouds that enclose the
limbs, leaving only the head free. Offerings are being made to
him; a huge bull's horn and two small images of black and brown
spotted bulls. In back of the dead man may be seen a painted
sarcophagus of the same shape as the one we are looking at, with
the same characteristic spiral painting of the corner posts. (To
judge by the form, these were, it would seem, originally carved
wood sarcophagi that were later imitated in clay.) The dead
man's conveyance in this world is a wagon drawn by horses,

represented at the foot of the sarcophagus; his team in the hereafter consists of griffins; their birds' heads and wings and their
feline bodies are plainly depicted at the head of the sarcophagus. The rear of the sarcophagus informs us of the nature of the
sacrifice. We recognize a bull trussed to an altar, its blood running into just such a vessel as the girls are carrying in the picture
on the front side of the sarcophagus. Obviously it is the blood of
the sacrificed animals that is being offered to the deceased; and
the sacrifice itself (the bull appears to be still alive) is performed
near an altar flanked by double axes at which a priestess is performing some office. The ceremony seems to be taking place in
the open air, before a brightly painted palatial building over-
shadowed by the crowns of trees. A musician accompanies the
proceedings on a flute.

"The separate panels on the sarcophagus represent the various
sites at which the cult of the dead was performed: sacrifice in
the open air, outside the palace of the dead; veneration and
offering within the burial chamber, where there would have been
no room for the whole ceremony of sacrifice. In his underground
vault (steps in the picture on the front of the sarcophagus indi-

FIG. 46 Hagia Triada sarcophagus: griffin wagon and sacrifice of bull.

cate the underground position of the burial chamber) the deceased receives only the horns of the bull, miniature models of
the sacrificed animals, and the blood—as proof that the sacrifice
was actually performed. Such models of sacrificed animals and
human beings (!) have been found in great numbers in the Cretan palaces; likewise vessels of all types and sizes for ritual purposes. The images of human beings frequently show typical
gestures of respect: the right hand raised to the forehead, or
above the heart.

"Human sacrifice must once have been practiced. The Greek tradition referred to earlier, that seven Athenian youths and seven maidens were offered to the Minotaur annually or every seven or nine years, certainly implies such sacrifices. And the numerous votive representations of human beings which accompanied the dead in later times were probably a form of substitution for the onetime human sacrifices. No doubt many less than well-to-do families had to content themselves with providing their dead with only model animals; genuine sacrifices must have been the prerogative of the prosperous.

"We might note that the deceased who is being carefully prepared for his voyage into the hereafter receives the offerings in upright posture. Later this seems to have been changed to a sitting position. Is it not strange that the selfsame cult objects depicted on the sarcophagus should have been found in, of all places, the so-called domestic quarters of the king in the Palace of Knossos? If so, that king was no longer among the living when he dwelt in these rooms! For the rooms identified by Sir Arthur Evans as living quarters evidently served for the performance of a ceremony such as is depicted on the Hagia Triada sarcophagus: the invocation and ritual veneration of a dead, not a living, person. And it is obvious that there was not just one such worshipful deceased in this palace, but a great many—as the numerous rooms of generally similar though somewhat less lavish appearance and appointments indicate. Countless others of the respected dead were venerated here—persons perhaps far less wealthy and high in station than the 'king'—and all of them in Knossos and the other similarly arranged Cretan palaces were the focus of ceremonies that to us seem macabre and almost incomprehensible. All were the recipients of similar offerings and in many cases bloody sacrifices while they were being prepared for their last rest, which in the ancient Cretan conception was not so much a rest as a continued life after death, with the body having some kind of presence in the hereafter.

"The palaces of Knossos, Phaistos, Hagia Triada, Mallia and Kato Zakro, therefore, were not the gay residences of peaceful and artistic rulers, as the imaginations of Sir Arthur and his successors have made them. In reality they were highly involved cult structures built for the veneration and burial of the dead. Sir Arthur—and innumerable visitors after him—have been deceived by the gracefulness of the frescos and by the above-ground and underground chambers, which recall the chateaux of baroque rulers. But reality was far less cheerful: a congeries of buildings meant for the ritual veneration and proper preservation of tens of thousands of dead from the better families of Crete. Instead of a joyous residence, these were funerary palaces where the dead were surrounded by pictures of the beauty of this world so that they might regale themselves with life's pleasures even after their departure.

"Etruscan tombs, too, frequently show gay, lively scenes of music, dance, hunting and daily life; they also depict matters such as physical love with a frankness that leaves nothing to the imagination. Such scenes were surely not intended for the general public. The idea was that the dead man, who in the view of the ancients had not really departed, would lack for nothing in the way of earthly pleasures in his tomb. We should therefore not regard the young women with bared breasts in the Minoan funerary palaces as early apostles of the topless fashion, and imagine that this was the type of clothing generally worn by women. Evans and along with him the Minoan professional archaeologists mistook the joyous and graceful sham world of the funerary palaces for the genuine world of the Minoan living. And in fact we must admit that the illusion is nearly perfect.

"Our cemeteries even today often present such a world of sham, with a great deal of emphasis on the dignity and serenity of death, though the tone is often marred by kitsch and tastelessness. But it is hard to conceive of an archaeologist in future millennia excavating one of our great cemeteries and interpreting its vaults, its chapels, its crematoria and administrative buildings as homes for the living; the funerary art, the urns and religious utensils as articles of daily life; and the *pompe funèbre* as an expression of our artistic feelings. In similar fashion the funerary palaces may well give a distorted picture of the authentic life of the ancient Cretans.

"In the light of this revelation we suddenly understand many things about the palace that seemed strange, and many of the traditions about King Minos's labyrinth. And the *pax Minoa*, that peaceableness of the Cretans at which the archaeologists have marveled, evidenced by the absence of walls and moats and bastions around Minoan palaces, now appears to us in a new light. It is nothing more than the peace of the graveyard. No one would dream of surrounding a cemetery—or a funerary palace—with defenses. The dead no longer need to be defended.

"On the other hand, the Cretan funerary palaces were more than mere cemeteries in our modern sense. The Minoans did have cemeteries (for poorer folk), as well as isolated temple tombs for important personages. Possibly the very occurrence of simpler graves and of artful vaulted tombs hewn into the rock cliffs around Knossos confirmed Evans in his belief that the buildings of the palace were intended for the living. But in fact all of Knossos with its two palaces, with its 'royal villa,' 'caravanserai,' temple and rock tombs, as well as its simple earth burials and its cave tombs further up the valley, constitutes an enormous realm of the dead on the slopes of a 'Valley of the Dead.' The development started with simple natural caves, went on to artificial caves, then to more and more cunningly crafted tombs, until it culminated in the funerary palaces 20,000 square meters in area. More than a mere cemetery, more even than the Etruscan necropolises (cities of the dead), these 'palaces' were institutions for commercialized care of the dead such as we will scarcely encounter anywhere in the ancient world outside of Egypt. The offerings to the dead, the conjurations of the dead, the veneration of the dead, the careful preservation of the body and provisioning it for the journey to the hereafter with all sorts of utensils, ornamentation and food (bowls of fruit and similar foods have been frequently found, charred)—all these things are alien to us today, and to some extent repellent. The dead were not simply buried in our modern sense, but were taken care of as though they were still animate. Only unimportant people and small children were rudely put into the ground. When bones of children were found beneath the pavements at Knossos, the archaeologists decided that Minoan children were buried beneath the floors of the living rooms! They interpreted the cist graves lined with alabaster in the 'magazines' of the palace as treasuries or as containers for grain.

"Personages of some rank were buried in clay sarcophagi (*lar-nakes*). In the course of time two types of larnax developed, the chest form and the bathtub form. An oval sarcophagus found in a burial chamber in the palace of Knossos, next to the Queen's Megaron, was promptly interpreted by Evans as a bathtub. But enough genuine and remarkably similar clay sarcophagi of oval shape, and even with remnants of bones in them, have been found in earth graves to leave no doubt about the true purpose of these 'bathtubs.' It can scarcely be assumed that the Minoans bathed in sarcophagi or had themselves buried in bathtubs, depending on the need of the moment!

"We will, therefore, have to part with the idea we all learned with amazement: that the Minoans were the inventors of the first refined bathing techniques in the history of civilization. The peculiar 'lustral basins'—shallow pits lined with alabaster—have been variously interpreted as underground shrines, bathrooms and cages for sacred snakes. In fact they were the display rooms for the sarcophagi of important persons—in other words, they were the actual burial chambers. The generally larger rooms adjacent to them, and frequently several stories above them (so that a great many stairs connected the upper rooms for worship with the lower-lying burial chambers), served for the cult of the dead and as places to keep the grave goods. The more distinguished and respected the corpse, the more stories it was necessary to descend to his burial chamber. In palaces of the living the finest apartments are situated at the highest point of a complex. In the palace of the dead this order is reversed. The Cretan

FIG. 47   Bathtub sarcophagus from Gurnia.

palaces had, after all, evolved from natural caves—with which Crete abounds. These caves originally served for burial and worship, and in western Crete were used in the same way as the palaces until well into the late palatial period. So was the Dikte Cave above the Lassithi Plateau. Given this origin, the urge to darkness and to depth is understandable. Since western Crete is particularly rich in natural caves, building artificial caves for the dead (palaces) was hardly necessary there.

"In addition to the ceramic sarcophagi man-sized artistically-ornamented ceramic vessels (pithoi) were used for burial purposes. Indubitable burial pithoi with remnants of bones in them have been found in cemeteries. Similar forms were in use in the Neolithic Age throughout the Mediterranean region as far as the Lipati Islands, north of Sicily. The palaces of the dead in Crete contain, as we have seen, pithoi in great numbers. But hitherto

FIG. 48   Chest sarcophagus, Palaeocastro.

everyone has followed Evans in calling these oil jars, since Knossos has been regarded as a palace of living kings. To be sure, similar large jars are still in use in the Mediterranean region, for example in Sicily, especially for olive oil. But they differ from the burial pithoi by their more stout-bellied shape, their plainer surface and the narrower opening at the neck. Since the wider the opening, the harder it is to seal, oil jars are deliberately shaped to be narrow at the mouth. They do not allow an adult to slip into them, as Luigi Pirandello has jestingly recorded in one of his Sicilian stories. Funerary pithoi, on the other hand, are shoulder-wide at their mouth; they belly out only slightly and narrow less sharply toward the bottom. These funerary pithoi may be found in virtually all the rooms of the palace. Some are arranged in long rows in the 'magazines,' others are single in chambers of their own, still others stand beside sarcophagi or in the corners of the '*megara*.' But again it is most improbable that the Minoans used such vessels for burials at one time and for oil storage at another, depending on the needs of the moment.

"But why are ceramic sarcophagi, funerary pithoi and earth burials found side by side? Why were not all the dead treated in the same way? The answer to this question is provided by Egyptian archaeology, which can supply us with vast amounts of information on the burial customs of the period. We shall return to this subject later; for the present a brief summary will suffice. According to Herodotus and Diodorus, the ancient Egyptians practiced three types of embalming. The first cost approximately $10,000 in modern currency (1 talent); the second could be had for 20 minas (about $2,500); and the third was cheap enough for the ordinary citizen. In the first method the intestines were removed and buried separately in what were called canopic vases, which had lids in the shape of human heads. The body cavity was filled with myrrh, cassia, resins and other aromatic and decay-inhibiting substances, and impregnated with soda and other alkaline salts. This practice of genuine mummification, so widespread in Egypt, seems hardly ever to have been used in Crete. At any rate, such mummies of people or of animals have not been found in the Cretan funerary palaces.

"The second, considerably cheaper method of preservation did not involve removal of the intestines. The body was filled with cedar oil. In the third procedure it was pickled. Both these more cursory methods of preservation seem to have been used in Crete. At any rate, the many funnel-shaped vessels called rhytons that have been found in the Minoan palaces along with brightly painted pitchers with extended pouring lips suggest that they were used for embalming. The rhytons were originally made of large, pointed triton shells whose ends were broken off so they could be used as funnels for pouring cedar oil. Later, when the right kind of tritons became rarer, artificial funnels in helical form were made, and artistic shapes based on the same motif were devised. Since Cretan ceramics have also been found on the Greek mainland, in Asia Minor and in Egypt we can deduce that the export of cedar oil probably was one of the most important sources of income for Minoan Crete. In Etruscan times the production of ointments and balm apparently shifted to the Greek mainland, for Greek ceramics occur frequently in the Tuscan tombs dating from about 700 B.C. By this time, possibly, the original wealth of cedar in the Cretan mountains had been so

FIG. 49   Wild goat rhyton. Representation of a shrine surrounded by high walls topped by sacred horns.

depleted that the production of balm (balsam oil) was diminishing. We might conclude that the wealth of Minoan Crete was also coming to an end—all the more so since the change in burial customs meant less and less demand for the ingredients needed for embalming.

"The cult of the dead seems to have been a profitable business in its heyday, as the prices for Egyptian embalming indicate. Hundreds of the Linear B tablets consist of lists of payments in kind, slaves, cattle, household goods and supplies. These were initially interpreted as tax lists; but if we consider that they were found in funerary palaces we shall be more inclined to regard them as bequests for payment of the funeral costs. The sheep was considered the unit of value; but in some cases the payment seems to have been made in the form of bronze bars, significantly cast in the form of a fleece, as the finding of numerous bars makes plain. It was distinctly expensive to be buried in keeping with one's social station in one of the celebrated funerary palaces.

"On the clay tablets we also find references to the artisans employed: incense burners, potters to make ritual utensils, makers of the ceramic sarcophagi for the embalmed bodies and funerary pithoi for the less important corpse, chair-makers for the special chairs found in several places. Of the last only those of sandstone or alabaster remain, of the type dubbed 'the throne of Minos.' The dead were originally venerated in upright posture, their eyes not closed but seemingly staring into eternity. But since they could no longer stand of their own accord, special chairs were used for the funeral ceremony. These chairs, originally of wood, later of stone, had typical high backs to give the upper part of the corpse's body firm support. Three indentations on either side apparently served for fastening supporting belts. Again, in order to give the body firmness on the seat, the seat was hollowed out; a ridge on the outer rim would have been troublesome to a living person, but it prevented the corpse from sliding off the seat. In addition, large numbers of female bath assistants are mentioned in the clay tablets. We can assume that the Minoans probably bathed and washed themselves while they were still able to. The ladies in question were probably engaged in washing corpses. In Pylos alone thirty-seven such attendants

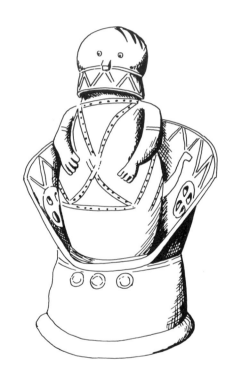

Fig. 50 Seats in the antechamber of the *Tomba degli scudi e delle sedie,* Cerveteri, Etruria. Etruscan tombs contain as many as five such chairs ("thrones") for ritual veneration of the dead during the months that the time of mourning lasts. The rounded form prevents the dead body from slipping sidewise off the seat. The actual burial vaults, whose doors are visible here, receive the dead only after completion of the prescribed period of mourning, which is simultaneously the period for drying out the embalmed corpse.

Fig. 51 Urn in human form on a chair, Chiusi, Etruria. Although the corpse was cremated, the urn suggests the wrappings that were wound like swaddling clothes around the mummified form of a body that was not, in the past, cremated. Before the practice of cremation came in, the bodies were embalmed and venerated on these "thrones" until, after the prescribed period of mourning, they were interred in the vault proper.

were employed to prepare the dead properly for the funeral ceremony and the hereafter.

"This necessity also explains the careful installation of wells, water pipes and drains in the Minoan palaces. What Arthur Evans and his associates took for a sign of the highest civilization—flush toilets—were nothing but a complicated arrangement for preparing the corpse for embalming.

"The supposed light wells that are said to have illuminated the deep interior of the palaces with 'magically indirect light' were probably ventilation shafts, without which the deep burial chambers would have been scarcely usable for lack of fresh air. Even so, without the burning of incense it would no doubt have been intolerable in the underground cult and burial rooms, for the smell of decay and of blood from the sacrifices must have been overwhelming. The fact that so many religious ceremonies still employ incense is a reminiscence—of which people today are unconscious—of this ancient cult of the dead practiced by all the Mediterranean cultures.

"But the question must be asked: Why did not Evans recognize the true function of the 'bathtubs' and the 'storage jars'? The answer is: Almost all of them were already empty before, smashed to pieces, they became embedded in the rubble of the palaces. Moreover, the Minoan sarcophagi had ventilation openings in the bottom (to help preserve the dried mummies), which Evans interpreted as drainage holes for the bathwater. Since, however, in the so-called bathroom next to the Queen's Megaron in the Palace of Knossos there are no indications of either water pipes or drainage tiles in the floor, bathing there would have been a difficult matter. The water would have had to be carried in and ladled out.

"But what happened to the tens of thousands of corpses that were once buried in the palace? Evidently the Cretan funerary

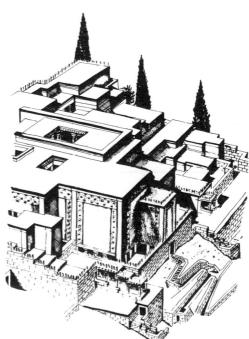

FIG. 52 Palace of Knossos: east wing. Reconstruction.

palaces, like most of the other tombs in Egypt and the rest of the Mediterranean world, were robbed in antiquity. Since it was dark and confined inside the labyrinth, the grave robbers smashed the sarcophagi and pithoi and carried the corpses, swathed in their wrappings, outside where it was easier to work. There they unwrapped the corpses in order to get at the jewelry and death masks. The result was that Evans found plenty of the religious vessels and votive figures that were worthless to the grave robbers, but only those few remnants of jewelry the robbers had missed. But the robbers must have found their work rewarding, for all around the palace, concentrated near the former exits, an agglomerate of bones and pithoi shards was heaped up several meters high. Possibly Sir Arthur thought these were refuse from the palace kitchens.

"The bones scattered all around the labyrinth helped explain why this place always seemed weird to the living. That is why legend made it taboo, so that no one wished to settle there (before the Turks of the seventeenth century)."

These are the essential passages from my essay, "The Secret of the Minoan Palaces," as it was published in the Spring 1971 issue of $n + m$. The article, as I have said, was intended as a trial balloon. I did not regard it as the definitive result of a carefully planned program of scientific research. The incompatibility of the sparkling picture Evans had sketched of the glory and destruction of Minoan culture with the geological facts had become a fascinating scientific problem to me. If the history of ancient Crete could not have been the way Evans had seen it, what had it been?

In the critical discussion of Evans's reconstructions the main issue is not such comparatively minor matters as bathtubs, water pipes, magazines of stores and domestic conveniences. These rather prosaic details acquire interest chiefly because of the extremely far-reaching deductions Evans drew from them in order to shape his picture of the early history of the eastern Mediterranean region which gave rise to a high civilization.

The development of Western man shifts one way or the other depending on how we view the position of the Minoan Age within the context of the Near Eastern and Egyptian empires, and within the cultures of the islands, Asia Minor and Greece, down to the relatively well-illuminated age of Homer. Evans placed his Minoan culture outside the stream of other cultures, according it a unique position and a special destiny. If we follow his argument, the millennium from the Early Minoan period around 2500 B.C. to the sudden extinction of the Minoan world by some catastrophe around 1450 B.C. was a golden age that left no mark.

Isolation, noncorrelation, uniqueness—a scientist who deals with the investigation of nature's laws finds it hard to accept this "individualistic" approach. Modern geology works principally with theoretical models of evolution. To be sure, the history of mankind obeys other laws—if it obeys any at all—than the history of the earth. But a geologist is also a scientist who thinks in historical categories, and something in him rebels when he is asked to accept a significant historical phenomenon such as the Minoan millennium as a kind of flash of lightning out of a clear sky, without antecedents and without consequences. That would constitute a unique and unparalleled exception from the general trend of evolution—and a physical scientist would be prepared to accept it only if it could be proved beyond the shadow of a doubt that the facts compel this interpretation which seems contrary to scientific "laws."

Minoan archaeology has not provided any such incontestable proof of the necessity of Evans's theory. My relatively simple geological and logical considerations, which were more or less forced on me when I confronted Evans's excavations and reconstructions in Knossos, inevitably led to doubts about the cogency of our traditional conception of Crete. Either those doubts had to be answered, or the problem of Minoan civilization had to be considered again within the framework of the whole cultural evolution in the eastern Mediterranean region, from which our own Greco-Occidental world has emerged.

In publishing my essay on "The Secret of the Minoan Palaces" I wanted to lead scholars to think through once again, without bias, the whole complex of questions surrounding ancient Crete, with the hope that in the end they might have a better basis for their picture of that society. What was intended as a spur to thought immediately set off vehement opposition. Shortly after publication of the article I returned from a trip abroad to find heaps of letters manifesting a public interest that I had never anticipated. In particular, physicians with a broad range of interests sent in a flood of questions and comments. There had been a number of additional notices in the press which had likewise aroused a lively response. And as is usually the case, readers who agreed wrote directly to me, while those who disagreed wrote to the press.

In the course of a year an extensive correspondence developed with specialists, amateur researchers and laymen in many parts of the world. I am grateful for their encouragement, objective criticism and useful suggestions. Inevitably, perhaps, there were also a good many venomous charges and personal insults fired at me, which did nothing to clarify the subject. I was to discover that Cretan civilization, at least in the visionary version presented by Evans, appeals so strongly to deep emotional needs in modern man that many people will not give up this dream and strike out wildly at anyone who disturbs it.

Interdisciplinary research often has to contend with wholly unscientific resistance. When revered doctrines of a greatly gifted founder are threatened, defensiveness against the heretical outsider is especially fierce. Perhaps that is because the endangered beliefs cannot be defended with rational arguments.

In order not to impede the train of thought in this book by a succession of digressions and repetitions I shall not go into the details of the controversy. Let us pursue our subject. If the Minoan palaces were not the residences of living kings, but funerary palaces for the dead who had not departed altogether into the hereafter, what does this new hypothesis do to our picture of the early history of the eastern Mediterranean region and of that phase when Europe was germinating?

13

Crete and Egypt

Onc of the few civilizations concurrent with the Minoan, likewise centered in the eastern Mediterranean region and already fairly well known during Evans's lifetime, is that of ancient Egypt. Evans was undoubtedly well informed on Egyptian finds and researches. He compared the findings of his own excavations with what had been discovered in Egypt. His conclusion, however, was that virtually no significant agreement existed between the Cretan and Egyptian cultures. The architectural and artistic findings seemed to him too different. It was precisely the lack of any such parallels that made him posit a "Minoan" civilization largely distinct from the contemporary eastern Mediterranean cultures.

This conception of Crete and Egypt as culturally without connection is well expressed in a letter sent to me by one knowledgeable reader of my articles:

> Egyptian and Cretan culture no doubt evolved at approximately the same time and attained great heights. But their ideas did not cross-fertilize each other. Both countries were completely separated, and only in later times were scanty trade relations established.

The letter goes on to discuss the Hagia Triada Sarcophagus, nd points out the lessons to be drawn from it:

There is no sign of Egyptian-style hired mourners, nor is any embalming of the corpse taking place. The dead man stands before his small mortuary, not as in Egypt before an impressive pyramid whose many chambers are painted with records of the ruler's military feats, and his hordes of prisoners, as well as with pictures of crafts and agriculture from which we can draw conclusions about the life of the ancient Egyptians. Nothing of the sort in Knossos. Not only is the bird of death absent but there are no traces of embalming of the dead. A long procession of figures bearing vessels, carrying themselves proudly and dressed in striking clothing, accompanies the visitor as far as the "Priest-King" at the entrance of the reception room. All the walls of these official chambers are richly decorated with paintings that give us an impression of the resplendent life that prevailed in the palace. By far the majority of the pictures are devoted to the religious games. . . .

Another correspondent, Hedwig Hinze, writes in the *Frankfurter Allgemeine Zeitung*:

But we also see a theater in Knossos. A long access route leads to a small theatrical area which is enclosed by wide, ascending tiers of seats. In the small Palace of Phaistos this row of seats in the theater is completed by a second row on the side. Among the religious games we must also mention the acts of the female snake charmers. Statuettes of them may be seen in the museum. . . . I should also refer you to the Harvesters' Vase, which depicts the singing and in some cases drunken harvesters returning from the gathering. It is an exuberant, cheerful picture with a strong emphasis on human characteristics. I have not seen such a joyous, cheerful atmosphere in Egyptian pictures, and it strikes me as strange to attempt to cite Egyptian cults as an interpretation of a Cretan palace.

FIG. 53
Fresco of
the procession,
Knossos.

Let us sum up the objections. Egypt is known for her pyramids, obelisks, temples, mummies, representations of military deeds, of crafts and agriculture, but there is no joyous and cheerful atmosphere in the somewhat stiff Egyptian pictures. In fact this stiffness pervades Egyptian painting even where scenes of daily life are represented, or where musicians or dancers are depicted, as in the graves of Nakht and of Nebamun in Thebes. At most a kind of cheerful serenity is attained in such paintings as the famous Walk in the Garden from the Amarna period (Berlin Museum), or in the mural showing the two daughters of Amenophis IV (Ikhnaton) from the palace adjacent to the Temple of Aton in Amarna, now at the Ashmolean Museum. Scenes of outright mourning are common, as are scenes of offerings to deceased persons on their funerary chairs, processions of offering bearers and of course the obligatory Judgment of the Dead scene. In the tomb of two Theban sculptors a mourning woman depicted at a funeral pours out torrents of tears.

FIG. 54   Procession of Keftiu, Tomb of Mencheperresenb, Thebes, fifteenth century B.C.

The Minoan pictures, on the contrary, are livelier, gayer, with a preference for animals and flowers and religious names. No mummies have been found in Crete, nor pyramids, obelisks or temples of the dead. Minoan architecture seems more human in dimension, although it lacks the symmetry and mathematical clarity of Egyptian buildings. Images of the gods and large-scale human figures are not found in Minoan Crete, unless we were to place representations of bulls and "snake charmers" in the first category. On the other hand religious games and theatrical performances seem to have been far more important in Crete than in Egypt. In other words, a considerable number of significant differences can be noted, differences that suggest the autonomy of Minoan civilization.

But was there really so sharp a separation between Crete and Egypt as is indicated in the words quoted above? There is considerable evidence to the contrary.

Thus, for example, Friedrich Matz states:

> The two kinds of flesh tone in [Minoan] painting—red or reddish brown for the men, white for the women—is a convention taken over from Egypt. In the paintings the men always appear almost undressed, except for an apron. In the warm season they really dressed that way, as they always did in Egypt. Those suntanned, bronzed bodies, which so effectively set off their flashing eyes, may therefore he regarded as authentic. [*]

Some further similarities are the pictures of processions, the small votive sculptures with whole herds of bulls and other animals, the great quantities of small male or female figures and the fondness for ceramic, carved stone or bronze imports.

A German expedition working in Egypt under Eduard Meyer brought back some extremely interesting photographs of typical Cretan processions painted on walls in fifteenth-century tombs in the Theban necropolis. Paintings of this sort were found, for example, in the tomb of Mencheperresenb, the tomb of Senmut and the tomb of Rekhmire. This would imply that the paintings were not accidental, isolated representations of some event, say, of a Cretan embassy "bringing tribute." Rather we are dealing here with an already standardized mode of tomb painting found in a whole series of different tombs.

---

[*] *Grosse Kulturen der Frühzeit, Kreta, Mykene, Troja,* 5th. ed. (Stuttgart, 1965).

FIG. 55   Keftiu: Tomb of
Rekhmire. Thebes, Eigh-
teenth Dynasty.

It is instructive to examine these figures more closely. To begin
with, they are plainly labeled *Keftiu*, that is, Cretans. In dress
and attitude they largely resemble their Knossan cousins, and
their gifts are the sort of Cretan artifacts with which we are
familiar: elegantly painted vases, bowls, big jars with one or
several handles, kraters with the Minoan spiral pattern, bucket-
like vessels with painted bulls' heads, even a rhyton resembling
the famous one found by Evans in the Palace of Knossos near
the grand staircase to the *piano nobile*. There are also copper
bars in ox hide form (that is, cast in the shape of an ox's hide),
small images of bulls (or possibly bull calves) and even whole
bulls' heads with mighty horns. In the tomb of Mencheperresenb
a priest in a long white garment walks in the van of the Cretan
procession, holding a tiny human figure (an offering, a votive
image?).

How does a Cretan procession such as we have already seen
in the Palace of Knossos, or rather how do several versions of
such Cretan processions, come to be in the tombs of courtiers
of the Egyptian Eighteenth Dynasty?

The official answer given in Egypt is: "They are bringing tribute to Pharaoh, as the supreme ruler of the land, from an island
that owes him tribute."

But how strange that rich Minoan Crete with its dominion
over the sea should have owed tribute to the Egyptian pharaoh.

The Minoans had a powerful navy, whereas the Egyptians supposedly had but little experience in sailing on the high seas. Why did not the Cretans simply stay at home on their sheltered island, out of reach of demands for tribute from pharaoh in his distant Land of the Nile?

The whole business becomes even more mysterious when we find listed on clay tablets from the labyrinthine Palace of Mari in the central Euphrates Valley utensils similar to those borne by the Keftiu processions in Thebes and Knossos. The tablets even mention that the objects were made by Cretan artists, and thus apparently imported from Crete. Did Crete also owe tribute to the lords of Mari in Mesopotamia?

And if these figures marching in procession were bringers of tribute, why should the ruler of Knossos depict a similar tribute procession in his own palace? Was this the megalomania of a petty sovereign who in reality was subordinate to others? But with the exception of the copper bars, most of the supposed tributary gifts have only artistic value. A boy, it is true, might be sent as a sacrifice in the place of an adult victim. Crete could then repay herself with those famous Athenian boys and girls that she received! But the bulls' heads and the ritual vessels scarcely represent the kind of material wealth usually demanded in tribute payments. And what is the meaning of this curious back-and-forth movement of double or triple tributes from Athens to Crete and from Crete to Mari and Egypt?

Indications of the presence of Keftiu are found in other Egyptian tombs besides those of Thebes. Thus vessels of Cretan provenance and fragments of authentic Minoan Kamares vases have turned up in the Egyptian necropolises of Abydos, Kahun and Illahun. Late Minoan Post-palatial vases have been found in Tell el Amarna, the residence of Ikhnaton, whose religious reforms initiated the relaxed and joyous Amarna style. Under his successors Sakere and Tutankhamen the ruling family returned to Thebes. The consequence was a religious and spiritual restoration under the dominion of the Theban priests of Amun. Along with this there was a reversion to the strict Egyptian style in art. The attempt at reform in art, religion and thought had been defeated. The priestly caste in Thebes once more sat firmly in the saddle, and managed to check all later attempts at reform. Egypt became a living museum in which Stone Age and Bronze Age religious notions were carefully preserved down to the period of the Roman Empire. Progressive thinkers may find this deplorable. But for scholars researching early history this museum without walls which was Egypt is of priceless value. Through it we can step directly into periods of humanity's intellectual and spiritual development which have elsewhere been so overlaid by new ideas and so altered in emphasis that the original outlines are no longer recognizable.

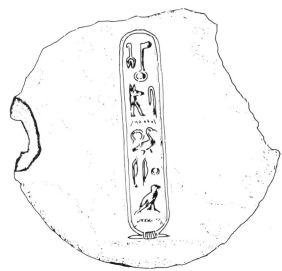

FIG. 56   Alabaster lid with cartouche of Pharaoh Chian (Seventeenth Dynasty), found at Knossos.

But let us return to the Cretan "payments of tribute" to Egypt. Our questions about the matter multiply when we examine the objects in the Herakleion Museum, which are clearly identifiable as Egyptian by their form or by their inscriptions. Among them are many Egyptian bronze statuettes, scarabs and offering bowls of hard crystalline stones that could not have been made in Crete because the stone was quarried in Egypt. In particular there is an inscribed diorite statue and the lid of a box formerly owned by Pharaoh Chian. In a grave in the port of Knossos an alabaster vase with the royal insignia of Pharaoh Thutmosis III (*ca.* 1490–

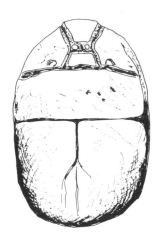

FIG. 57 Egyptian scarab (Middle Kingdom), Knossos. Scarabs were often inserted into mummies in place of the heart. The real beetles supplied cantharidin, at once a poison and an aphrodisiac.

1436 B.C.) has been found. These finds indicate reciprocation: the Cretans paid "tribute" to the Egyptians, who expressed their gratitude by return gifts from the royal possessions. Obviously such dealings went on between equals; this was not a case of real tribute.

Or were the two parties simply engaged in trade, and do the processions show Keftiu merchants arriving in the presence of Pharaoh? But then what is the meaning of those curious "wares" in the hands of the Cretans and why are these things particularly found in tombs? And, moreover, in tombs in both Egypt and Crete! If the items were bales of cloth, a trade agreement would seem indicated. But such a grab-bag of peculiar works of art hardly suggests sober and honorable merchants. Or are these processions a kind of national spectacle? Possibly a parade of Cretans with their odd utensils may have had the attraction of novelty and foreignness in Egypt. But then, why would King Minos have had an exactly similar procession painted in his own palace? Wouldn't he have preferred the spectacle of Egyptians, since he had his own people before his eyes every day?

But let us take a closer look at one of these processions of Keftiu. In the tomb of Mencheperresenb the first person behind the leader in the long white "priestly garment" (with the "sacrificial boy" in his hands) is a reddish figure dressed only in a loincloth, the "bearer of the bull's head." On a platter he holds aloft a reduced image of a Cretan bull, only the head and horns. We know these images of bulls from the Cretan palaces. An especially fine specimen was found during Nicolas Platon's excavations at Kato Zakro: a rhyton of black steatite in the form of an animal's head. It is now in the Herakleion Museum. The piece was once painted and gilded. The inside is hollow and there is a small spout at the mouth. Obviously it is a ritual drinking vessel of the kind used in Minoan consecrations.

Let us reflect on this: Minoan cult objects in Egyptian tombs; Egyptian votive pieces, amulets and statuettes in Minoan tombs and palaces! What was that statement we cited above: "Egyptian and Cretan culture . . . did not cross-fertilize each other. Both countries were completely separated, and only in later times were scanty trade relations established." The finds in the tombs of both Crete and Egypt prove the opposite.

Otherwise why would typically Cretan cult objects be found in tombs consecrated to Egyptian beliefs in the hereafter? And how are we to explain the similarity of the processions in the Theban tombs and the Palace of Knossos except as proving the close connection between certain religious ideas? Do they not indicate a relationship between the Minoan palace and Egyptian funeral rites?

What the archaeologists explained as a Cretan payment of tribute to Pharaoh must be seen today as a procession within the framework of a major Egyptian burial ceremony. The procession

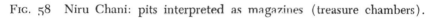

FIG. 58 Niru Chani: pits interpreted as magazines (treasure chambers).

is, of course, not moving toward a living pharaoh, but toward a deceased high official of ancient Egypt who sits on his funeral chair in the traditional pose of the venerated corpse. The figures in the procession are rendering homage to the owner of the tomb himself; and they have not come under compulsion, because they owe tribute, but voluntarily. In other words, they have been invited not to amuse the common folk or to pay tribute to a worldly power, but because Egypt has nothing like them. These figures depict Greek, or more specifically Cretan, healers who possessed power over death, who by their art could preserve the deceased for eternal life. As late as the era of the Roman Empire the grandees among Mediterranean peoples had themselves treated by Greek physicians. And when medical art failed to save them, Greek embalmers preserved their bodies for eternity. To this day the snake of Aesculapius serves as the symbol of the medical profession. It was not the Egyptians themselves who developed the art of embalming to its height, but disciples of the experienced Greek physicians—whom the Egyptians then heaped with gifts from the wealth of Pharaoh in gratitude for their services. The Egyptian *taricheutes* (embalmers) were merely apprentices of the Knossan art of medicine and embalming, assistants who remained at the artisan level.

I have been accused of inventing out of hand Minoan mummification and the rites of the funerary cult as practiced in the Cretan palaces. But in the museum at Herakleion we can still admire the bronze medical equipment of one such disciple of Aesculapius. The embalmer had to be thoroughly familiar with human anatomy, for otherwise he would mutilate the corpse and fail to arrest the processes of decay. In the next chapters we shall learn how the embalmers went about their work. The Cretans were greatly aided by nature in this respect, especially by the vegetation of their country. The cedar still grew on their island, supplying the dry distillate known as cedar oil, the *kedrion* of the Greek physicians. With ladanum, a resin obtained from various types of rock roses or cistus grown on Crete, loss of hair was prevented; it was also used as an astringent drug. The fruits and roots of *Punica granatum*, the pomegranate tree, were employed medicinally. Thus the pomegranate constantly appears on Mediterranean tombs (it may be seen, for example, in the small classical mortuary in the Palermo archaeological museum). The distillate of bridal myrtle (*Myrtus communis*) supplied a popular beauty elixir ("angel water"), and the big-leafed myrtle (*Myrtus c. var. romana*) was used to make wreaths and garlands for the dead. We shall have much to say later about the famous Cretan honey.

It was not easy to pour the various medicaments into the openings of the body. Evidently the funnel-shaped rhyton, which seems to have been mandatory in the equipment of a Cretan procession, served this purpose. Application of fluids to the exterior of the body was done in special tubs such as are used to this day in institutes of anatomy—shallow basins in which the body was laid for specific periods of time. A group of German physicians who visited the Palace of Knossos in June 1971 under the guidance of prehistorian Helmut Thierfelder of Münster looked rather closely at those built-in pits in the substructure of the palace, "small and medium-sized chambers with walls about half a meter high, which look like small baths." They came to the conclusion "that these facilities were like arrangements for mummification, of such construction that the body could be laid in a brine 30 or at most 50 centimeters deep."

But if this was the case, why did the custom of mummification not persist in Greece, and why do we not have a single well-preserved mummy from Greece when we have endless numbers of them from Egypt? During the restless times of the "Dorian Migration" and the "Invasion of the Sea Peoples" toward the end of the second millennium B.C. robberies of tombs and necropolises became more and more common. In order to forestall desecration of the grave the custom arose of cremating the body, and with it all the grave goods. (In the beginning, at least, careful anointment of the body preceded cremation.) Moreover, Greece's damp Mediterranean climate was far less favorable to the preservation of mummies than the desert climate that prevailed throughout much of Egypt (except for the thickly-settled Nile Valley). The great Egyptian necropolises were built on the margin of the desert.

The tomb paintings of Upper Egypt show us all the stages of the ancient rites of the dead, as Herodotus observed and described them in the Hellenic Age. By this time the Egyptian practices had long since been abandoned in Greece and were felt to be strange. More than half a millennium, after all, separated the age of Herodotus from the Minoan Age, and the Egyptian technique of mummification had undergone further development and therefore deviated further from the Cretan procedures.

An essential part of the Egyptian funeral processions were flocks of sacrificial animals, funeral ceremonies with music and dancing, a banquet, competitions of naked boxers or swordsmen, spearing fish on the Nile and finally crossing of the river to the realm of the dead in the West. Small clay or bronze statuettes were given to the deceased as servants for the afterlife. Those who could afford it made sure of having 365 of these votive figures, one for every day in the year.

In Knossos and other Minoan sites hosts of such terracotta "servants" have been found, as well as vast quantities of votive animals for sacrifice, mostly in the form of bulls. But whereas the Egyptians stressed clarity and symmetry in their architecture, but were careless about numbers where sacrificial beasts were concerned, the Greeks were extremely pedantic about having the precise numbers of animals for sacrifice. Thus on Linear B tablet Kn Db 1099 we find mention of ninety rams and ten ewes; on Kn Dg 2180 (both from the Palace of Knossos) there are thirty-nine young, ten old and forty yearling rams, and eleven sheep. In both cases the sum of animals on a tablet adds up to exactly a hundred.

Werner Ekschmitt comments:

> It is a peculiarity of most Cretan sheep herds, at least on the Linear B tablets, that they amount to exactly 100 animals. It is even more remarkable that these herds consist for the most part of males. Perhaps such herds can be found in the Land of Decipherers; but it is patent that in all of present-day Greece not a single such herd exists, nor did it exist in antiquity. Readers of the Bible may recall Jacob's reconciliation gift to his brother Esau when he returned: 200 goats, 20 bucks, 200 ewes, 20 rams, etc. (Gen. 32:15). In round numbers such figures give the natural proportions of a normal herd. Thus, we cannot believe the palace administration was listing normal herds; these animals can only have been sacrifices (hecatombs).

The Greeks in Homer also sacrifice such hecatombs—a hundred old ewes and rams no good for further breeding—to both the

gods and (deceased) human beings. The clay tablets found in
the Palace of Knossos therefore contain (in part) lists of hecatombs. We know similar lists from the Egyptian papyri. One
especially comprehensive list of this type is contained in the
"great papyrus Harris I" in the British Museum. Günther Roeder*
describes it as follows:

> When the death of Ramses III was approaching, or had perhaps
> already taken place, the royal chancery issued instructions to
> all the temples to hand in a report on the status of their pos-
> sessions and to list gifts that had accrued to the temple during
> the ruler's reign. . . . The royal chancery wrote an introduction
> which is placed on page 1 of the papyrus preceding the entire
> document. . . . The document was dated on the day of King
> Ramses III's decease. The royal chancery pasted the reports
> from the three major temples, which had been written on a
> strip of papyrus of the prescribed format, side by side in the
> original, without having them copied. A copy was made of the
> reports from the other temples.

The entire work thus provided an inventory of the king's sacrifices and donations.

> As king I have built you a temple; payments flowed into its
> magazines; I donated grain for your temple; I listed my dona-
> tions for your temple on two bronze tablets; I adorned your
> statues with amulets and necklaces; I made you a secret chapel
> out of the stone of Elephantine; I made you mighty decrees
> with secret words, set forth in the hall of writings of Ta-Meri,
> engraved on steles of stone, graven with the chisel, to admin-
> ister your venerable house unto eternity, and to administer
> your pure establishment of women I annually had the collectors
> deliver honey and incense to your temple; I set up magazines
> of grain for your temple; I donated royal figures with gift-
> offerings. . . .

This lengthy document was given to the deceased pharaoh to
take with him into the afterlife as written proof of his generous
gifts to his father, the venerable god Ptah, throughout his lifetime: Ptah, "the mighty one, south of his wall, lord of Anch-tawi,
Ta-tenen, father of the gods, tall in feathers, pointed in horns,
beautiful in face, dwelling in the great place."

---

* *Die ägyptische Gotterwelt*, Vol. I (Zürich and Stuttgart, 1959), p. 21.

Knossan Linear B tablets were also lists of the frequently lavish offerings made by the deceased to the gods and their ancestors. These inventories enabled them to prove in the hereafter how much good they had done to the gods, just in case the gods might have forgotten. The offering lists served as testimonial to a life pleasant to the gods and as letters of recommendation that should win them the best possible reception into the world of the "living dead." That hoards of such tablets have been found in more than fifty places in the Palace of Knossos (and only those accidentally baked by fire have survived!) proves that the labyrinth served as a burial place for vast numbers of prosperous citizens.

The royal chancery was not located where the dead man's papyrus or clay tablets were found—that is, in the tombs—but in the dwellings of the living. Possibly, however, a special scribes' office was attached to the larger funerary palaces to draw up such "books of the dead" and to carry on the correspondence from the living to the dead.

The Keftiu priest-physicians with their assistant healers; their sacrificial boys (for every life that was to be saved or preserved for eternity another life, either of a boy or a girl, had to be sacrificed); their libation cups and unguent vessels, rhyton funnels, vases of kedrion, ladanum, myrtle, pomegranate and honey; their bronze surgical instruments and their skilled hands, were always welcome, awesome and well-paid guests. With their implements and their medical knowledge of the vital organs, which had to be removed before embalming lest they cause the body to decay too swiftly, these Cretan priests must have made a tremendous impression on primitive minds. The mere appearance of one of their processions probably had a curative psychological effect. And once a person died, such a Keftiu procession created a tone of elegance, supernatural magic, mysterious powers and cosmopolitanism—in short, a *pompe funèbre* that could scarcely be surpassed. That is probably why the Keftiu were painted on the walls of a tomb even if they had not been present for the actual funeral ceremonies.

We find Cretan traces in Egyptian graves over a lengthy period of time in the important Eighteenth Dynasty (*ca.* 1560–1309 B.C.). Interestingly enough, the influence persists whether the priestly caste of Thebes is in power or whether religious reforms have been launched under Ikhnaton. Whether the supreme god was called Amon or Aton, the dead wanted to continue living in the hereafter; and no one understood the business of the dead as well as those mysterious Keftiu.

These visits to Egypt profited the Keftiu in a number of ways. In addition to the tokens of gratitude pressed upon them for their medical aid (some of which gifts ended up in their own tombs), in addition to certain Egyptian products used in their mortuary rites (such as natron, asphalt, incense and myrrh), they also must have brought back new ideas. Thus Greek legend tells us that Daedalus, the builder of the Knossan labyrinth, modeled his structure on a then famous Egyptian building, the labyrinth of Amenemhet III. This pharaoh, also known by the name of Ammenemes, reigned during the Middle Kingdom as the sixth ruler of the Twelfth Dynasty (1839–1791 B.C.). He is considered the colonizer of the Fayum, a fertile region within the Libyan Desert, southwest of Memphis, the capital of Lower Egypt. His labyrinth, a temple of the dead where funerals and memorial services were conducted, was situated in the vicinity of his pyramid tomb at Hawara, 8 kilometers east of Medinet el Fayum.

Describing the labyrinth of Fayum, I. E. S. Edwards has written:

> Ammenemes III had been immortalized by the classical historians as the constructor of Lake Moeris in the Faiyum and as the builder of a labyrinth in the neighborhood of the lake, which was considered to bear comparison with the older labyrinth of Minos at Knossos in Crete. . . . Ammenemes III's connection with the labyrinth has been proved . . . as Petrie was able to show in 1888–9 when he excavated this king's second pyramid at Hawara and discovered that its mortuary temple was, in fact, designed as a kind of labyrinth. It was a large construction, covering an area of about 1,000 feet in length and 800 feet in breadth. In plan, it differed from every known mortuary temple, consisting not of a series of courts and corridors leading to a sanctuary, but of a large number of separate courts arranged in rows. Few architectural details could, however, be recognized by Petrie, so complete had been its destruction.[*]

[*] *The Pyramids of Egypt* (New York: The Viking Press, 1947, 1961), p. 174.

We can obtain some idea of the appearance of this labyrinth from the testimony of ancient writers. For instance, the geographer Strabo, a widely traveled popular writer who wrote in Greek, around 25 or 24 B.C. accompanied the Roman prefect M. Aelius Gallus to Syene, to the frontiers of Ethiopia and to the Red Sea. Some time around A.D. 18 he compiled the seventeen books of his *Geographica,* based on his own observations and the writings of others. In the last book he describes Egypt and Libya in the following terms:

> We have here also in the labyrinth, a work equal to the pyramids, and adjoining to it the tomb of the king who constructed the labyrinth. . . . There is a table-shaped plain, with a village and a large palace composed of as many palaces as there were formerly *nomes* [districts]. There are an equal number of aulae [courts], surrounded by pillars, and contiguous to one another, all in one line and forming one building, like a long wall having the aulae in front of it. . . . There are long and numerous covered ways, with winding passages communicating with each other, so that no stranger would find his way into the aulae or out of them without a guide. The surprising circumstance is that the roofs of these dwellings consist of a single stone each, and that the covered ways through their whole range were roofed in the same manner with single slabs of stone of extraordinary size, without the intermixture of timber or of any other material. On ascending the roof—which is not of great height, for it consists only of a single storey—there may be seen a stone-field, thus composed of stones. Descending again and looking into the aulae, these may be seen in a line supported by twenty-seven pillars, each consisting of a single stone. . . . At the end of this building . . . is the tomb, which is a quadrangular pyramid. . . . They built, it is said, this number of aulae, because it was the custom for all the *nomes* to assemble there together according to their rank, with their own priests and priestesses, for the purpose of performing sacrifices and making offerings to the gods, and of administering justice in matters of great importance. Each of the nomes was conducted to the *aula* appointed for it.*

---

* Strabo, *Geographica*, Book XVII, I, 37 (Bohn). Quoted in *ibid.*

Thus Strabo, writing around the beginning of the Christian era, described the Egyptian labyrinth, probably from direct personal knowledge. He found many of the structures in a tumbledown condition.

Barely half a millennium earlier another Greek had traveled in the land of the Nile: Herodotus, the Father of History, whose description of immigration into Crete we have cited earlier. We have no precise dates for the life of this famous man. It is said he was born around 484 B.C. in the city of Halicarnassus in Asia Minor and died soon after the beginning of the Peloponnesian War in 430 B.C. in the colony of Thurii on the Gulf of Tarento in southern Italy. Herodotus led the life of a scholarly globetrotter. His voluminous work entitled "Account of Research" (usually known as *The Histories*) fortunately has been preserved. It is a lively book, richly studded with anecdotes and adventures. What this narrator had to say, often from his own observations, about the history, customs and arts of strange peoples in distant lands of the ancient world remains highly readable to this day. Herodotus visited Egypt after the Persian reconquest of the country, that is, after 448 B.C. His visit took place in the autumn months, when the Nile waters were receding.

In the second book of *The Histories* Herodotus describes how he visited the labyrinth of Hawara. In his introductory remarks he speaks of the builders as twelve "kings." (He means the district commanders of the Delta region; the number twelve is probably unhistorical.) These twelve kings were united by intermarriage and "governed in mutual friendliness on the understanding that none of them should attempt to oust any of the others." Herodotus continues:

> To strengthen the bond between them, they decided to leave a common memorial of their reigns, and for this purpose constructed a labyrinth a little above Lake Moeris, near the place called the City of Crocodiles. I have seen this building, and it is beyond my power to describe; it must have cost more in labor and money than all the walls and public works of the Greeks put together—though no one would deny that the temples at Ephesus and Samos are remarkable buildings. The pyramids, too, are astonishing structures, each one of them equal to many of the most ambitious works of Greece; but the labyrinth sur-

passes them. It has twelve covered courts—six in a row facing north, six south—the gates of the one range exactly fronting the gates of the other, with a continuous wall round the outside of the whole. Inside, the building is of two storeys and contains three thousand rooms, of which half are underground, and the other half directly above them. I was taken through the rooms in the upper storey, so what I shall say of them is from my own observation, but the underground ones I can speak of only from report, because the Egyptians in charge refused to let me see them, as they contain the tombs of the kings who built the labyrinth, and also the tombs of the sacred crocodiles. The upper rooms, on the contrary, I did actually see, and it is hard to believe that they are the work of men; the baffling and intricate passages from room to room and from court to court were an endless wonder to me, as we passed from a courtyard into rooms, from rooms into galleries, from galleries into more rooms, and thence into yet more courtyards. The roof of every chamber, courtyard, and gallery is, like the walls, of stone. The walls are covered with carved figures, and each court is exquisitely built of white stone and surrounded by a colonnade. Near the corner where the labyrinth ends there is a pyramid, two hundred and forty feet in height, with great carved figures of animals on it and an underground passage by which it can be entered.*

That "white stone" of which the courts are "exquisitely built" we have good reason to believe was "alabaster," or possibly ordinary gypsum, for Egypt is poor in marble.

Given all the interconnections, we can scarcely go on regarding Crete as an isolated civilization. Rather we see that the island fitted into the general cultural and civilizational context of the rest of the eastern Mediterranean region. In earlier chapters we called attention to the various ties with Etruria. The conception of a Minoan civilization rising to a solitary height, autonomous of all the other cultures of the area until it succumbs to geological and military catastrophes, leaving no traces upon the later civilized world, can no longer be sustained—for archaeological reasons. All we need do is to look beyond the specialized

---

* Herodotus, *The Histories*, translated by Aubrey de Sélincourt (New York: Penguin Books, 1955), pp. 160 f.

boundaries of Minoan, Mesopotamian, Egyptian or **Etruscan** archaeology and seek the interconnections. Egypt offers the unique advantage that for over a long period of time it preserved ways of life and forms of culture that had long been abandoned in Greece and the rest of Europe. Thus Egypt already struck Herodotus as an alien world, although it was not Egypt but Europe that had come such a distance from a shared stock of Stone Age and Bronze Age ideas.

Anyone who takes the disparate artistic styles as proof that there could have been no link between Crete and Egypt ought to consider what stylistic differences also exist between the Minoan and Helladic eras, although we know today that they were closely connected linguistically and in other ways. In the one case there is a geographic separation, in the other a gap in time, the interval being occupied by the Late Bronze Age and the Early Iron Age, and dominated in art by the protogeometric, geometric and archaic styles.

Nevertheless, all these styles are linked by a continuous stream of transitions. Linguistic and mythological tradition winds a narrow band around Minoans, Mycenaeans, Late Bronze Age

FIG. 59 Evolution of styles rather than a break in continuity, exemplified by pottery. 1 and 2: Late Mycenaean (thirteenth–twelfth centuries B.C.), from Mycenae. 3: Submycenaean (twelfth–eleventh centuries B.C.) and 4: Protogeometric (eleventh–tenth centuries B.C.), both the Kerameikos Cemetery, Athens.

and Iron Age Greeks. To be sure, our knowledge of the Minoan and Mycenaean periods is fairly recently acquired, and but for the excavations in Crete and the Peloponnesus we might never have known about them. But this does not mean that the period of classical Hellas was without contact with the supposedly vanished preceding cultures.

The preserved frescos found in the Palace of Knossos show us what importance cult games had in Minoan life. Here is one tradition that was undoubtedly intensively cultivated in classical Greece in the form of religious festivals in honor of the heroes. And it is precisely in this tradition of the Hellenic Age that the heroes of ancient Crete live on side by side with those of the Greek mainland and islands. The tradition of Minoan Crete was not lost; it survived, just as the traditions of Mycenaean Greece survived, in mystery plays and festivals.

It is significant that ancient Egypt also had such mystery plays. Günther Roeder writes:

> The Egyptians did not only read their mythological tales (given the restricted nature of Egyptian education, few were able to do so), but also saw them as dramatic performances. Those with religious belief or dramatic talent participated as actors or singers. . . . The mystery plays of Osiris in Abydos were famous; one portion of them, the mysteries of Isis, survived and attracted seekers well into the Christian era. . . . A festival play given at the accession of pharaoh represents the pharaoh as an embodiment of Horus who took over the rule of the earth from his father Osiris.

A stone memorial found at Edfu in Upper Egypt ° carries an inscription on the life of the actor Meheb: "I am he who followed his master on his ways and who did not fail in reciting. I played opposite my master in all his recitations. If he was a god, I was a ruler. If he killed, I brought back to life." The wall enclosing the Temple of Edfu showed, in eleven scenes, episodes of the ancient mystery play of "Horus Stabs his Antagonist Setech as a Hippopotamus."

One significant difference between the Egyptian and the Greek theater lay in the Egyptian concentration on the life of

---

° See Étienne Drioton, "Le théâtre égyptien," Revue de Cairo, 1942.

the gods. Heroes, that is, great men sprung from the people, were hardly ever glorified. But the Greek theater characteristically featured plays about heroes (as well as mystery plays).

To put the matter in modern terms: Egypt was unacquainted with stories of the "self-made man of the people" who by his own efforts rose to divine station. Egypt in fact offered practically no chance for common folk to rise in the world. Her heroes were gods or princes, not men of uncertain origin who later had to claim one god or another as their father because they could not point to any earthly father (quite often because they were children who had been begotten or born in a temple). In Egypt it seems the children of the temple prostitutes were usually exposed—partly as a measure against overpopulation. In Greece even those without a biological father of high rank could attain to high honors.

The Greek myths relate how this was done. What was involved in the Greek stories (in Teutonic stories also) was usually a visit to the underworld, where the hero encountered all sorts of dangers, but from which he might also return home with a "hoard" (guarded by strange, fabulous animals, underworld figures and "dwarfs")—that is, richly laden with treasures. To put this in blunter language: a hero won power and wealth by plundering a temple treasury or the gravegoods of a tomb shrine. Such a deed did not require a warrior spirit, since it was not so much an armed enemy as terror of strange, unknown powers that had to be contended with. And once the hero had the cash in hand, everything else might well arrange itself—a wealthy heiress could be found, smoothing the path to a further rise and helping to establish a dynasty.

Egypt had no such heroes. The country was too orderly for such exploits, too much under the control of a centralized government. Not that the Egyptians were any more successful than the Greeks in curtailing grave robbing. But if they caught the "robber heroes," they would bring them to trial and punish them as common criminals. Under Ramses IX the stonemason Hapi, the skilled artisan Iramun, the peasant Amenemheb, the water carrier Kemwese and the Negro slave Ehenufer were captured, and after torture (they were beaten on their hands and feet with a double switch) they confessed:

We opened their coffins and their coverings in which they
were. We found the august mummy of this King. . . . There was
a numerous string of amulets and ornaments of gold upon it;
the august mummy of this King was overlaid with gold throughout. Its coverings were wrought with gold and silver, within and
without; inlaid with every costly stone. We stripped off the gold,
which we found on the august mummy of this god, and its
amulets and ornaments which were at its throat, and the covering wherein it rested. We found the King's wife likewise; we
stripped off all that we found on her likewise. We set fire to
their coverings. We stole their furniture, which we found with
them, being vases of gold, silver, and bronze. We divided and
made the gold that we found on these two gods, on their mummies, and the amulets, ornaments, and coverings, into eight
parts.[*]

Rich booty was found in tombs, as Heinrich Schliemann and
Howard Carter were to discover. In the twelfth century B.C.
precious metals already had commercial value; before that period
gold had been used chiefly for the cult of the dead. Amulets,
too, and possibly parts of mummies had magical and curative
properties. Whatever was not needed was discarded or set afire
(possibly the traces of burning in tombs come from such fires).
It was impossible to prevent grave robberies; and because of
this, as we have said, there was a gradual changeover to the cremation of corpses in the protogeometric period of ancient
Greece. Egypt, always fixed in its religious ideas, would not
adopt the new-fangled practice. In Greece, however, the "Heroic
Age" ended when there was no longer an underworld to force,
no hoards to be won. All the grave goods were now burned up
along with the body. Quite often bronze utensils in tombs were
smashed before the burial and placed in pottery vessels (there
are such "deposit finds" at the Lipari Museum). Or the bronze
was melted down and poured into the form of bars, like the bars
that weigh 29 kilograms each from Hagia Triada, or the similarly shaped bars of the Keftiu processions shown in the Egyptian
Eighteenth Dynasty tombs at Thebes.

[*] C. W. Ceram, *Gods, Graves, and Scholars,* second revised ed. (New
York: Alfred A. Knopf, 1970), p. 159.

The Minoan altars with rounded hollows, and the shallow bowls with raised rims and pouring spouts found in many Minoan sites, have their parallels in the altars and libation bowls found in Egyptian tombs. Minoan archaeology, however, has identified these bowls, which were intended for libations, as either lamps or basins for oil mills (depending on size). The curse the Egyptians imposed on those who did not obey their testaments or who violated their graves read: "May their offering stone remain empty and the libation for the dead be denied them."

From a letter written by the widow Merti to her deceased son (Upper Egypt, First Intermediate Period, between the Old and the Middle Kingdoms, 2280–2050 B.C.) we learn that beer was brewed in Egypt as early as the third millennium B.C. and that it was used as a libation for the dead. The procedures connected with brewing, such as the malting of barley, are thus very ancient—this accounts for the barley reapers noted in the hieroglyphic and Linear B inscriptions.

In malting, the barley is roasted after it has begun to germinate, thus preventing further growth of the sprouts. Following the roasting, the malt, with certain additives, is fermented into beer. It does not take very much ingenuity to guess that the process of malting was invented comparatively early, simply as a method for preserving the grain in grave goods for the afterlife, experience having shown that it quickly sprouted because of the effects of moisture in the underground storage places. But when the roasted barley was again subjected to moisture, the process of

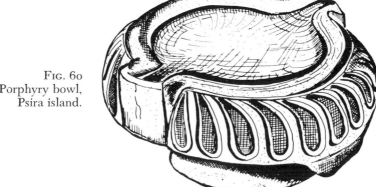

FIG. 60
Porphyry bowl,
Psira island.

fermentation necessarily began, ultimately producing an intoxicating product whose effects may well have contributed significantly to the ancients' fantastic notions about the afterlife. Ultimately the beer thus accidentally brewed was deliberately reproduced and found its way into the profane world.

For malting, comparatively large vessels are needed, and these must be fireproof. It may be that the astonishingly voluminous round bronze containers of the Late Palatial period, now in the Herakleion Museum, represent the oldest malting coppers in the world that have come down to us, from an age before wine had become the usual libation in Greece. The recent spread of beer consumption in the Mediterranean region (and beyond), partly as a result of mass tourism, is thus merely a return to a beverage that was brewed as long ago as the Bronze Age—though a good part of the beer then was undoubtedly intended for the consumption of the dead in the afterlife. In the time of Strabo *zythos* (barley wine) was generally drunk in the taverns of Alexandria.

An odd kind of resemblance between early Crete and ancient Egypt is to be found in their faulty arithmetic: there are errors in addition in Linear B and in the Egyptian hieroglyphic writings. Werner Ekschmitt in his criticism of the Linear B decipherment [*] devotes a page and a half to discussion of such an arithmetical error in the famous Pylos tablet Py Ab 553. The text is supposed to deal with rations (wheat and wine) for "bath personnel." All that is quite definite is the number of individuals, their sex and the quantity of victuals to be distributed to this group. The figures do not balance; Ekschmitt shows that the sum of what was issued to each individual comes to a quantity of only 654 liters instead of the indicated 666 liters. Any such deviation in a tax register or in palace records seems incompatible with orderly bookkeeping. Ekschmitt uses this disparity as one of his major reasons for finding the texts "on closer examination contradictory and incredible, and that all the more so since efforts are made to gloss over these contradictions by arbitrary tricks of printing, calculation and interpretation." We can well understand how Ekschmitt's sharp criticism would evoke from the Ventrisians equally sharp retorts, the first two of which have already

[*] *Die Kontroverse um Linear B* (Munich, 1969).

appeared in print. But this is not the place to discuss this controversy.

Nor do we wish to discuss the more general question of the extent to which tax lists and other such records are free of error even (or especially) in the age of computer technology. But it is pertinent to our subject that in the bequest made by Pharaoh Sheshonk I (*ca.* 950–929 B.C.) for his father Namirt's funerary services there are no less than five arithmetical mistakes, although the accounts deal not with a ludicrous few bushels of wheat or figs, but with silver and a servant. (The missing amount of silver is at least 70 grams.) Any serious administration would unquestionably have straightened out such arithmetic errors. Ekschmitt might also charge the Egyptologists with contradictory and implausible decipherments when in fact the mistakes were made by the scribes of the original texts. The point is that these were not figures intended for serious administrative purposes; the calculations were for the cult of the dead, who were not likely to check them. In fact exaggerating the numbers was probably not unwelcome to the donor interested in his reputation. We certainly cannot apply the standards of a modern bureaucracy here.

I should like to conclude this comparison between Minoan Crete and Egypt with a digression, an argument I put forward with circumspection and a warning to the reader that for the present it remains wholly hypothetical.

Digression: Who was Minos?

Arthur Evans named Minoan civilization after the legendary first King of Crete. The myth runs: Minos, Rhadamanthys and Sarpedon are sons of Zeus, begotten in Crete on the Phoenician Princess Europa. Europa afterward marries the native ruler Asterios who adopts her three "sons of the god." Minos drives out his rival brothers and becomes king. He marries Pasiphaë, a daughter of Zeus and the nymph Krete—that is, his half-sister. The *Oxford Classical Dictionary* says of Pasiphaë (in the article on Minos): "Her name, 'all-shining,' has been interpreted as that of a moon-goddess, which is unnecessary, as it fits a fully human child of the sun-god (*cf.* Phaëthon); but that both kings and queens of Minoan Crete were regarded as partly or wholly divine is quite possible." The same article suggests that "Minos" may be a dynastic name or title.

Diodorus Siculus distinguishes two kings: Minos I, the son of Zeus, and Minos II, the son of Lykastos. He makes Minos II out to be the grandson of the first Minos.

The trouble is that in the mythographic tradition there is a gap between Minos I and his grandson Minos II of no less than two hundred years. A gap of one hundred years between the lifetimes of grandfather and grandson is conceivable, but certainly not two hundred. There is a strong temptation to resolve this puzzle by assuming one or more Minos dynasties in the early history of Crete. "Minos" then would be both a personal name and a title.

In this context I wish to mention a delightful *aperçu* by H. Thierfelder, professor of ancient history at the University of Münster. In conversation Professor Thierfelder called my attention to the similarity, perhaps not accidental, between the names Minos and Menes. Menes is the Hellenized form of the Egyptian royal name Meni. Since the vowels are not given in Egyptian script, there is no way of telling what the word sounded like to Egyptian, Cretan and Hellenic ears.

If—and I would stress once more that for the present there can be no certainty about these matters; we must rely on suppositions that perhaps cannot be proved but that may stimulate us to further reflection—if the name "Minos" for the ancient Cretan dynasty should be derived etymologically from the Egyptian name Meni-Menes, we would have here an early example of the generalization of a proper name. An important human being lives on in his legitimate or usurping successors, who deck themselves with the potent magic of his name and thus become, after a fashion, his heirs. This dynastic "trick" is a common phenomenon in world history. The most familiar example is the transformation of the name underlying all the Kaisers and Czars of the Occident. These titles all derive from the barely republican or perhaps already monarchistic Roman Gaius Julius Caesar.

Now who was Menes?

Menes was the unifier of the first empire, the Old Kingdom, of the Egyptians. In 2950 B.C. he united Upper and Lower Egypt under his rule. He was the oldest and thus the most revered great majesty of the ancient world, and reigned over an empire whose extent and population is imposing even by modern standards.

The Egyptians of around 1700 B.C. did not speak of their rulers as "pharaoh"—this term comes from the Bible. They used the traditional elaborate title: "Horus who established the two lands, Horus victorious over Nubti [a reminiscence of the victory of the prince of the southern Falcon District over Nubt], Lasting in love, Son of Re [in Memphis this would be Son of Ptah, in Hermopolis Son of Thoth], Hawk and Serpent [corresponding to the gods of Upper and Lower Egypt]." Or: "Beloved of Osiris, the First in the West, Lord of Abydos"—thus went the title of Noferhotep, for example. It was not until the New Kingdom, after the fourteenth century B.C., that it became customary in Egypt to use the term Great House (Egyptian *par-ó*) to designate the royal palace, the court and finally the king. Apparently there was trepidation about naming the king himself, so instead people spoke of "the court." It is surely not by chance that it was in this period that the enormous mortuary temples with attached palaces (the Ramesseum, Medinet Habu, etc.) were built.

From *par-ó* came the "pharaoh" of the Bible which we use today to denote the entire line of Egyptian kings from Menes to the Ptolemies.

Yet official titles remained; e.g., for Thutmosis III (1490–1436 B.C.) Egypt's greatest warlord: "Strong Bull, Shining in Weser [Thebes], Felicitous in Royalty as Re in Heaven, Mighty in Strength, Glorious in Crowns, King of Upper and Lower Egypt, Lord of the two Lands [Menchoper-Re], as Son of Re." Or for Ramses II (1290–1223 B.C.), known for his many buildings: "King of Upper and Lower Egypt, Strong is the Truth of Re [*Woser Maat Re*, for which reason he is called King Usermare in Greek tradition], Son of Re, Beloved by Him, Lord of the Crowns, like Re Gifted with Life in Eternity, Beloved of Osiris, the Lord of Abydos." The titles of Ramses III (1181–1150 B.C.), the builder of Medinet Habu, add another note: "King of Upper and Lower Egypt (Strong is the Truth of Re, Beloved of Amon), Life, Health, Hail, the Mighty God."

From the "Son of Re," Ramses II, "a mighty god" has come:

in other words, the deification of the pharaohs gained ground from the nineteenth to the twentieth Dynasty. This accounts for the reluctance of the Egyptians (and, obviously, of the Hebrews as well) to pronounce the names of these divinities openly. The euphemism used was "at court," "in the Great House," "in the palace": *par-ó.*

In the early dynasties it may be that the popular term for "pharaoh" was the name of the first of the line, Menes. But if the Cretan title Minos was really equivalent to Menes—that is, was the name of the office—then the established notion of an autonomous "Minoan" culture would be stripped of its meaning. It would be a "Menean," that is, an Egyptian culture. But in spite of the similarity in sound, we ought not to go that far.

14

Balsam and Honey: Mummification

W e can pick up a goodly amount of information on the
burial rites of ancient peoples of the eastern Mediterranean region from the Bible (Gen. 50), from Herodotus (*The Histories*,
Book II, 85, and Book IV, 26), from Lucian (*De Luctu*, 21),
from Diodorus (I, 91–92) and from Porphyrius (IV, 10). Among
more recent modern sources is the wealth of medical studies on
mummies.

On the orders of his son Joseph, Jacob's body was "embalmed"
by physicians familiar with the art; "And Joseph commanded
his servants the physicians to embalm his father, and the
physicians embalmed Israel. And forty days were fulfilled for
him; for so are fulfilled the days of those which are embalmed;
and the Egyptians mourned for him seventy days." Jacob's embalmed body was taken to Canaan and buried after a further
seven days of mourning. (The number seven was considered
sacred in ancient Egypt.) Joseph, too, was embalmed after his
death (at the age of 110), but he was buried in a sarcophagus in
Egypt.

Even at the time of the New Testament rubbing the body with
unguents and spices was still practiced: "And when the sabbath
was past, Mary Magdalene, and Mary the mother of James, and
Salome, had bought sweet spices, that they might come and
anoint him" (Mark 16:1). The Church of the Holy Sepulcher in

Jerusalem still contains the *kline* (the bierlike platform in the rock tomb) on which the anointing is said to have been performed.

The Syrian sophist and satyrist Lucian of Samosata (*ca.* A.D. 120–180), who wrote in Greek, declares in his treatise *On Mourning:* "The Greek burned his corpses, the Persian buried them, the Indian coated them with *hyalos* [rock salt? isinglass?], the Scythian devoured them, but the Egyptian made them into mummies."

Concerning the *hyalos* used by the Indians and the Ethiopians, Herodotus says (III, 24):

> The method the Ethiopians follow is first to dry the corpse, either by the Egyptian process or some other, then cover it all over with gypsum and paint it to resemble as closely as possible the living man; then they enclose it in a pillar of *hyalos* which has been hollowed out, like a cylinder, to receive it. The stuff is easily worked and is mined in large quantities. The corpse is plainly visible inside the [transparent] cylinder; there is no disagreeable smell, or any other cause of annoyance, and every detail can be as distinctly seen as if there were nothing between one's eyes and the body. The next-of-kin keep the cylinder in their houses for a year, offering it the first fruits and sacrificing to it; then they carry it out and set it up near the town.[*]

Who, reading this passage, will not be reminded of Lot's wife, who perished during her flight from the burning city of Sodom and "became a pillar of salt" (Gen. 19:26)? That is, she was apparently buried in a *hyalos*, in keeping with this oriental custom.

Since rock salt is soluble under moist conditions and readily clouds on exposure to air, the material is more likely to have been easily workable isinglass, that is, transparent gypsum, or possibly mica (muscovite) sheets.

Herodotus also speaks of the strange custom of eating the dead (IV, 26):

> Some knowledge of the practices of the Issedones has come down to us: for instance, when a man's father dies, his kin bring

---

[*] Herodotus, *The Histories, op. cit.,* p. 184.

sheep to his house as a sacrificial offering; the sheep and the
body of the dead man are cut into joints and sliced up, and
the two sorts of meat, mixed together, are served and eaten. The
dead man's head, however, they gild, after stripping off the hair
and cleaning out the inside, and then preserve it as a sort of
sacred image to which they offer sacrifice. This service of son to
father may be compared with the Greek ceremony of Genesia,
or commemorative offerings. In other respects the Issedones
appear to have a sound enough sense of the difference between
right and wrong, and a remarkable thing about them is that
men and women have equal authority.*

Herodotus tells this tale of the Central Asian Issedones' funeral
customs with some reservations, but he does give us a very
realistic picture of the procedure of mummification in ancient
Egypt. In addition, as mentioned, we can draw upon two other
classical writers. One of these was Diodorus Siculus of Agyrium,
in Sicily. All we know about this writer's life is that he lived for
a considerable time in Rome and in Egypt around 60–56 B.C. For
thirty years he wrote away on his *Bibliotheke* ("World History"),
a history of man from the very beginnings of recorded knowledge
to Diodorus' own time, when Caesar was undertaking his Gallic
Wars. We may be certain that Diodorus, when he speaks of
Egypt in the first of his forty books, was giving us authentic
recollections of his own experiences in that country.

The other classical writer to whom we are indebted for information about the customs of mummification in Egypt is
Porphyry. The real name of this versatile and knowledgeable
philosopher and prolific writer was Malchus. He was born *ca.*
A.D. 234 in Phoenician Tyre, 75 kilometers southwest of present-
day Beirut in Lebanon. For ten years (until 262) he studied
philosophy in Athens under Longinus, then became a disciple of
Plotinus in Rome, where he probably remained until his death
between 301 and 305.

From the information given by these three writers we may put
together the following picture of mummification in ancient
Egypt, although we must also consider that the procedure
changed considerably during the long period from about 2000

---

* *Ibid.*, pp. 250 f.

B.C. to A.D. 200, and that what was done in the various places of
Upper Egypt (which comprised the temples of Amun in Karnak,
the temples of Luxor, the mortuary palaces and rock tombs, and
the Valley of the Kings in Thebes West, on the left bank of the
Nile) varied somewhat from what was done in Lower Egypt
(which comprised the capital Memphis, 20 kilometers south of
Cairo, the pyramid tombs of Giseh, Sakkara and Dahshur, and
the temples of Ptah and the sacred Apis bull).

Let us hear the testimony of Herodotus first (II, 85):

> When a distinguished man dies, all the women of the house-
> hold plaster their heads and faces with mud,° then leaving the
> body indoors, perambulate the town with the dead man's female
> relatives, their dresses fastened with a girdle, and beat their
> bared breasts. The men, too, for their part follow the same
> procedure, wearing a girdle and beating themselves like the
> women. The ceremony over, they take the body to the embalm-
> ers [taricheutes].† Embalming is a distinct profession.‡ The
> embalmers, when a body is brought to them, produce specimen
> models in wood, painted to resemble nature, and of three pos-
> sible grades; the best and most expensive kind is said to rep-
> resent a being whose name I shrink from mentioning in this
> connexion; the next best is somewhat inferior and cheaper,
> while the third sort is cheapest of all. After pointing out these
> differences in quality, they ask which of the three is required,
> and the kinsmen of the dead man, having agreed upon a price,
> go away and leave the embalmers to their work.§

° A light, sticky clay that according to Diodorus was not removed during
the entire seventy-day period of mourning. Possibly this custom went back
to the use of fertile Nile mud as a symbol of future fertility. During the
mourning period the relatives took no baths, avoided wine and tasty dishes,
restricting themselves to the simplest, most essential foods, and dressed
in dark clothes.

† But the bodies of young girls and women were kept at home until
decay set in, for fear that the embalmers might violate the corpse.

‡ According to Diodorus the embalmers comprised a caste, the work
passing from father to son. According to the Bible embalming was a profession close to that of medicine; the men were familiar with "pickling" the
flesh, "sewing up" the corpse and treating it with "spicy stuffs."

§ Herodotus, op. cit., p. 133.

According to Diodorus:

> The body is now placed on the ground, and first the marker
> [*grammateus*] indicates on the corpse's left hip how much ought
> to be cut through. Thereupon the "slitter" [*paraschistes*] takes
> the Ethiopian stone that he holds in his hand [a nephrite or
> flint blade] and cuts through as much as the law commands,
> of the flesh, and then hastily flees while the kinsmen pursue him,
> throwing stones at him, cursing him, and as it were heaping
> upon his head all the sinning that is being done against the
> body. For they believe that anyone who commits violence upon
> a body of the family, wounding it or hurting it in any way, is
> hateful.

According to Diodorus, the *taricheutes* or embalmers hold the
same position and rights as priests. He continues:

> When the embalmers have assembled for the preparation of
> the opened body, one of them inserts his hand into the opening
> cut into the corpse as far as the cavity of the chest and takes
> out the intestines, up to the heart and kidneys [he "trieth the
> heart and reins," so to speak]. Another cleans the intestines
> piece by piece and washes them in Phoenician wine and spices
> [*thymiamata*]. Then they prepare the body with cedar oil and
> myrrh and cassia and other medicaments, which not only pre-
> serve it for a long time but also make it sweet-scented [evi-
> dently the drugs mentioned by name were generally applied,
> whereas the "others" remained a trade secret of particular fam-
> ilies of embalmers].
>
> Thus every part of the body is preserved so unharmed that
> even the hair on the eyelids and eyebrows remain, the entire
> form of the body continues unchanged, and its shape can be
> discerned.

Herodotus goes into greater detail on the matter of the three
classes of Egyptian mummification. For the most expensive:

> As much as possible of the brain is extracted through the
> nostrils with an iron hook, and what the hook cannot reach is
> rinsed out with drugs [*pharmaka*; a syringe or funnel would
> have been necessary for this]; next the flank is laid open with a
> flint knife [as Diodorus reports] and the whole contents of the
> abdomen removed; the cavity is then thoroughly cleansed and

washed out, first with Phoenician [palm] wine and again with an infusion of pounded spices. After that it is filled with pure bruised myrrh, cassia and every other aromatic substance with the exception of frankincense, and sewn up again, after which the body is placed in natrum [sodium carbonate, Na_2CO_3—the Greeks called it *litron*], covered entirely over, for seventy days —never longer. When this period, which must not be exceeded, is over, the body is washed and then wrapped from head to foot in linen cut into strips and smeared on the underside with gum [*kommi*, a plant resin], which is commonly used by the Egyptians instead of glue [*kolla*]. In this condition the body is given back to the family, who have a wooden case made, shaped like the human figure, into which it is put. The case is then sealed up and stored in a sepulchral chamber, upright against the wall.*

Here Herodotus is confusing the effigy of the mummy which was set up in the *serdab*, a special room in the tomb, with the actual sarcophagus in its inaccessible burial chamber. Incidentally, the rectangular tombs of the Egyptian Old Kingdom resembled, when covered by drifting sands, the benches outside houses and have therefore been called by the Arabic word for such benches, *mastabas*.

The embalmers took particular trouble with this "perfect" method of embalming, and charged a great deal. According to Diodorus, this first-class burial cost a talent, or something like $10,000. The method was used chiefly in Thebes (Upper Egypt), but sometimes also in Memphis (Lower Egypt). Its drawback lay in the fact that the septum was destroyed, which resulted in a slight flattening of the nose. This phenomenon has nothing to do with the possible appearance of syphilis in ancient Egypt, as suggested by F. Kuchenmeister in 1885.

According to Czermak, another technique was used in Lower Egypt which avoided this destruction of the septum. There the practice was to remove a brain by an incision at the back of the neck at the level of the atlas, and then fill the brain and spinal cavities with pitch from the asphalt springs of the Dead Sea and Asia Minor. The pitch was liquefied by heating. If pitch

* *Ibid.*, p. 133.

were also used to fill the abdominal cavity, it would not be necessary to sew up the incisions in that part of the body. In some
cases the intestines were placed in wooden boxes and thrown into
the Nile; in other cases they were replaced in the body after having been cleaned (a custom that persisted until the nineteenth
century in the funeral rites of some parts of India, where the
body was first embalmed and then burned). One peculiar custom was that of stripping the skin from the soles of the feet
(and sometimes from the palms of the hands as well). Possibly
this was connected with the application of painted or gilded
ornamentation on the hands and feet. The stripped skin has been
found enclosed in pitch inside the abdominal cavity, along with
pieces of intestine.

The surface of the body was coated with a thick black layer of
mummy resin. Sometimes the linen bandages on the body were
also covered with resin. The extremities were wrapped separately;
the bandages can be unwrapped in layers and sometimes run to
2500 meters in length. Male mummies had their arms crossed
over their chest; women's arms were placed at their sides, palms
pressing against their thighs. Concavities in the body were stuffed
with wads of cloth; women's breasts were pressed flat against
the thorax. Skull measurements differ widely ("Egyptian," "Semitic," "Pelasgian," etc.), so that it is impossible to speak of
any one racial stock. Body hair was either removed or fell out
during the pickling process, with the exception of eyelids and
eyebrows, which did not come into contact with the pickling
solution.

The ceremony on the day of the corpse's transfer to the tomb
(eternal dwelling) included the voyage in the funerary ship
across the Nile to the graveyards, mortuary temples, mastabas
and pyramids. The deceased had also to face the Judgment, conducted by more than forty judges of the dead sitting in a semi-
circle around him. The Judgment served to expiate the sins of
the deceased, who could find rest in his eternal dwelling only
after his obligations in the world of the living had been fulfilled
and any wrongs he had committed atoned by his family according to the customs of the country. This fear that the ghosts of
the unshriven dead might return was also common in the European Middle Ages. To this day customs involving the judgment of

the dead are said to crop up occasionally in the Arab world. In ancient Egypt the realm of the dead was strictly separated from that of the living (except during the mourning period of up to one year). The graveyards were located across the river on the edge of the desert—west of the Nile at Memphis and Thebes, on the eastern side of the river at Beni Hassan and Tell el Amarna —as a rule on the sides of the hills that rise behind the narrow, fruitful valley of the river.

Those of the deceased who did not pass Judgment, and also pawned mummies, could not set out on their voyage across the river until all their obligations in the world had been met. Failure to redeem pawned mummies was considered a grave disgrace upon the mummy's entire posterity, and even after the passage of generations the children's children would do everything in their power to assure such mummies decent burial by redeeming them. If the deceased was of high rank, the embalming and veneration took place across the river in the valley temples below the pyramids or in the mortuary palaces outside the Valley of the Kings. Important corpses such as those of pharaohs had several funerary dwellings, tombs and cenotaphs in various parts of the kingdom. It seems likely that the preservation of the body was not only a matter of individual interest; the Egyptians apparently believed such preservation was necessary for the fertility and prosperity of the country, on which man and beast depended—including, of course, all the deceased's descendants. Here was a country whose tillable area and wealth were governed solely by the variable height of the annual Nile flood, which depended on unknown elements, for the highlands where the Nile had its sources were inaccessible. Early in Egypt's history, accordingly the belief took shape in a direct connection between the well-being of the local and national gods, both living and dead, and the welfare of the country. This was particularly the case with Osiris, the god of vegetation whom the pharaoh personified and whom the goddess Isis awakened to new life. Every pharaoh was also regarded as the god Osiris, as the death masks and the inscriptions on the mummy wrappings testify. And it was every Egyptian's firm belief that if insufficient respect were shown for the god Osiris, in the form of the living or dead pharaoh, the country could expect drought, poor harvests and famine. Constant fear of failure of the Nile flood, or even of too sparse a flood, drove the Egyptians to the most lavish death cult of the Stone and Bronze ages. Similar trains of thought, however, were probably common to most of the human race in that remote age.

Concerning the two cheaper types of mummification, Herodotus writes:

> When for reasons of expense the second quality is called for, the treatment is different: no incision is made and the intestines are not removed, but oil of cedar is injected with a syringe into the body through the anus which is afterwards stopped up to prevent the liquid from escaping. The body is then pickled in natrum for the prescribed number of days, on the last of which the oil is drained off. The effect of it is so powerful that as it leaves the body it brings with it the stomach and intestines in a liquid state, and as the flesh, too, is dissolved by the natrum, nothing of the body is left but the bones and skin. After this treatment it is returned to the family without further fuss.*

According to Diodorus Siculus, the charge for this second procedure was 20 minas or about $3000.

In the third method of embalming, used by the poor, the body was simply rinsed out with *syrmaia* and then kept in natrum for seventy days, after which it was returned to the family. Herodotus earlier (II, 77) defines *syrmaia* as a strong purgative which the Egyptians were in the habit of using for three days out of every month "in the belief that all diseases come from the food a man eats." F. Kuchenmeister believes that the *syrmaia* might have been the juice of fresh radishes which, he says, when consumed in sizable quantity produces "drastic effects."

Diodorus Siculus indicates that the third-class "poor man's" embalming was quite reasonable in price, but he gives no figures. One other advantage of this simpler method seems to have been that no violence was done to the corpse, since it did not have to be opened by incision. But undoubtedly the Egyptians regarded the second and third classes of treatment as inferior because the external form of the body was not so well preserved, and because the intestines were destroyed, whereas in the first method they

* Herodotus, *op. cit.*, pp. 133 f.

were returned to the abdominal cavity after cleansing. It is only natural, though, that with increasing density of population the process of mummification would have had to have been rationalized. Hence the development and the promotion of a simple treatment using chemicals in solution. Since these methods meant that sizable profits could be made from the masses, the composition of the reagents remained a secret. Neither Herodotus nor Diodorus was able to find out what substances were used. Czermak assumed they were largely concentrated solutions of sodium hydrate to which cedar oil or radish juice were added, partly to conceal the smell. To test this theory F. Kuchenmeister carried out experiments on animal brain tissue and discovered that such tissue was in fact most quickly dissolved by such a mixture. This reagent works better than a mixture of potassium and sodium hydrate or of potassium hydrate alone, whereas a solution of saltpeter in pickling solution (two parts of saltpeter and one part common salt) made the brain tissue harden, and a mixture of salt and radish juice produced no effect. Natron was abundantly available in Egypt from the salt deposits of Wadi al Natrun and other dry basins of the interior. But the cedar oil from the mountains fringing the eastern Mediterranean must have been extremely expensive (especially in larger quantities) and therefore an important commodity of commerce—as were myrrh and incense.

It is at any rate clear that strong solutions of alkalis, assisted by a goodly dash of cedar oil, soon reduce the brain and other tissues of the human body, including the intestines, to a soaplike mass easily soluble in water. The resultant matter can be removed from the abdominal cavity by rinses of lukewarm water. After the abdominal cavity dried, it was partially filled with liquid pitch in order to prevent a subsidence of the body. What resulted was not a homogeneous mass of pitch; the pitch coagulated in many irregular lumps, suggesting a degree of lingering moisture inside the body.

On the whole, Egyptian mummification proves that the *taricheutes* had a great deal of empirical knowledge concerning the application of reagents. Inevitably they also acquired a sound knowledge of the interior of the human body; after all, in the course of Egyptian history hundreds of thousands of corpses were available to them for experimentation. From the hygienic point of view, mummification must be recognized as a good method for preventing the spread of harmful germs and toxins.

Since only some of the requisite ingredients for embalming were to be found in Egypt, the embalmers were dependent on imports, probably secured by barter. The principal ingredients involved in this commerce were cedar oil from the mountains of the eastern Mediterranean and incense and tincture of myrrh from the arid areas of southern Arabia, east Africa and India.

There were also some other ingredients used for the preservation of corpses. According to Aemilius Probus (whose statement is confirmed by Cicero), corpses were often embedded in honey or wax. That was done, for example, with the bodies of Spartan kings. King Agesiuaus of Sparta, who died in 360 B.C. in Kyrene (Cyrenaika), was preserved in honey like Alexander the Great. Alexander was temporarily coated with honey in Memphis and subsequently taken to Alexandria where his mummy was still on display during the lifetime of St. Augustine (A.D. 354–430).

FIG. 61   Twentieth-century crouching mummy. Prepared by Australian aborigines in 1904.

FIG. 62   Australian mummy, side view.

Finally we ought to mention mummification by drying, which has been practiced by various peoples all over the world. The Peruvian Indians mummified their dead by leaving the corpses out to dry in the almost germ-free air of the high Andes. The body was bound up in a crouching position, chin and knee touching, to make a handy package. This practice continued at least down to the last century. Among the Guanches of the Canary Islands (again a region largely free of airborne germs) dried mummies were likewise produced, dried in air for the poor and by artificial means for the wealthy. The drying time amounted to fourteen days. The body cavities were emptied and then filled with aromatic herbs. The body was then tied up with goatskin thongs and deposited in volcanic caves such as the Baranco de Herque on Teneriffe.

In 1905 H. Kaatsch reported on the smoking (*corroboree*) of King Narcha, a North Queensland chief from the Boenje district near Cairns, Australia. The man, tall in stature and a brave fighter in the Australian aborigines' struggle against the invading white pioneers and gold prospectors who in the 1890s had pitilessly shot down native men, women and children, was mummified after his death in 1904. Kaatsch describes the process as follows:

> The corpse was buried for several days, then exhumed and the decaying epidermis removed, as well as all hair. The abdomen was cut open and the body slowly dried on a rack of tree-trunks, over a fire. The natives smear the hair with the fat and blood that drips from the body. They then twine it into bundles to form that peculiar mourning costume (in their English they call it "devil-devil-hair") that attracted attention when worn by the last Tasmanians. The body is then put into its final position (arms and legs pressed close against the body in a tight crouch, knees at the chin, hands behind the ears, making a handy package of approximately 80 centimeters in length and 40 centimeters in width and depth—a photograph of the front and side view accompanies this report of the find. The extremities are tied close to the torso with cowhide thongs. The resulting position seems to me to imitate the attitude of the fetus in the uterus.[*]

[*] *Zeitschrift für Ethnologie*, 37: 772–781 (Berlin, 1905).

No chemical reagents are used to produce such Australian mummies. The process is essentially nothing more than slow smoking. Kaatsch continues:

> The custom of making mummies seems, in the old days, to have been the predominant way of treating corpses in the vicinity of Cairns as far as Cooktown to the north and Townsville to the south. . . . The drying of bodies over the fire is also reported from other regions, e.g. South Australia.*

Kaatsch bought the mummy of King Narcha from the natives in exchange for "lavish donations of tobacco, clothing and food," and turned it over to the Berlin Anthropological Society. It had been in the possession of the natives for only eight months.

Vestiges of embalming ceremonies have also been reported by Max Muller, along with a description of the cremation ceremonies practiced by the Brahmins of India. In describing the preparations for cremation, he writes:

> The hair of the head, the beard, the body hair, and the nails of the corpse are cut. It is then anointed with spikenard and a wreath of spikenard is placed on its head. The intestines are excised, cleaned of filth and stuffed with milk and butter. They are then replaced in the abdomen. Then a hem is cut from an unused piece of cloth for the sons to keep. The deceased is covered with this shroud, the remaining hem pointing to the west. The feet are left uncovered. . . . Then the kinsfolk bring fire and sacrifice implements to the burning pit. . . . This was followed, if an animal was to be burned with the corpse, by a cow or a monochrome goat, in some cases black. . . . In the north a dead man's wife was placed on the pyre, and if he were a warrior his bow also, until the brother-in-law . . . a foster child . . . or an old servant led the woman down from the pyre (reciting the words of a sacrificial spell).†

Once, it would appear, the wife was also burned, but in later times she was rescued from the pyre by a substitution spell. The dead man was covered with numerous offerings of implements,

* *Ibid.*
† *Zeitschrift der deutschen morgenlandischen Gesellschaft Band,* 9: 1 ff. (1855).

vessels, idols, mortars and pestles, all presented in a specific way:

> Everything that is made of iron, other metal and clay, as well as the two stones [which are at first laid on the dead man's teeth] are to be taken by the son. Then the priest cuts the fat of the animal intended for covering and lays it upon the dead man's face . . . then the kidneys, placing the right one into the dead man's right hand and the left one into his left hand, and laying the heart on the dead man's heart . . . and then the entire flayed animal, fitting limb to limb, upon the dead man, covering the whole with the animal's skin.*

The bones of the cremated corpse are gathered on certain specific days and placed in a funerary *kumbha*, a vessel with a breastlike swelling in the case of women and without such a swelling in the case of men. The *kumbhas* are afterward buried in the ground, to the accompaniment of certain rites.

* *Ibid.*

15

Burial in Mycenaean and Pre-Mycenaean Times

❁

I n 1903 a Bavarian archaeological expedition under the direction of Bulle and Furtwängler conducted excavations in Orchomenos, north of the Boeotian capital of Levaida. They named the culture they found there "Minyan," for it seemed intermediate between the Minoan and the Mycenaean. Among the remains they found (aside from the so-called Treasury of Minyas, a Mycenaean *tholos* 14 meters in diameter) were simple round structures of air-dried bricks set on circular or oval clay foundations. Beneath the floor pavement of these structures were tombs in which the dead were buried in a crouching position, with knees drawn up to the chin. Concerning these burials J. Zehetmaier writes:

> Following the age-old Indo-Germanic custom, the dead person was here given to the earth inside the human habitation. The dear departed, who has been so close to his loved ones in life, had to remain among them in death also and share the family's joys and sorrows, food and drink. While living he had enjoyed his nightly rest under the roof of the simple round hut in a crouching posture; dead he surely preferred to sleep the eternal slumber in the same position, beneath the domestic hearth.°

° *Leichenverbrennung und Leichenbestattung im alten Hellas* (Leipzig, 1907).

These round mud-brick buildings may be regarded as the forerunners of the later domed tombs of the Mycenaean period, although the *tholoi* were built of stone. Common to both was the rounded or oval shape and the doming that used the so-called false arch or corbel technique, in which ring upon ring of wall edges in further and further as the vault rises until at last it is closed. (In the genuine arches of the Roman period segment-shaped blocks distribute the pressure of the vault to the outer walls or pillars.) In the Mycenaean *tholoi* corpses were frequently buried under the floor of the vaulted chamber itself rather than in the actual burial chamber, which was an additional room off to the side. Similarly, the crouching corpses of Orchomenos, contrary to early reports, were not always buried under the floors of dwellings, but in specially constructed vaults of mud brick. Zehetmaier's picture of Minyan funeral customs is evidently based on his confounding tombs with genuine dwellings. The mistake is understandable when we realize that the remains of burnt offerings and grave goods can easily be taken for a "domestic hearth" and household utensils.

Graves with crouching corpses laid on their sides have been found in Argos, in Lefkas and on the southern slope of the Acropolis in Athens (in 1899).

Grave sites identified by the excavators as pre-Mycenaean have been found in Thorikon on the southeast coast of Attica, together with simple round and rectangular foundations of buildings; likewise in Aphidnai, northwest of Marathon, and near Tiryns. In all of these graves the dead were buried in large ceramic pithoi. A perfectly preserved specimen from Aphidnai measured 1.15 meters in height and .32 meters in diameter at its opening. The pithos had three handles. Its ornamentation of a wavy band in relief resembled those of the pithoi found in Tiryns and on Crete.

Similar recumbent corpses in the fetal position were found in graves under the citadel of Volo in Thessaly. These were interred in shaftlike cist graves. Others were found in a shaft grave in Corinth, buried in two oval vaults hollowed out to either side of the shaft. Among the grave goods were vases, jugs, cups and bowls of simple, rather rough clay.

At the Temple of Aphrodite at Aigina on the Saronic Gulf

graves with pithos burials have been found, as well as *osteothekes* in the walls. These are niches filled with human bones. Recumbent skeletons in the fetal position are again found in the Cycladic culture of the islands; here the dead were buried in curious trapeze-shaped graves lined with plaques. The rear measures approximately 110 centimeters, the front (where the knees and elbows fall) 90 centimeters; the side fitting the head and lower thighs is about 80 centimeters, and the depth some 50 centimeters. Among the grave gods are obsidian knives, broken marble vessels, boxes of green soapstone ornamented with spirals, the concave part of a hand mill (or offering bowl), potsherds, masklike jar lids, bronze spearheads, saucers made of an alloy of lead and silver, clay wortels for spinning and whetstones made of sandstone. Extensive graveyards have been found on Amorgos, Paros, Antiparos, Despotikes and other islands of the group. On Syros, on the other hand, as in Minyan Orchomenos, the round *tholos* tomb dominates; it is generally circular to elliptical, but sometimes becomes almost trapezoidal or rectangular in outline. The corbeled vault is closed at the top with a flat slab. Among the grave goods found with the skeletons were marble idols of naked females with arms crossed under the breasts; vessels of white marble; bowls and cups of clay; rather large clay boxes with lids and tube-shaped appendages; engraved ornamentation of concentric circles with lines; shards of pithoi with similar decoration; slate box lids; and small bronze implements shaped like slender chisels.

Near Palaikastro in eastern Crete graveyards were discovered at the beginning of the twentieth century. Because they obviously belonged to a pre-Mycenaean culture they were identified as Minoan. In them were ceramic vessels resembling the Kamares ware found in the cave tombs of Kato Zakro. In a rectangular area fenced by stone walls five parallel corridors separated by walls (almost 10 meters long and 2 meters wide) were found filled with more than seventy skulls and the principal bones of human skeletons. These were in small heaps surrounded by ceramic vases. One vessel contained the bones of a child. Nearby were found obsidian knife blades and a small bronze axe.

Evidence of pre-Mycenaean cremation has been found in an urn burial from Eleusis.

From *Mycenaean* times we are familiar with shaft graves, domed vaults, chamber tombs and cremation—that is, all the forms of burial that had existed, albeit in simpler form, in pre-Mycenaean times. The tombs, as structures, underwent improvement but there seems to have been no fundamental change in the mode of burial. Mycenaean tombs developed consistently out of the pre-Mycenaean, as we have already suggested in connection with Orchomenos in Boeotia.

No doubt the most famous shaft graves are in the lower citadel of Mycenae (Schliemann discovered five of them in 1876; a sixth was found by Stamatakis the following year). Within a ring-shaped area 26.5 meters in diameter, tombs of rectangular outline, 3 to 6.75 meters in length and up to 5 meters in depth were hewn into the rock. The interior was dressed with stone slabs, while copper-clad wooden beams were laid over the top. These beams supported the roofing slabs, which were covered

Fig. 63
Shaft grave
stele, Mycenae.

with earth. Schliemann identified the slab-lined circle of the lower citadel as the "agora," the forum of Mycenae; on this point he was following the description given by Pausanias in the second century A.D. Chrestos Tsuntas, who excavated at Mycenae for the Greek Archaeological Society between 1886 and 1902, thought the double circle of slabs must be the substructure of a tumulus (mound grave) that had once been heaped over the shafts. But Zehetmaier points out that the slab enclosure might also be compared with similar arrangements of stones in northern Europe. These are the cromlechs, quite common in England, where they outline a sacred precinct. For the shaft graves were originally marked by grave steles; above Grave III at Mycenae the bones of sacrificed animals were found.

In the shaft graves themselves Schliemann came upon clear signs of burnt offerings, which suggested to him that the corpses had been cremated:

> The quantity of ashes from the robes that cover them and from the wood that had entirely or partially cremated their flesh, furthermore the color of the lower layer of stone and the traces of fire and smoke on the stone casing of the grave, could leave no doubt in this regard. In fact, the unmistakable evidence of three different pyres was found.

Zehetmaier comments on this:

> It is curious that a man could have been so utterly obsessed that he saw even the smallest detail of the culture that shines forth from the Homeric epics confirmed before his eyes! In spite of the natural position of the well-preserved skeletons, even in spite of the traces of actual flesh still clinging to several of the skulls beneath the face mask, Schliemann for the sake of his Homer preferred to regard what he saw as incontrovertible proof of cremation.

Dörpfeld has surmised that the corpses were not burned (*kata-kaiein*), but singed (*kaiein*), that is, lightly exposed to fire in order to preserve them.

At a depth of 5 meters in Shaft Grave I Schliemann found three female corpses, separated from the rock beneath by a layer of gravel and also covered with gravel. Three large gold diadems, forty smaller gold ornaments, a copper ring, a knife blade, a

fragment of a vase, other ceramics, beads of blue glass, a fragment of bone box and two clay female idols had been given to
the dead for grave goods. In Grave II the gravel under the single
corpse had also been blackened by fire; a thick layer of ashes
covered the dead. Lanceheads, swords, gold cups, gold bracelets,
three vases of Egyptian faience "porcelain" and two painted ceramic vessels were given to the dead. Grave III contained the
remains of two children along with three women's bodies: "The
bodies were covered with gold." Found were: two large gold diadems, a dozen gold pendants, amulets, earrings and hair clips, more
than seven hundred gold platelets for ornamenting the garments,
another two hundred objects of gold, gold masks on the faces of
the children (whose hands and feet were wrapped with beaten
gold), four silver vases, alabaster and bronze vessels, three
bronze cauldrons, a bronze knife, sardonyx and amethyst gems,
agate beads, amber beads, a shard from an Egyptian pot with
a warrior's head and a ceramic jug. Above the caved-in roof of
this grave several human skeletons were found. According to
Zehetmaier, these, just like the skeletons found outside the doors
of other tombs, for example the chamber tombs in the Mycenaean
Lower City, are those of hapless slaves or prisoners of war who
were slaughtered at the grave of their master or at some hero's
grave."

Grave IV had a stone altar in the center, under which were
three male and two female skeletons. Among other objects the
following had been given as grave goods for the women: two
gold crowns, seven gold headbands, one armband, gold hairpins,
fifty-six amulets of beaten gold, bulls' heads with double axes
between the horns, two gold seal rings, three tiny gold temples
of Astarte, many small objects and innumerable amber beads.
For the men there were three gold face masks, a gold breastplate,
swords, daggers and spears (all of bronze), obsidian points, a
copper axe, five dagger blades inlaid with gold and silver, gold
sword belts, parts of shields, buttons, a silver bull's head with
gold horns, nine gold cups, an alabaster vase, a silver and a gold
jug, many ceramic vessels and shards of vases, thirty-four copper
jugs and cauldrons, a zoomorphic vessel (a stag with an open
back made of a lead-silver alloy) and much more.

Grave V held three male skeletons, but only two wore gold

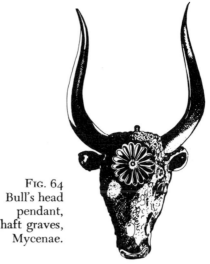

Fig. 64
Bull's head
pendant,
shaft graves,
Mycenae.

face masks. Schliemann reported: "The round face with all the
flesh was wonderfully preserved under the gold mask. There was
no trace of hair, but both eyes were plainly visible, likewise the
mouth, which was opened wide under the great weight pressing
upon it and showed its thirty-two fine teeth. In addition to
many amber beads, more than three hundred gold pommels and
sword bosses were found, twelve square gold plates, an armband, oyster shells and boars' teeth (probably worn as part of
a headdress of the kind preserved in the Herakleion Museum in
Crete), four cups and fragments of a silver vase, three gold
cups, two alabaster vessels, copper cauldrons and pitchers, ceramic vases, sixty bronze swords and daggers, some with inlaid
gold and silverwork showing hunting and battle scenes, remains
of shields and—quite astonishing—an ostrich egg.

No conclusive explanation has yet been offered for the presence of an ostrich egg in one of the shaft graves of Mycenae. It
is noteworthy, nevertheless, that whole bowlfuls of hen's eggs
have come to light from graves approximately a millennium
more recent dug up in the vicinity of Paestum in southern Italy.
These eggs are now preserved in the museum at Paestum. We
are naturally inclined to think first of eggs as provisions for
the journey into the hereafter. But in the ancient tradition of
the Jewish Passover eggs are a symbol of mourning. This might
have a bearing on the eggs in the Mycenaean and Lucanian
graves: many eggs mean much mourning, and of course a huge
ostrich egg would mean great mourning. Perhaps this symbol

also explains the use of egg-and-dart borders as ornaments on
classical funerary structures and temples. From the Jewish Passover the egg passed into the rituals of the Christian Easter, where,
however, it lost its original meaning. A Passover Eve custom is
to hide a piece of mazzoth (unleavened bread), which is then
hunted for by the youngest member of the family; in the Christian church this hide-and-seek tradition was shifted to Easter
eggs.

FIG. 65
"Queen's
bathroom,"
Knossos.

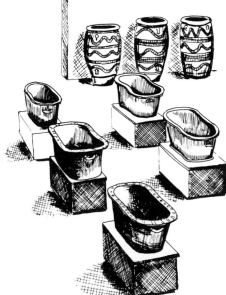

FIG. 66
Hall of
the Sarcophagi,
Herakleion
Museum.

The theme of resurrection is closely connected with the symbol of mourning. The ostrich egg that hangs in Coptic Orthodox churches in front of the iconostasis (the wall covered with icons of the saints) is probably meant to be a symbol of resurrection. Here, too, the Christian tradition obviously is linked to far older traditions. In Mycenaean times such imports as ostrich eggs probably reached Europe by the regular trade route between Greece and Egypt.

Shaft Grave VI, which was excavated by Stamatakis, held fewer precious grave goods but two very well preserved male bodies. Helbig [*] believes there is ample evidence that embalming preceded burial; on the basis of certain passages in Homer he considers that the method of preservation must have involved the use of honey. According to *The Iliad*, Book XXIV, Hector's corpse was not consigned to the flames until the twenty-second day after his death; and Book XXIV of *The Odyssey* indicates that Achilles' body was kept for eighteen days. According to Herodotus (I, 198), the Babylonians also used honey for preserving corpses. According to *The Iliad* (XXIII, 170), amphorae of honey and fat were placed on the pyre for the Greeks who had fallen in the battle for Troy. The nineteen corpses in the Mycenaean shaft graves were buried in a half-sitting (somewhat fetal) posture with raised heads. Near the circle of slabs of the Lower Citadel still other, rather simple shaft graves have been detected; these were later built over and it was not possible to dig without destroying the later structures.

In addition to shaft graves, rock tombs were in use in Mycenaean times. These usually had a rectangular entrance (*dromos*) either cut into the rock or built up of stone and sealed with earth. Depending on the type of main chamber, these are spoken of either as beehive tombs (*tholoi*) or chamber tombs, the latter being rectangular with flat roofs.

Of the nine known beehive tombs near Mycenae, the Treasury of Atreus, with its diameter and height of 15 meters, its 5.8 meter-high entrance and its *dromos* 35 meters long and 6 meters wide, is the biggest. To the side of the beehive vault is the actual burial chamber (*thalamos*), a square more than 8 meters on each side,

---

[*] *Das Homerische Epos*, pp. 53 ff.

hewn into the rock. At the Tomb of Clytemnestra, excavated by
Sophia Schliemann in 1876, instead of a *thalamos* a shaft grave
has been dug out inside the *tholos*—which, however, may be more
recent than the rest of the site. Traces of a double door suggest
that the entrance (*stomion*), 5.6 meters high and equally wide,
may once have been closed by doors. Another beehive tomb, 14.5
meters in diameter, is situated to the northwest of the Lion Gate;
this was discovered in 1892 inside the city wall. Beehive tombs
have also been found in ancient Amyklai near Sparta, in central
Greece (Thorikos, Menidi, Acharnae, Orchomenos, Eleusis and
Delphi), in northern Greece (Dimini near Volos [Ioikos] in
Thessaly, Gura of Phthiotis, Ossa northeast of Larissa), in the
Kephallenian Islands, in Mykonos and especially in Crete.

Long before the excavation of Minoan places on Crete had
begun, many small and large beehive tombs were known.° Some
of the dead had been buried without coffins or sarcophagi, on
the ground, laid upon a heavy layer of sand mixed with seashells,
or on *klines* hewn out of the rock, or in *larnakes* shaped like
chests or bathtubs.

In Chapter 4, while we were making our tour of the Palace of
Knossos, we came upon the room called the "queen's bathroom."
At that point we broached the technical problem: What good
was a "drain hole" in the ceramic "tub" if there were no drains
in the floor to carry off the water? How was the tub emptied?

Now we shall confront another question: What really distinguishes this bathtub in the "queen's bathroom" from the numerous ceramic sarcophagi of the Minoan period that have long been
known and have been found in many sites all over the island?
In the Hall of the Sarcophagi of the Herakleion Museum, just to
the left of the main entrance, there are long rows of such tubs
lined up four to a row, each one on a low platform. All of these
tub sarcophagi are highly imaginative. Some of them are color-
fully painted; they have handles at the head and foot and on
both sides, and belly out more or less plumply; one is flattened
at the lower end. They slope upward toward the head at vary-

° Anoia Messaratiks, 4.5 meters high, *dromos* 5 meters long; Milatos,
2.3 meters diameter; Kurtes near Phaistos, with well-walled *dromoi* up to
12 meters in length; Heraklea; Burlia; Praisos in the eastern part of the
island; Angathia near Palaikastro, etc.

ing pitches, with rims of varying widths. But all are remarkably small, between 80 and 120 centimeters long. When we looked at the supposed bathtub in the "queen's bathroom" we had worried about that. But if it is small for a bath, it seems quite impossible to have stuffed an adult corpse into so wee a vessel.

Were only children buried this way? But in that case larger sarcophagi for adults would turn up. Yet even the chest sarcophagi—made of clay but, to judge by the form, modeled on a wooden chest with four corner posts—are not noticeably longer than the tubs. Yet in a good many of these remnants of bones were found—not the bones of the children but of adults.

A fetal-position grave in the same hall of the Herakleion Museum gives us a clue: the dead were not laid to their eternal rest in outstretched posture, but with their knees drawn up against their chin. In this position even a large man takes up barely a meter of space. Fetal-position burials have a tradition stretching back into the Stone Age, and apparently this tradition continued to be observed in Minoan Crete.

Nowhere in the entire museum is there any indication of which tubs were used for bathing and which were solely for burials. Nor are there any guidelines on characteristics of shape or ornamentation that would help distinguish bathtubs from sarcophagi. A guide told us that a broad, flattened rim would have served as a base for a sarcophagus lid, whereas bathtubs would have a curved lip. But in the Hall of the Sarcophagi there are several tubs with curved lips without any indication that they were bathtubs—and one of them actually has some bones in it.

Did the Minoans bathe in sarcophagi, or did they have themselves buried in their bathtubs? Is it really conceivable that no distinction was made between such utterly different uses? Did the oval form of the "all-purpose tub" seem to them so ideal that they wanted no other? But then, why the rectangular coffin-chests? Or did considerations of thrift cause them to bury the dead in their own bathtubs? That hardly seems to fit into our conception of an extremely wealthy country in the Bronze Age.

Incidentally, all the sarcophagi in the Herakleion Museum, whether they are oval or rectangular, have drain holes! The tub-shaped ones have the hole at the foot; the chest-shaped sarcopaghi have holes in each of their corners.

In the Hall of the Sarcophagi there are not only tub-shaped and chest-shaped ceramic sarcophagi, but also large ceramic vessels about a meter and a half in height; the pithoi, which were used for burials. They come from tombs in various parts of the island. In them, too, obviously, the dead were buried in the fetal position. The opening, scarcely 30 centimeters across, with a bulging rim, is barely large enough for a corpse to be squeezed through. The excavators report that in many cases a good deal of force had to be exerted; if the shoulders would not pass through the opening, the bones were broken. The custom of burial in pithoi was not restricted to Minoan Crete; it is also known from Asia Minor, from the Greek islands, from Sicily and from Lipari.

Minoan funerary pithoi are distinguished by characteristic ornamentation. There are usually a goodly number of handles, shaped like the eye of a needle, on the upper and lower rims. Running around the vessel and usually in three rows are serpentine patterns. Here again is that snake motif we have already encountered in the statuettes of the snake goddesses in the west wing. How can we fail to recall the legends of Aesculapios and Polyeidos with their snakes? These were the famous physicians who brought young Glaukos back to life—and, as the Romans believed, Hippolytos also. Snakes are, as we have seen, the symbol of resurrection, of conquest of death—and consequently logical as ornamentation for a funerary pithos.

But it was just such pithoi, ornamented with the serpentine motif and exactly of the same size and shape as these funerary pithoi, that we found filling the magazines in the Palace of Knossos! Not only that, they were even to be found in the queen's living room! In the palace they are said not to have served as funerary vessels, but to have been filled with olive oil, honey or other stores; and it is even alleged that they served as substitutes for wardrobes. Doubts, much like those we had about the bathtubs, begin to creep over us. Did those Minoans make no distinction between an oil jar and coffin just because they had found the ideal form of an "all-purpose container"? But we know that they used simultaneously at least two different types of ceramic sarcophagi. Or did those Minoans, for the sake of simplicity, push their dead into the very same vessels in which the deceased during their lifetimes had kept their food supplies? Perhaps the idea was that the dead person would be able to nourish himself in the afterlife from the selfsame jar that had provided for him during his life. But then, did the living have death before their eyes every time they took a handful of fruit, a cup of olive oil or a bowl of honey from one of the storage pithoi? What curious ideas Minoan archaeology tries to sell us! We know that the serpentine motif was distinctly connected with certain notions about death; was it also supposed to promote the keeping qualities of foods when used on storage vessels? And when someone died, would a storage vessel be cleared out in order to bury the corpse in it?

But let us return to the question of how the Minoans could stow the corpses of adults in the relatively small "bathtubs" or squeeze them through the narrow necks of the pithoi. In Heraklea a corpse was found in the fetal position with legs drawn up even though there was ample space—1.90 meters—to bury him outstretched. The fetal position was preferred regardless of available space—and this explains why the *larnakes* could be relatively small. A bathtub-shaped coffin from the same tomb measured 1.04 meters long at the top, .95 at the bottom, .58 wide and .54 deep. The measurements of two others from Anoia Messaratiks were .99 and .80 long, .42 wide, .64 and .54 deep. The museum in Herakleion has large numbers of such sarcophagi with almost exactly the same measurements. Here and there much smaller sarcophagi, the so-called children's bathtubs, have been found.

Given an interior length of barely a meter, it is obvious that even with a population of comparatively small stature the dead could only have been placed in such containers in an extreme fetal position, with the knees drawn up very tightly and the head more or less bent. It would also have been important to reduce considerably the volume of corpulent bodies. Treating the bodies with fire draws out virtually all the fluid in the tissues and the fatty substance, so that what is left is largely skin and bones. In the beehive tombs near Phaistos traces of fire indicate that "a mighty fire" was kindled inside; yet the remains of the bones are scarcely singed. It is quite possible that a form of dry mummification was practiced, fire being used just as the aborigines of Australia used it down to the twentieth century.

There have been numerous reports of traces of fire in the Minoan palaces. But from our own studies of the alabaster slabs that are used for dressing the walls it is evident that no extreme temperatures were reached. Insofar as these fires do not represent traces of burnt offerings, we might also attribute them to such procedures as mummification by drying. On the other hand there is good reason to think that other modes of mummification, using liquid chemicals (as the Egyptians did), were also practiced. The extensive drainage systems, the numerous funnellike rhytons and other utensils useful for such purposes—tubs, basins in the floor, jugs with pointed spouts and so on—do suggest chemical treatment of the dead. That seems all the more likely since active contact between Crete and Egypt is proved by the articles of Egyptian origin found in Minoan tombs and palaces, and by the Kamares ware shards in Egyptian temples and tombs.

In the beehive tombs of Angathia heaps of bones were found gathered together, each heap crowned by a skull. In *tholos* necropolises in central Crete the dead have been found crouching upright, merely leaning with their backs to the wall (Erganos). In Menidi actual urns of ashes have been found.

Among the grave goods found in the Cretan tombs were bronze weapons, stirrup jars and other ceramic vessels, bronze bracelets, spirals of gold and beads. One chamber tomb near Chania contained, alongside the skeleton of a woman, two gold rings, a bronze mirror, a stone vessel, bracelets and three shattered bronze vessels. In Palaikastro a body was found with a gold breastplate and a sword with gold inlay work. A "Geometric" urn from Knossos which contained burned human bones may possibly have been a later burial in an old vault; the height of the vessels with lid was 40 centimeters.*

What relationship there may be between beehive tombs in the western Mediterranean region and Cretan-Mycenaean civilization has not yet been clarified. There are such structures at Matrensa near Syracuse (in which were Mycenaean vases), near Florence and near Lisbon (Palmella), even on Sardinia and in the Balearic Islands.

* See Paolo Orsi, "Note on a Mycenaean Vase and on some Geometric Vases of the Syllogos of Candia," *American Journal of Archaeology*, pp. 254 ff., Vol. I, No. 3 (1897).

It is, again, at Mycenae that the best-appointed beehive tombs of Greece have been found. Up to 1896 ninety-nine of these had been excavated in the Lower Citadel. Tsountas, digging in fifteen of them, found in 1895 eight bronze swords, two axes, a lance head, two alabaster vessels, a gold band, a belt of beaten gold, a gold diadem composed of fifty-nine parts, small gold beads, fourteen gems, two gems of glass paste with representations of animals, six gold rings, five gold brooches of wound and twisted wire, a silver bowl, two bronze vessels and four stone vessels with handsome ornamentation. Even larger chamber tombs with *dromoi* up to 8 meters long and the interior measuring 4 by 4 meters were found in the necropolis of Kato Paigadiu near Mycenae. Quite often bodies without grave goods were buried in shafts dug into the floor of these chamber tombs. Apparently the grave goods were placed on top of the shafts, once they had been sealed with slabs of stone.

Further chamber tombs were discovered at Nauplion; according to Strabo, these had already been robbed in antiquity. There are others at Epidauros, Phoris, Sphettos, on the eastern slope of Mount Hymettos in Attica, at Halike near Athens, at the Shrine of Artemis in Brauron, at the port of Prasiai, on Melos, Cyprus and elsewhere. Evidences of Late Mycenaean cremations have been found at Eleusis, Athens, Dimini, Menidi, Halike and Argos.

16

Burial Rites
in Classical Times

❀

It is said of the Assyrian King Assurnasirpal I that in 883 B.C., out of fear of the besieger Arbakes, he killed himself and had his body burned as follows:

The pyre in the midst of the court of the palace was piled to the height of 4 plethra (about 130 meters). Upon this 150 gold beds and an equal number of gold tables were placed. Inside the pyre was a square wooden room with sides of thirty meters, and inside a large bed and several small beds. In the one he placed himself and his wife, in the smaller ones the concubines (he had sent the children away). That room was roofed with great thick beams. In it he also heaped up his treasures—ten myrads of talents [of what? gold?], 10,000 talents of silver and a large quantity of purple dresses and robes. Heavy wood was laid close around the room, so that exit from it was blocked. The pyre is said to have burned for fifteen days.

Achilles also had a mighty pyre built for the funeral of his dead friend Patroclus. The Achaeans

built a pyre a hundred feet long this way and that way,
and on the peak of the pyre they laid the body, sorrowful
at heart; and in front of it skinned and set in order numbers
of fat sheep and shambling horn-curved cattle; and from all
great-hearted Achilleus took the fat and wrapped the
corpse in it

from head to foot, and piled up the skinned bodies about it.
Then he set beside him two-handled jars of oil and honey
leaning them against the bier, and drove four horses
        with strong necks
swiftly aloft the pyre with loud lamentations. And there were
nine dogs of the table that had belonged to the lord
        Patroklos.
Of these he cut the throats of two and set them on the
        pyre;
and also killed twelve noble sons of the great-hearted Trojans
with the stroke of bronze, and evil were the thoughts
        in his heart against them,
and let loose the iron fury of the fire to feed on them.°

Earlier the Achaeans had shorn their hair and laid the hair
on the bier of Patroklos. The still glowing ashes were quenched
with wine, the dead man's bones gathered up and wrapped in
"a double fold of fat" which was placed in a golden jar. A mound
was reared above the site of the pyre, but it contained only the
burnt remains of the grave goods, no bones of the honored
corpse. Funeral games in honor of the dead man followed; as
prizes for the games Achilles fetched from his ships cauldrons
and tripods, horses, mules, massive bulls, fair-girdled women
and gray iron.

Achilles himself was burnt, after a mourning period of seventeen days. In order to keep the corpse from decaying during this
(probably prescribed) period of mourning, embalming was necessary. In the Heroic Age of Greece this apparently could be
done only by a few high priests, priestesses or even goddesses,
since they alone seemed to possess the technical knowledge. Thus
we read in *The Iliad* of the heroic struggle around the *corpse* of
Patroclus; for the requisite funeral ceremonies could be carried
out only in the presence of the dead friend's body. We read also
of Achilles' anxiety "that flies might get into the wounds beaten
by bronze in his body, and breed worms in them, and these
make foul the body. . . ." But his mother Thetis, of divine descent,
hastens up: "and meanwhile through the nostrils of Patroklos

° *The Iliad*, translated by Richmond Lattimore (University of Chicago
Press Phoenix Book, 1970). Book XXIII, lines 164–177.

she distilled ambrosia and red nectar, so that his flesh might not spoil.° Thus the corpse was "embalmed" even for a mourning period of only seventeen days. Here we encounter the nectar and ambrosia, the traditional food of the Greek gods, in their real function as anointing oil and honey for the preservation of the dead. The gods, once also of "human" kind, are made "immortal" by nectar and ambrosia. That is, the methods of preservation so widespread in the Aegean region made them so. The same "imperishability" could be achieved by those whose families and descendants could afford an expensive funeral. Embalming was a way to buy a share in immortality.

According to Homer, the other fallen Greek heroes of the Trojan War were burned, as were in later times Plutarch, Solon, Alcibiades, Philopoimen and King Pyrrhus of Epirus, who was reputed to have been a descendant of Achilles. The bodies of the Athenians who died in the plague of 429 B.C., among them Pericles, were likewise given to the flames. Nevertheless, cremation does not appear to have been the original form of burial practiced in Greece. In the cases cited, it was usually practiced for warriors who died in battle or for people whose deaths occurred in other exceptional situations. Possibly the general population tended to practice the custom of cremation rather more in times of war and rather less in periods of peace.

The Kerameikos Cemetery in Athens has been in constant use for an extraordinarily long period. According to Manolis Andronikos,† sparse signs of cremation begin in sub-Mycenaean graves, whereas in the Protogeometric period (ca. 1000–900 B.C.) cremations predominate. This is the period after the Trojan War, whose long duration, cultural and political importance, and large numbers of participants contributed to the codification of mores. This was all the more true because the memory of the period was kept alive in the epics. During the ninth and eighth centuries B.C. graves with skeletons in them recur; these are especially common around 750 and grow rarer once more in the seventh and sixth centuries. Particularly large numbers of cremation graves of the Geometric period are known from Crete; the urn

° *Ibid.*, pp. 392–393.
† "Totenkult," *Archeologica Homerica*, III (Göttingen).

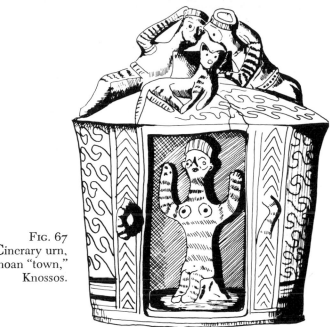

Fig. 67
Cinerary urn,
Minoan "town,"
Knossos.

found in Knossos at the end of the last century belongs to this period.

Cremation could not have been introduced into Crete by the Dorians, for it was practiced before the Dorians appeared on the scene. Urns found in Horizon VI of Troy, which has been dated as from 1900 to 1300 B.C., show that cremation was practiced then.

From *The Iliad* we gather that cremation was used to dispose of the victims of plague quickly and as far as possible to avoid the danger of contagion (I, 52). But the bones of fallen heroes were supposed to be brought back to their families at home (VII, 332 *ff.*). Given the length of the voyage, the bodies had to be cremated. The Trojans also burned their dead. Moreover, they did so outside the gates of the city (VII, 408 *ff.*), whereas the dead Danaeans were given to the flames on the beach in front of the assembled ships. The huge casualties on both sides during the first battle made a kind of sanitary clearing of the battlefield necessary, such as was undertaken in similar fashion in modern times (1870–1871) at Sedan, with fire as the sanitizing agent. The treatment of Hector's corpse is important evidence both for the genesis of *The Iliad* and the softening of manners with time. In the older, Aeolian Book XXIII his corpse is torn to pieces by dogs, whereas in the younger, Ionian Book XXIV the burning of

his body on the pyre is described in detail. After the flames have
been quenched with wine the kinsmen wrap the remains in soft
purple robes and place them in a golden casket. This *larnax*,
of the type known from Crete and also from the Early Geometric
necropolis of Hissarlik, was lowered into an earthen grave lined
with slabs of stone (a *kapetos*) and covered over with a barrow.

Even in case of death at sea the corpse had to be brought to
land and burned there, according to *The Odyssey* (III, 285),
and historical fact bears this out. Thus after the naval battle off
the Arginusae in 406 B.C. death sentences were meted out to ten
Athenian commanders for their failure to recover the bodies of
the fallen.

At Troy, it is quite clear, the bodies had to be embalmed
before cremation if they were to last during the long period of
mourning. Aside from the nectar and ambrosia used on the body
of Patroklos, the same purpose was served by the "ambrosial
garments" that the daughters of Nereus wrapped around the dead
Achilles. Apollo himself took charge of Hector's corpse. In this
embalming we must recognize ritual residues of the interment
that had once been customary; external preservation of the body
had once been requisite, though of course it was not possible in
times of war and pestilence. That cremation was not the sole
manner of disposing of corpses at the time the Homeric epics
were composed can be deduced from the verses in which the
Greek word *tarchyein* (according to Zehetmaier from *taricheuein*:
dry, smoke, pickle, embalm) occurs (*The Iliad* VII, 85; XVI,
454–457). Dörpfeld* assumed that in both classical and Mycenaean times virtually the same burial rites were followed, consisting of "burning" (or drying for better preservation of the
corpse) along with interment. Only during war, he believed, was
the body completely burned (*katakaiein*); in normal times it was
merely singed (*kaiein*) to slow decay. In fact innumerable tombs
of the Minoan and Mycenaean period show signs of such singeing
at temperatures of below 120°C. (as determined by the method
described earlier, from the presence or absence of bituminous
strata in gypsum slabs used for dressing walls). As we have seen,

---

* "Über Verbrennung und Bestattung der Toten in alten Griechenland,"
Zeitschrift für Ethnologie, 37 (Berlin, 1905).

drying over a slow fire is one of the two methods for preparing relatively durable dried mummies. Manolis Andronikos, it is true, argues that there is an etymological and semantic difference between the two words *tarchyein* and *taricheuein*. But fire was certainly present in many Mycenaean and Geometric tombs throughout the Greek world; and in those cases where full cremation did not take place we may infer mummification by drying. That would also be true for the Stone Age fetal-position burials. The use of fire both for drying and for cremation also suggests why the Greeks from the Mycenaean to the Classical era saw little fundamental difference between the two ways of treating corpses.

According to *The Iliad* (XVI, 456), the dead body of King Sarpedon of Lycia would scarcely have any prospect of being carried back to his native land and buried there in the ground with a barrow and the customary pillar raised above his grave if some measures were not taken to preserve its external form during the slow journey. Zeus himself requests Apollo to anoint the body with ambrosia and wrap it in an "everlasting pall." Both words, *tarchyein* and *taricheuein*, do in fact seem to go back to the same root. Since *taricheutes* was the Greek word for the Egyptian preparers of mummies, *taricheuein* probably meant mummification in the Egyptian sense (using chiefly chemical methods of pickling, with removal of entrails), whereas *tarchyein* possibly was equivalent to drying of the body (dry mummification over a low fire).

Archaeology also supports the tradition concerning Homeric rites for the dead. Cenotaphs (empty tombs), usually taking the form of barrows above funeral pyres, have been found in many places; some of them, however, were in later times used for burials such as were customary in tumulus graves. Possibly the Geometric urn from Knossos should be viewed as such a subsequent burial. The barrow of In-Tepe on Cape Rhoiteion (near Troy) was considered in antiquity to have been the tumulus grave of Aias. In the time of Emperor Hadrian the presumed bones of Aias were washed out by the waves. The emperor gave orders for them to be reinterred in a new mound adorned with a temple and statuary. Temples of the Greco-Roman period likewise crowned the hill of Hissarlik (= palace), which Schliemann identified as the site of Troy and excavated. Sixteen tumuli excavated by Schliemann contained no bones or urns to indicate cremation. Probably these must be regarded as cenotaphs.

According to Chrestos Tsountas, charred matter may be found in almost all Mycenaean tombs. Evans attributed the traces of burning found in such tombs to ceremonies of ritual purification. Now it is true that purification of buildings was practiced in Roman times, but what was purified was the dead man's former home, not his tomb. Indications of early cremation are also found in the excavation of the mound of Jericho. A beehive tomb near Praisos opened by Nicolas Platon and assigned to sub-Mycenaean IIIc provides further evidence that interment and cremation existed side by side. The tomb contained two sarcophagi; in one was the funerary urn for the ashes of a man, the other held an unburned corpse.

Archaeology has also provided direct testimony about the practice of human sacrifice in the cult of heroes. In Cypriot tombs skeletons of men bound hand and foot have been found; they were killed and placed in the tombs as "doorkeepers" (although face down). Other corpses have been found alongside stone altars with drains in them for the blood to run off. In other places the real "doorkeepers" were replaced by statues (like those in the tomb of Tutankhamen). There is ample evidence of animal sacrifices at funerals. Skeletons of horses have been found in graves from the Middle Bronze Age on, and thus also in Minoan sites. In Oxylithos on Euboia the bones of cattle, sheep, goats, pigs and dogs were found above those of almost every human corpse—samples of virtually all the former owner's domestic animals. Certain portions of animal bones are also sometimes found together with human bones in amphorae turned up in the Kerameikos Cemetery of ancient Athens.

Pits and grooves in tombs are also quite common in Greece. There are examples in the Tomb of Clytemnestra, in Beehive Tomb 2 at Malthi, in Damania Monophatsiou in Crete, in Prosymna, in Pylos and in Trogana. Given the small size of many of these tombs it is obvious that these could not have been the wheel ruts of carts, as has been suggested. A likelier explanation is that the grooves served to allow the blood of sacrifices to run off. Incidentally, similar grooves have come to light in front of the pithoi found in the new excavations at Mallia, Crete.

Furthermore, *kylikes* (libation vessels) for pouring the drink offerings at or in the tomb, as well as pierced vessels for libations, are often found in the upper part of the grave shaft. The tripods that are frequently mentioned in Homer are used to support urns in depictions of funerals. Clay idols were placed around the chest-shaped or bathtub-shaped *larnax*, such as was in use in Crete, in Mycenae and in central and Ionian Greece during the Archaic period. These idols represented female mourners with raised hands and breasts only partially covered.

Similar female idols have been found in great numbers in Crete, not only in such "sanctuaries" as Gazi near Herakleion or such "country houses" as Kannia near Gortyn. They have also been found in the Palace of Knossos itself (in the Sanctuary of the Double Axes). The representations of female mourners frequently show, or at any rate suggest, bared breasts—reminiscent of the accounts in the ancient writers of the conduct of Egyptian mourners who likewise bared their breasts to bewail the death of a member of the family. As for the snakes shown in conjunction with mourning females, these immediately call to mind, of course, the famous "snake goddesses" of the Palace of Knossos. These, too, might very well be nothing but grave goods, clay figures of mourners.

The bathtub shape of many Cretan ceramic sarcophagi has suggested to E. Cahen the idea of an "eternal bath." But we question whether the cramped and awkward clay sarcopaghi

FIG. 68
Hut urn
from Verulonia,
Etruria.

ever served as bathtubs. For bathing purposes the Minoans probably used wooden tubs, which are more practical by far, since even full-sized ones are light enough to be handled.

Among the interesting finds of gold in Crete are gold mouthpieces to serve as props for the jaw, keeping the mouth from dropping open when *rigor mortis* sets in; these resemble the mouthpieces found in ancient Greek tombs. A scrap of gold jewelry ("bracelet") found on the small island of Mochlos in Mirabello Gulf, off the northern coast of Crete, may be part of such a mouthpiece.

The usual stylistic division into Mycenaean, Protogeometric and Geometric might further the impression that each successive period represents the advent of a new population with entirely different manners and mores. But cemeteries showing continuous occupation prove that this was not the case. Zehetmaier comments:

> The beginning of the period of the Greek Middle Ages link directly with the end of the era of Mycenaean civilization. At the sites Mycenaean shards are often mingled with those in the Geometric style. That is so, for example, in the Eleusinian necropolis and in the cemetery of Sparta, so that it is often quite difficult to assign the graves and their types of burial to one or the other period of time. In the Greek motherland and on Crete the two cultures passed gradually from one to the other, the older Mycenaean culture being replaced by the so-called Greek Archaic Period.

Since such fluid transitions between Minoan culture in Crete and Mycenaean culture must also be recognized, and since the Minoan civilization of the Bronze Age developed out of Neolithic beginnings, there obviously can be no question of a sudden, catastrophic extinction of the ethnic "carriers of culture." Despite all the changes in stylistic feeling and in artistic and technical detail, a certain cultural continuity is preserved. It is true that Minoan and Mycenaean culture seems to have been wealthier and incomparably more artistic than that of the Geometric Age, so that archaeologists and historians have spoken of a breakdown in the feeling for art. But that must be attributed to a general evolutionary trend rather than to a sudden extinction of the ancient population in the Aegean region. Instead of a few wealthy families in the Bronze Age who buried their dead with precious possessions, making enormous sacrifices of jewelry, food, animals and even human beings—in full accord with the spirit of the ancient Mediterranean cult of the dead—there appears a rapidly increasing population of solid though not rich burghers with commercialized tastes. The consequence is a stylistic descent into mass production, a turning away from authentic artistic as well as religious feeling, and a conversion of the ancient death rites into acts of bourgeois display and status seeking. In place of the fine ancient handwork we find mass-produced ceramics; in place of the original mortuary, rock or tumulus grave, simple grave mounds; in place of authentic sacrifices to the dead there are more and more worthless "grave goods," models that substitute for the valuable pieces of personal property the dead were formerly entitled to.

But this development had its good side. Who would complain that instead of genuine sacrifices of men and animals, idols and votive images were gradually substituted; that "companions," "doorkeepers," women, slaves, servants, horses and cattle were no longer immolated in flesh and blood, but in the form of bronze or clay statuettes; and that instead of the distinctly macabre methods of dry and wet mummification simple interment was practiced, along with cremation of soldiers on the battlefield or of the victims of tyranny and epidemics? The fetal position of the dead, so widespread in ancient times, remained customary in the oblong shaft graves in the cemetery of Eleusis deep into the Greek Archaic period, although the number of such graves seems to diminish slowly as we come closer to the Classical period, so that ultimately burials in outstretched posture by far predominate.

Burial in jars (pithoi) was longest reserved for children in Eleusis, deep into the Geometric period. Aside from the bones of unburned corpses, there are also clay vessels of small dimensions with grave goods and a number of smallish clay spheres. Adults were apparently partially burned, as the nineteen pyre sites (*pyrai*) found near Eleusis indicate. The size of the *pyrai* of the Mycenaean period in the eastern part of the necropolis visibly diminishes as we approach the Geometric period in the western part of the area. Sites at which the charred bones were not gathered but covered over obviously represent the simplest form of such burial. More important corpses received *osteodocha angeia,* funerary urns with Geometric motifs. These were often handsomely ornamented amphorae, whose shapes were never so simple as the pithoi used for corpses. Such vessels were buried upright in the ground, either without further provision or in the midst of a stone casing or even a stone casket which would itself have been sufficient to hold an uncremated corpse. On the other hand the pithoi of the Eleusinian necropolis are usually buried in the ground lying on their sides, a slab of stone or ceramic or a bronze lid being used to close the opening.

At Vurva in eastern Attica a mound grave was found with signs of seven cremations, dating from the seventh century B.C. Possibly this was the burial site of a family of local nobility, whereas the ordinary population of this period practiced earth burial. In the Bronze Age it was frequently assumed that preserving the body was a prerequisite for preserving the soul; the soul had indeed freed itself from the body, but sometimes might return to it. However, this belief changed; due in considerable part to the influence of the great poets from the Homeric to the Classical Age, it gradually became accepted that the soul was not destroyed by fire. Nevertheless, deep into the Hellenistic Age tumulus graves such as that of Eretria were built, with vaulted burial chamber and stone biers that look like benches (*klines*). Formerly, however, the dead had been laid on the kline or venerated on the mortuary chair. Now the procedure changed; the klines and chairs were hollowed out and filled with the ashes of the dead, even though the klines—as large as 1.9 meters long and .9 meter wide—would have been quite large enough for laying out uncremated corpses.

Finally the idea became more and more established that the soul, after leaving the perishable body, could utilize the grave goods only if these were burned also (that is, also transformed into an invisible, ethereal form). Thus Herodotus relates (V, 92) how the Corinthian tyrant Periander sent an inquiry to an oracle, whereupon his deceased wife Melissa appeared to the oracle and complained that she was naked and cold in the underworld because the clothes that had been buried with her had not been burned. Periander promptly assembled all the women of Corinth in the Temple of Hera and made them strip off their clothes, which were burned to appease the ghost of Melissa.

At the cemetery before the Dipylon in Athens unburned corpses were buried laid out on their backs as early as the seventh century B.C.; they were surrounded by various articles they had needed in life (sword, lance, diadem, etc.). But on the islands (Thera, Neandria) pithos burials continued here and there into the sixth century B.C. Along with this practice there may be found in the necropolises coffins, clay sarcophagi, tile coffins, tube sarcophagi in the form of drainpipes, chamber tombs (some with klines), *ossilegia* (for the collection of unburned bones transferred from some other place), *osteothecae* (small, shallow hollows cased with terracotta slabs for the preservation of bones and ashes), oblong graves for earth burials or for the burying of funerary urns (although in many cases the grave would have been big enough for an unburned corpse) and tumuli. As was later done in Rome, the lawgivers of Athens took pains to check wasteful expenditure on funerals. Solon explicitly forbids the slaughter of cattle over graves.

It is at any rate well established that in ancient Greece earth burial and cremation were practiced simultaneously. According to Zehetmaier, for the period from 600 to 300 B.C. simple earth burial seems to have been the predominant mode, even in times in which the "heroic" procedure of cremation was quite widespread. As we have seen, the situation was different on battlefields. It has proved possible, for example, to localize the cremation sites at Marathon and Plataiai; at the latter site members of the different tribes were burned with their own tribesmen. Those who fell at Marathon were buried on the spot after cremation, but the ashes of the dead of Plataiai were transported to Athens where—like the fallen heroes of other campaigns—they were buried with military honors. The dead Macedonians of Chaironia, where Philip II won a victory over the Athenians and Thebans in 339 B.C., were first cremated, then interred under a barrow 70 meters in diameter and more than 7 meters high. The burnt stratum itself was .75 meter thick and extended over a diameter of 10 meters. When 100 square meters of the surface

FIG. 70 Up to the fourteenth century B.C. Egyptian mortuary structures had zigzag corridors and several stories. Examples of such angled corridors: Giseh, the Valley Temple below the Pyramid of Chephren (Fourth Dynasty). Sakkara: Mastaba of Prahhotep (Fifth Dynasty). Thebes West: Rock Tomb of Amenophis II (Eighteenth Dynasty).

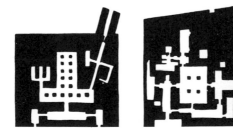

Fig. 69 Structure of several stories, with rooms for worship in the upper story and burial vault in the lower. Compare this with Herodotus' account of the two floors in the Egyptian labyrinth.

were exposed and examined carefully, it was discovered that
only the thickest bones, the bones of the arm and the thigh,
remained. The ashes and bones of the fallen had not been collected in urns; instead vases and small cups of fine light clay
with a black glaze had been added to the barrow.

The custom of marking the grave site with a stele, or placing
a vase over the grave, goes back to the Pregeometric period. Such
vases would have their bottoms pierced or broken so that offerings could be poured into the loose soil that filled the grave.

We are at the end of our digression, which has ranged so far
afield in space and time. Our investigation of the funeral rites
and burial techniques of the ancient peoples of the Mediterranean world may strike some readers as macabre. One scientist
with rather unscientific ire has even charged that my view of
the Minoan palaces as mortuary palaces has driven me to necro-
mania, even to necrophilia. It is best to ignore this feeble pun.
An allegation of this sort is on a par with accusing someone
who has written on the problems of pathology of hypochondria.

Our journey into the past should have made this much clear:
The attitude of pre-Christian man toward death was fundamentally different from our own; the dead person played an enormously important part in the world of the living; and religious
ideas and customs concerning death affected many of the peoples
of the eastern Mediterranean in much the same way. Ethnic
origins, different languages, political forms, the stage of culture,
seem to matter little compared to the tremendous force exercised
by the cult of death in this area over very long periods of time.
This should not be surprising. The Christian religion, with its
special expectations about the hereafter and its contempt for this
world, has after all affected the thought and conduct of billions
of human beings down to the smallest details of their daily life
for twenty centuries.

A somber and eerie light now falls upon the Cretan finds. We
can no longer believe in that gay and festive Minoan world con-
jured up by Evans and his disciples. But on the other hand we
now recognize how logically and consistently Minoan Crete fit
into its geographical and cultural surroundings. The dream of
Minoan Crete has come to an end. The reality of Minoan Crete
rises before us, transformed, but no less beautiful and entrancing.

BOOK THREE

In the Shadow
of the Minotaur

17

Tales from a House
of the Dead

Let us recall, at the risk of repetition, Strabo's and Herodotus' descriptions of the Egyptian labyrinth at Hawara. Strabo spoke (see p. 186) of:

> a table-shaped plain, with . . . a large palace composed of as many palaces as there were formerly nomes. There are an equal number of *aulae*, surrounded by pillars, and contiguous to one another, all in one line and forming one building, like a long wall having *aulae* in front of it. . . . There are long and numerous covered ways, communicating with each other, so that no stranger would find his way into the *aulae* or out of them without a guide.

And Herodotus:

> Inside, the building is of two storeys and contains three thousand rooms, of which half are underground, and the other half directly above them. I was taken through the rooms in the upper storey, so what I shall say of them is from my own observation, but the underground ones I can speak of only from report, because the Egyptians in charge refused to let me see them, as they contain the tombs of the kings who built the labyrinth, and also the tombs of the sacred crocodiles. . . . The baffling and

> intricate passages from room to room and from court to court
> were an endless wonder to me, as we passed from a courtyard
> into rooms, from rooms into galleries, from galleries into more
> rooms, and thence into yet more courtyards. . . . Each court is
> exquisitely built of white stone and surrounded by a colonnade.

It would be hard to find a better description of the impression
the Palace of Knossos must once have made on its visitors (and
still does on the open-minded tourist, provided he has not
equipped himself with one of those charts for sale at the entrance
to the site). The description fits, even to the zigzag corridors
with their "spirit traps," the central courts, the pillared ante-
rooms and the "white stone." The abrupt bends served, in the
minds of the builders, to block the path of baneful influences,
whether from inside to the outside or vice versa. Anyone familiar
with the intricate ground plan of the Palace of Knossos would
have been able to grope his way to his destination, but evil
spirits in or around the palace would not be able to find the right
way. Or so it was hoped. Obviously the ritual shields—which
were there for protection—were not considered entirely effective.

We must also consider that the Egyptian labyrinth was much
bigger because it served all twelve districts of Egypt, whereas
the Palace of Knossos met the needs of a relatively small population living in the area of cultivated land around Knossos. But
given the more limited conditions of Crete, the Knossos labyrinth
is confusing enough.

Herodotus clearly emphasized one principle of the structure:
many of the rooms are "double," that is, there is one above and
one beneath the ground. In Knossos, too, we find this principle
of duality in the Queen's Megaron, in the House of the High
Priest and in other places. The upper room is connected by stairs
with the lower. Entry to the upper rooms is permitted; these are
the ceremonial rooms. In the lower chambers rest the dead,
whose earthly bodies have been transformed and may not be
disturbed. "The Egyptians in charge refused to let me see them
as they contained the tombs of the kings," Herodotus says of
these underground rooms, and he takes care to ascribe his description of them to the Egyptians. But could there have been
so many kinds? Nearly fifteen hundred? That number would
have sufficed for all the pharaohs from the first to the last of the
thirty dynasties. We know, however, that most of the pharaohs

were in fact buried elsewhere. By "kings" the Egyptian guides did not mean "pharaoh" at all, for had they been referring to *them,* they would have spoken of "gods." In hieroglyphic texts the form of address for a pharaoh runs approximately as follows: "In the fourteenth year in the third month of the second season on the sixth day the Osiris, King Usermare [Ramses II], was brought here to be reburied in the tomb of the Osiris, King Menmare Sethos [I] by the High Priest of Amun, Pinutem." In the Hawara labyrinth the pharaoh, as King of Egypt, was simultaneously a god and Osiris himself, the god of vegetation and of the dead, as well as the son of Ptah, who was both the creator god and the local god of the city of Memphis. All life in the land of the Nile depended on vegetation. The lines between the fruitful Nile Valley and the desert, hostile to all life, on either side,

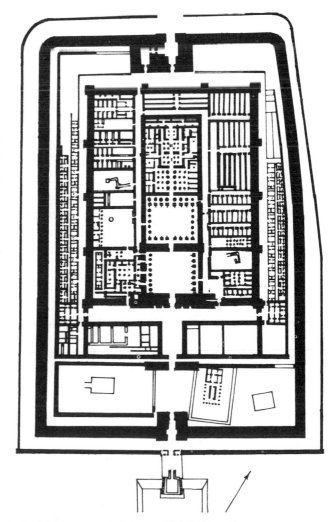

FIG. 71 Medinet Habu: Ramses III's mortuary palace. This did not serve as the dead pharaoh's tomb (he was laid to rest in the Valley of the Kings), but to venerate him in death and equip him for the hereafter. In contrast to tombs, therefore, the access corridors do not twist and turn, but run in straight lines. Note the magazines.

look as if they had been drawn with a knife. The purpose of the costly pyramids and mortuary temples involved in the worship of the dead pharaoh was to propitiate Osiris, to win the favor of the god of vegetation.

The fifteen hundred burial vaults and dwellings for the dead in the labyrinth were meant for provincial sovereigns, princes of the blood and similar highly placed personages of the Twelfth Dynasty of the Middle Kingdom. The labyrinth, therefore, was not a mortuary *temple* in the strict sense of the word. By that is meant, in Egypt, a structure for the cult of the dead but not a burial place. Examples are the valley temples at the foot of the pyramids for ceremonies in honor of the dead, or mortuary temples like the Ramesseuum in Thebes West for according divine honors to the deceased; images of him are placed in the temple, but he himself is interred in a rock-hewn tomb in the Valley of the Kings.

The vast mortuary temple of Medinet Habu in Thebes West, built for Ramses III (1181–1150 B.C.), was inhabited and maintained by a total of only ten persons: an overseer, two scribes and seven servants who carried out the daily service for the dead. This small group was virtually cut off from the city in which people lived on the eastern bank of the Nile. It frequently happened that the servants, feeling deserted and fearing the ghosts of the hereafter, fled to the eastern shore of the Nile and had to be brought back by the police. Papyrus No. 10,494 of the Berlin State Museum (which vanished after 1945), reports one such case and describes the overseer's loneliness in his dreary post: As for us here, I live in the temple area of [Medinet Habu]. You know the conditions in which we live here, both inside and outside. As for the sons of the Cher necropolis [on the West Bank], they have arrived in Nowet [the city on the East Bank] and have settled down there. I live here all alone with the scribe Zaroy and the scribe of the soldiers, Penta-hit-nacht. Would that you may cause the men of the necropolis to be captured; would that you may have them brought to me on this bank. . . . But if any of the big youths happens to rebel, send him here. . . .*

---

* Published in the *Proceedings of the Society of Biblical Archaeology*, 31 (London, 1909).

Being compelled to live in the deserted necropolis of Cher on the west bank of the river was akin to banishment. And it was altogether unthinkable that a living pharaoh might hold court there. The palaces attached to the mortuary temple were not intended to serve as a residence for the living pharaoh, but as a dwelling for the dead pharaoh's immortal soul.

By "labyrinth" we should understand a structure for the ceremonies for the dead, the sacrifices to the dead, and also for the preservation of the dead. That is why in my initial publications on the subject I spoke of mortuary *palaces* in deliberate contrast to mortuary *temples*. In the Cretan palaces temples in the proper sense of the word are at most found as late annexes, such as the Temple of Rhea at Phaistos.

But a labyrinth is not a necropolis. By necropolises we mean *cities* of the dead in which the dead are placed singly or together in dwellings or tombs. Necropolises may be attached to labyrinths. But a labyrinth has, in addition to its primary function of serving as a residence for the dead, quite a few additional functions: it is the spiritual center of the surrounding settlements, a religious site, an assembly point; an arena, archive and scriptorium; a place of judgment, execution and sacrifice; and so on. The great courts and subsidiary buildings serve these purposes, as well as the prime purpose of holding impressive funeral ceremonies, which were accompanied by religious dramas and competitive games complete with music, dancing and banquets.

In antiquity the usual meaning of a labyrinth as a structure in which the dead rested in the underground rooms was well understood. Though Herodotus' eyewitness account makes it quite plain that the Egyptian labyrinth was not a residence for living kings, modern scientists have overlooked the precise information furnished by the Father of History.

So marvelous were the Knossan finds, as interpreted by Evans, that no one even looked for parallels, let alone earlier examples of what seemed to them unique. And even when the Kamares and Postpalatial pottery turned up, and the fresco processions of Keftiu in Egyptian tombs, no one wanted to abandon the already established, pretty and beloved picture of a Minoan paradise with its enchanted palace. That accounts for the purely Minoan (Greek) reading of the word "labyrinth" as the "palace of the *labrys*," the double axe. Yet Pliny the Elder not only wrote of the Egyptian and Cretan labyrinths, but also applied the same name to structures in Lemnos and Etruria. The double axe, however, is a cult symbol that was largely limited to Crete, and even there primarily to Knossos, and could certainly not have had anything to do with the Egyptian labyrinth at Lake Moeris.

There is, to repeat, no doubt that in antiquity the use of labyrinths as burial structures was known. The thick walls and dark corridors, the virtual absence of windows, the airshafts and propylaea, suggest that less importance was placed on good light than on ample supply of air. Hence the Widow Merti, more than four thousand years ago, wrote the following words to her deceased son to whom she applied for help in obtaining the aid of the gods and of dead souls against a wicked relative: "May Osiris, First of the Western Ones, give you millions of years by blowing wind [fresh air] into your nose, and bread and beer for nourishment. . . ." Fresh air in fact was essential to the dead; mummies kept better in the dry west wind. The dead in the labyrinth received fresh air through the air shafts, and food and water from temple servants who filled the offering bowls and grooves. It was not until the end of the Hyksos period (*ca.* 1650–1542 B.C.) that the Egyptians moved from their customary primitive dry mummification to the more complicated procedures of embalming in which the Minoan Keftiu had led the way. Eventually the Egyptian *taricheutes* themselves became masters in performing operations and preserving corpses. The oldest preserved royal mummy is that of Sekenenre (*ca.* 1550 B.C.). This dating corresponds to the Late Minoan period.

In the labyrinth the dead were not "out of this world." They could not be visited directly; that would have disturbed their rest and their transformation in the grave. But members of the family could come to the upper cult rooms to leave sacrifices and to converse with the dead directly, or even better by letter, and tell them their cares and concerns and ask for help from the "western ones."

In parts of black Africa such a conception of the "living dead" has survived to this day in popular beliefs. Professor John Mbiti of the University of Kampala uses exactly that term, the "living dead," in his book on African religion and the concepts of death, a book based on his own profound knowledge and experience as a black African. From the *sasa*, this present world, the living dead move on to the *zamani*, the past, or eternity. In the *zamani*, however, they remain alive as long as some one of their kin brings them water and food, such as cola nuts, daily. At the grave an old woman will speak aloud with her dead, will sing something to them, tell them about the family and neighbors; she may also rail against them if things are not to her liking. "Ghosts" are of two kinds: the ghosts directly created by the gods, and the souls of people long dead who have no living relatives. "Africans are notoriously religious," says John Mbiti. I would add that they have preserved a kind of religious feeling that once upon a time was very widespread in the Mediterranean region and far beyond it. Europeans, it is true, have moved a considerable distance from this primeval religious attitude. Evans should properly have compared the Minoan world not with the British monarchy at the turn of the century, with its palaces and country houses, but with the practices and thought of Africa, where attitudes toward death are age-old and bear a strong resemblance to those of ancient Egypt.

Only a few years ago the people of Burundi, who had expelled their king for political reasons, were much concerned with recovering the body of the dead ruler. Only if the king were buried in his capital city would he be appeased and look with favor upon the living. An unreconciled dead king was a highly dangerous force. In African belief we even come upon the bird of death known to us from ancient Egypt and from the Minoan Hagia Triada sarcophagus. Its form has changed, however; in Africa bats appear at the time of the king's death to accompany him into the hereafter.

Such observations can be made to this day—but not at excavation sites. Moreover, the cult of the dead among contemporary Africans is considered the province of anthropology rather than archaeology. Particularism in science is often not so much a matter of modesty as of self-imposed narrowness, and this kind of narrowness in science, as in politics, is intensely chauvinistic. To be sure, it was enormously gratifying to archaeologists to behold the achievements of their own high civilization as preexisting in the millennially ancient monuments of an aristocratic island kingdom. Yet to have followed that line of thought was profoundly unhistorical. It is methodologically more proper and scientifically more profitable to compare a newly discovered archaeological complex with neighboring or kindred cultures. We come closer to the truth when we investigate the survivals, in other parts of the earth, of old rites and ways of life that might serve better to illustrate a certain stage of man's thinking and behavior than do twentieth-century patterns in western Europe. When adherents of the Evans school accuse me of drawing conclusions by analogy, I am not in the least disconcerted. After all, this criticism applies even more pointedly to them.

While I am on the subject of criticism and accusations, let me say a word about one of the pet jibes directed against my Minoan studies: "Here comes the Däniken of archaeology." My secret hope that Erich von Däniken (author of *Chariots of the Gods?*) will someday let his cat out of the bag is probably doomed to disappointment. But at the risk of betraying Däniken's secret strategy and spoiling his joke, I venture to assert that he is the most important and most brilliant satirist in German literature for at least a century. It really doesn't matter what this subtle intellect writes about cosmic visitors who have set up, for their amusement, a global terrarium on earth with experimentally "enriched" apes. Däniken's wit is implicit not in the exact shape of his fantasies, but in his biting satire of an influential school of scientific thinking. This master literary spoofer and creator of a new genre of cosmicomic books is merely carrying to the extreme a method that has been pursued by eminent archaeologists, and that even Arthur Evans was guilty of. At the turn of the century bathrooms and flush toilets were among the symbols of modern progress. In old Berlin the bathtub from the Hotel Adlon used to be carried to the Royal Palace whenever His Majesty wished to take a bath. Evans promptly found bathtubs and toilets in his excavations. A short while ago a fad for home grills swept West Germany. Sure enough, grills were soon found in the Büdelsdorf excavations of a Neolithic site. Today space travel is the *dernier cri* of civilization; therefore Däniken finds evidence for it in the excavation sites of cultures going back to the Stone Age. A glorious jest!

The landscape that frames the Cretan palaces has probably

changed significantly in three and a half millennia. Excavators and restorers see the palace sites within the context of present-day agricultural patterns, without considering that a considerable portion of the vineyards that today surround the hill of Knossos were planted only since the immigration of Greeks from Turkish Asia Minor after the end of the First World War. As has been mentioned, those immigrants, within a relatively short time, enormously increased the production of grapes and raisins on the island.

Today the surroundings of the palaces are like a garden, thanks to steel agricultural implements that were unknown in Minoan times. The Minoans had no iron hoes and plowshares; consequently, as we pointed out earlier, tillage and the planting of orchards were largely confined to the rich, friable soils of the flood plains. The hard, stony soil of the slopes could not be exploited for agriculture, and so the Minoan palaces—just like the Egyptian mortuary temples—were originally situated outside the land susceptible to settlement, in wasteland outside the ecumene. To locate a heavily populated royal residence on such an escarpment would make sense only for reasons of defensibility; but the Cretan palaces were patently not conceived as fortresses. Logic tells us that the homes of a Bronze Age peasant population whose highest good consisted of its herds would not have been built far from springs of water and agricultural land.

Recent stratigraphically careful excavations at Knossos have determined that the palace stands upon the site of Neolithic mud-brick structures, under the floors of which the bodies of children were buried. (This is similar to the observations made by the Bavarian archaeological expedition in Orchomenos at the beginning of the century.) Archaeologists have concluded that these finds also are dwellings. In fact they assume that intra-muros burial was customary in the Stone Age, in spite of the fact that all ancient peoples manifested strong fear of the return of the dead and maintained a strict separation between the realms of the living and those of the dead. Thus it seems much more reasonable to assume that the mud-brick structures that preceded the building of the mortuary palace were likewise morgues and tombs in which the corpses were partly inhumed (especially the bodies of children), partly buried in jars or on *klines,* until ultimately a more lavish cult of the dead led to the construction of the palaces.

Why, then, have no bones been found in the excavation of these sites? In reply to that question let me point out that no bones were found in the Egyptian mortuary palaces, although the Egyptians developed the most elaborate technique of mummification and could rely on their unique climate for the preservation of mummies. After all, virtually every single site (including the relatively well-preserved Tomb of Tutankhamen) had been visited by grave robbers. Moreover, mummies themselves were probably subject to theft; until recently even our occidental pharmacies carried "mumia" as a curative. Mummy powder was considered to have supernatural medicinal powers. In Arabia the dead are still placed in underground chamber tombs, where they often disintegrate so completely within a few years that the tomb can be used again. And a modern "grave robber" (one on a scientifically acceptable level), Heinrich Schliemann, could only look on helplessly as the bodies from the Mycenaean shaft graves fell to dust before his eyes, although an instant before the mummylike, discolored faces under the gold masks were perfectly preserved. Not even the teeth could be saved once the bodies were exposed to air.

It has been established that the building of the Egyptian labyrinth at Hawara was contemporary with the Middle Minoan period as defined by Evans (more specifically, with Middle Minoan Ila), equivalent to the Palaeopalatial period in Nicolas Platon's chronological system (Phase II, *ca.* 1900–1800 B.C.). It is difficult to determine whether a similar older structure existed at the site of the Hawara labyrinth before the reign of Amenemhet III, or whether this Twelfth Dynasty palace (*ca.* 1839–1791 B.C.) is of completely new construction. Cretan datings are also not so precise that the actual building of the labyrinth can certainly be dated back to the period before 1839 B.C., that is, before the beginning of Amenemhet III's reign. The question of who suggested the labyrinthine mode of building to him must therefore be left open for the time being. But the parallels are plain to see.

At the time the newer palaces of Crete were being built (Platon's Neopalatial period), the vast mortuary palace of Thebes

West, below the Valley of the Kings where the pharaohs of the Eighteenth Dynasty were buried, was also under construction. Egyptian archaeologists do not feel it is calumny to identify these structures as mortuary palaces. On the contrary, Egyptian specialists have long since abandoned the initial interpretation of the buildings as royal residences. To this day only a few fragments of genuine residential palaces in Egypt are known. The reason is that these were made of air-dried bricks, as perishable a material as that used for the housing of the pharaoh's subjects. Given the relations between Crete and Egypt, for which we have indubitable proofs in the funerary finds in both countries, why should we refuse to accept an analogous interpretation of the Cretan mortuary palaces? It is true that in Crete there is no glorification of individuals in paintings, sculpture and writing, such as we find commonly in the Egypt of the New Kingdom. But this can scarcely be taken as a serious argument against this interpretation.

We may also consider the possibility that palaces of the Knossos type may have served both as residences and as temples for the cult of the dead, their upper stories being used as a domestic wing and their lower stories as burial vaults. The difficulty with such an idea is that stairways and air shafts connect all the stories. Given the traditional fear of returning ghosts, such easy communication between the realms of the living and the dead seems highly improbable.

Our argument, then, can be summed up: The British archaeologists recklessly projected their picture of life in England at the turn of the century upon Knossos. As they saw it, none but the royal family could have lived in the palace. In the same spirit they decided that the villas scattered around the countryside must have been the dwelling places of the nobility descended from the king. So far, no element in this conception has been proved. Who lived in the palaces, who in the stately villas, who in the three-story dwellings of the cities? My answer remains, after I have once more intensively reviewed all the facts: No living Minoans inhabited these places, but the venerable dead of ancient Crete, provided with all the equipment they would need for eternity.

18

Symbol of Joy
or Token of Mourning?

❁

Even in their interpretations of the frescos and art objects found in the Palace of Knossos the excavators seem to have imagined that they could proceed from the psychological impression such works of art make upon people today. It did not occur to them that images of *joie de vivre* and tokens of mourning might have undergone changes in three and a half millennia. They decided that the frescos of birds, beasts and fish in the palace celebrated this earthly life and all its joys. But they could have offered such an interpretation only by ignoring the iconography of the age, by failing to grasp the meaning of certain images for the people of that time.

According to ancient belief, birds, fish and dolphins accompany the souls of the dead into the hereafter. Images of birds, fish and dolphins are repeatedly found painted on the outside and inside of the ceramic sarcophagi of the Minoan period and of later times. Hecate, goddess of the underworld, is often depicted with a dolphin on her belly. Deep into Roman times representations of dolphins are found on cinerary urns. The color of mourning was generally blue. Roman columbaria, where cinerary urns were kept, were generally painted blue.

The decor of the Queen's Megaron in the Palace of Knossos would have struck the people of antiquity quite differently from the way it strikes us today. We see dolphins gaily disporting, surrounded by light-blue ornamentation. To us, such a picture seems a charming bit of natural history. But for the people of antiquity the dolphins were symbols of the soul's liberation from its earthly body, comparable to the Christian sign of the cross as a symbol of salvation; and the blue would correspond to our black. For a proper understanding of the effect that such a fresco would have made at the time we must imagine paintings of crosses instead of dolphins, and a background of black instead of blue. This would suddenly bring home to us the tomb-like nature of the building.

Bull-leaping games and festive assemblages, such as are represented on other frescos in the Palace of Knossos, were probably held for a variety of reasons. But it is established beyond doubt that competitive games of all kinds, and general gatherings, were held in honor of the dead throughout the ancient world. Bullfights are pictured on Roman cinerary urns, as are griffins and other fabulous monsters such as we encounter in the Knossos Throne Room.

For light on the many questions still posed by Minoan archaeology we can profitably turn to what we know of the Etruscans. In Mallia deep shafts with central pillars have been discovered and identified as cisterns. This seems to me a totally arbitrary conclusion, inasmuch as similar findings in Casal Marittima have been recognized as shaft graves. Moreover, there would have been no need for cisterns in Mallia, where the groundwater level is so high that a single dug well would yield an abundance of water, making water storage unnecessary. Similar shafts have also been found in the Little Palace in Knossos and in Phaistos; again, these have been labeled cisterns. But no one who has seen the offering shafts (*mundi subterranei*) of Cuccumella and Marzabotto in Etruria could miss the strong resemblance between these and the aforementioned cisterns. In Etruria, too, we find decorated underground chambers that are incontrovertibly tombs. And there again are frescos repeating the fish, flower and bird motifs, as well as the griffinlike fabulous beasts familiar to us from Knossos.

Among the grave goods we have come to know from many early cultures are specimens of black, extremely thin-walled pottery to which a "metallic" look has been given. Etruscan art provides countless examples. We have already mentioned the Regolini Galassi tomb in connection with the ritual shields found there. The Gregorian Collection in Rome has considerable quantities of such "metallic" ware, of the type known as *bucchero sottile,* from that tomb. The vessels are extremely thin-walled, glistening black in color, with a metallic sheen, and are no doubt meant to represent genuine metal vessels. They occupy the same place in Etruscan funerary art as the Kamares eggshell ware does in Minoan culture. Cretan eggshell ceramics, so called because of their pronounced delicacy and fragility, were regarded by Evans as signs of an overrefined culture and of supreme artistic perfection.

The well-known Etruscan scholar O. W. von Vacano, one of the foremost German specialists on the archaeology of Etruria, some time ago raised the same question in regard to *bucchero sottile* ware that we have raised in regard to eggshell ware: whether such fragile vessels could ever have been intended for daily life.

The imitation of metal is particularly distinct in Minoan vase saucers with repoussé flowers, and on similarly made kraters in the "barbotine" technique. An excellent specimen of this type from the Old Palace of Knossos (Kamares style, Middle Minoan

FIG. 72　Kamares krater, Old Palace of Knossos. Note the remnants of chain links on the upper left rim, a ceramic imitation of metal and hence not intended for practical use.

II, *ca.* 1800 B.C.) actually shows two links of a metal chain imitated in ceramic. Pottery easily lends itself to such shams. Thus early Minoan ceramics, like the double-cone cup from Pyrgos in central Crete (now in the Herakleion Museum), are executed in imitation of woodwork and basketry (*ca.* 2500 B.C.) A whole school of pottery seems to have followed the patterns of vessels commonly made of wood or woven of wicker. But this does not mean that with the development of pottery wooden vessels were no longer wanted. On the contrary, ordinary household utensils continued to be made of wood well beyond the Bronze Age. Wooden dishes and wooden spoons could be made cheaply and quickly, and they lasted well, did not break when dropped and were considerably lighter and handier than pottery utensils. In addition, gourds were probably used as vessels quite frequently, as well as woven containers lined with leather and wineskins. Throughout this era warm meals probably consisted of flatcakes baked on hot stones and meat roasted on a spit. Not until the Bronze Age would there have been large cauldrons for cooking.

For the dwellings of the dead, however, wooden vessels, basketry and skins were not sufficiently durable. Here pottery took their place as a material suitable "for eternity."

Countless rhytons, those typical funnel-shaped vessels carried in the processions of the Keftiu, pitchers with the heads of bulls and all the other zoomorphic vases, beaked jugs, seashell shapes and so on, were produced for the cult of the dead and for the arts of healing and embalming. After grand burials such utensils were left behind in the tomb. Other vases, bowls and pithoi were intended as grave goods. Offering stones concave in shape served to receive the food for the dead, while flat stones with rims and drainage grooves on the side were meant for the daily libation of water, beer or wine at the grave. Such articles have been found in abundance and classified as lamps or saucers for oil mills.

Besides the famous tripod of the Linear B tablets, other peculiar objects are pictured or mentioned in those texts whose function remains a mystery. Palmer coined the designation "ghost forms" for such problematic items, and intended the phrase to cover all those baffling words and phrases that have cropped up in the decipherment of Linear B. The phrase was apter than he

imagined. Many curious things stand in the glass cases of the
Herakleion Museum and are reported to serve this or that common household use. In fact, like the so-called lamps and oil mill
saucers, they have been transferred from the spirit world to the
secular world. When we give them back to the ghosts for
whom they were meant, we find that various enigmas connected
with Minoan civilization are suddenly a good deal more intelli-
gible.

As we have seen, one of the most intriguing elements in the
newly discovered world of the Minoans was the frequent appearance, in frescos and statuettes, of women with bared breasts.
It was at once alleged, and in the most authoritative terms, that
such exposure was the fashion for ladies in ancient Crete. The
matter was stressed in every account of Minoan civilization, and
pictures of the open-bodied Cretan beauties appeared in countless histories of art. Far-reaching conclusions were drawn, on
the basis of this one detail, concerning the nature of the Minoan
social system and the unusual freedom, not to say progressive-
ness, of the Cretan mind. It seems strange that no one should
have recalled Herodotus' observation that Egyptian women bared
their breasts as a sign of deepest mourning. The statuettes from
Minoan palaces of women with upraised arms, sometimes with
hands held over the face or holding aloft a child, are not to be
interpreted as images of worshipers or priestesses, but as representations of mourning women. An instructive parallel exists in
the form of an ancient Greek sarcophagus which shows such
mourners surrounded by snakes. And significantly enough, some
of the Minoan mourning women are clasping snakes, which are
standard signs of grief. Such statuettes were promptly dubbed
"snake priestesses" or "snake goddesses."

Egyptian tombs repeatedly show the motif of women with
bared bosoms as a sign of mourning (see, for example, the funeral procession in the tomb of two sculptors of Thebes, Eighteenth
Dynasty, (ca. 1370 B.C.). The women are rending their garments
and beating their breasts.

In the Late Minoan palaces the original fate of widows was
alleviated by placing surrogate figures in the form of terracotta
mourning women outside the burial chamber. These terracotta
figures (there are some, for example, from the Sanctuary of the

Double Axes in the Palace of Knossos that date from before 1300
B.C.) have been interpreted as goddesses or idols. The torso
emerges from a round, bouffant skirt, the waist is narrow, the
breasts emphasized; large arms are raised high, the face is rather
broad, primitively painted, with a staring look. These figurines
represent the wives of the dead, who could thus escape the utterly exhausting duties of obligatory mourning, which went on
for weeks. In later specimens, dated around 1300, the breasts are
still emphasized but are partly covered.

Whereas the Hebrews rent their garments, the Egyptian women
bared their breasts; this same gesture of mourning may be seen
on Roman sarcophagi, and is also recorded among the Celts and
Germans. But for what is probably the most moving literary
description of this kind of mourning we must turn to Homer.
In Book XXII of *The Iliad* he tells how Priam, Hector's aged
father, tries to save his son from certain death in the struggle
with Achilles. When he realizes that all his supplications will be
vain, that his beloved son is determined to seek death in the duel
with his superior adversary, Priam

> in his hand seizing his grey hairs
> tore them from his head, but could not move the spirit
> in Hektor
> And side by side with him his mother in tears was mourning
> and laid the fold of her bosom bare, and with one hand
> held out a breast. . . .°

Here we find the baring of the breast symbolizing utmost despair
and grief. Homer is speaking out of the ancient Greek tradition,
which clearly reflects modes of behavior common to the Aegean
region toward the end of the Bronze Age. It is hardly possible
to doubt the meaning of this particular gesture among almost all
the peoples of the ancient world. Yet in Crete, we are told,
manners were just the opposite: there the bared breast must be
understood as a sign of joyousness and emancipation!

I would submit that the Cretan women did not bare their
breasts except when they they were in deep mourning. Nor was

° *The Iliad*, translated by Richmond Lattimore (University of Chicago
Press, Phoenix Book, 1970) Book XXII, lines 77–81, p. 437.

the male costume normally a kind of kilt displaying the men's reddish-brown skin to good advantage. All those russet male figures in the Minoan frescos do not show the ancient Cretan men in their normal appearance. Rather, their bodies have been reddened with cosmetics and they have stripped off their clothes for the ritual play. In Etruscan tomb frescos, too, we encounter some of these kilted, red-painted mourners. They are not shown manifesting our present-day gestures of mourning, but playing the flute, moving drunkenly, even dancing. However, anyone who applies contemporary standards to these pictures is bound to come to the wrong conclusions.

The snakes we have met with on the Greek sarcophagi, and that we see clasped by the so-called snake goddesses, are found stylized into undulating lines on the huge jars that fill the magazines at Knossos and stand about in the other rooms. Evans and his successors identified these jars as storage vessels for olive oil and other foodstuffs, and archaeologists claim to have found traces of wheat and lentils in some of them. We have already expressed our doubts of this interpretation of the jars. Now we have still another cause for doubt, for the presence of the snake motif certainly seems to suggest that these jars had some more solemn purpose than that of serving as the royal larder.

To be sure, large storage jars are to some extent still used in the Mediterranean region. But it is also true that ancient Greek funerary pithoi have been found in considerable numbers on the Greek mainland and the islands. It is advisable to study both types carefully and to distinguish between them. The pithoi, it soon becomes apparent, are wider at the mouth and less swelling at the waist than the storage jars. They are also characterized by bands of undulating lines (the snake motif), whereas the storage jars are left unornamented. As for the contention that the pithoi contained food or other goods, some personal possessions and provisions for the journey into the hereafter would have been placed in the funerary pithoi along with the cadaver—the same sort of grave goods that were generally put into graves. To be sure, most funerary pithoi have been found laid on their sides and covered with earth, whereas the pithoi in the Minoan palaces were found standing upright, lined up in rows in carefully constructed underground chambers. But this difference is easily explained. To cover a pithos 1.5 meters tall with a meter of earth, a very deep hole must be dug—a pit nearly 3 meters in depth. Given the rocky soil of Greece and the high level of the groundwater in the coastal plains, that was impracticable. Hence the jars were laid on their sides.

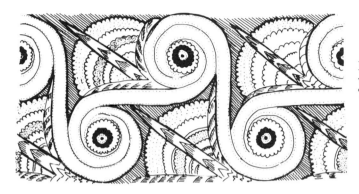

FIG. 73   Spiral fresco with lotus blossoms, Tiryns.

FIG. 74   Burial vault, Orchomenos: ceiling decoration with rosettes, spirals and lotus blossoms.

It is conceivable that some of the great jars in the Minoan palaces were indeed filled with food, which would have been apportioned to the more illustrious deceased for their journey to the hereafter. But food for the living would scarcely have been kept in such vessels. The snake symbol alone would have frightened away the people of that age.

Even such seemingly harmless symbols as the rosettes that often appear in bands on the pithoi, or in conjunction with the double axe, bear out this point. For the rose was no mere pretty blossom like others. In antiquity the rose was sacred to Aphrodite. By ancient custom the graves in Greece and Italy were strewn with rose petals and planted with roses. In our own millennium rosettes can still be found on Israelite, Turkish and Arab gravestones. In the Christian world the cult of Mary took the place of the ancient cult of Aphrodite; thus roses are now an attribute of Mary. In central Europe the "rose hedge" or rose garden signified a holy area in which rites for the dead and religious games were performed. (The fairy tale of Sleeping Beauty preserves this aura of death implied by the hedge of thorny roses.) Frequently these games consisted of duels to the death. In the great Rose Garden Epic Kriemhild invites the thanes of Dietrich of Bern (Theoderic) into her "rose garden" for the fatal struggle. Persephone is gathering roses and crocuses when she is abducted by Hades, who carries her off to the underworld to be his wife. And this motif of flower gathering turns up again in Knossos, of all places—in the famous fresco that has been interpreted as either a youth or a monkey picking flowers.

Another motif that constantly recurs in Minoan and Mycenaean sites is the spiral. We have met with it in Cycladic culture, where it serves to decorate soapstone boxes and the mysterious Cycladic "frying pans." On Crete a spiral frames the inscription on the Phaistos Disc. We find it on Kamares ware, on the edges of the Hagia Triada sarcophagus, and also on the altar and tomb depicted on that sarcophagus. There is the spiral fresco and the background of the shields in Knossos. In Tiryns the motif turns up as a border on frescos and on ceramic vessels, in Mycenae in the form of architectural or ornamental borders, on grave steles, on gold discs from the garments of the dead in Schliemann's shaft graves, on sword hilts inlaid with gold, on silver jugs and on ceramics. In the subsequent Geometric period the spiral line changes to a meander, a broken spiral. But it continues for a long time as a favorite device on cinerary urns, vessels of all sorts and friezes.

The spiral motif was also prevalent in Egypt. Sometimes the spiral is associated with snake imagery, as when used to orna-

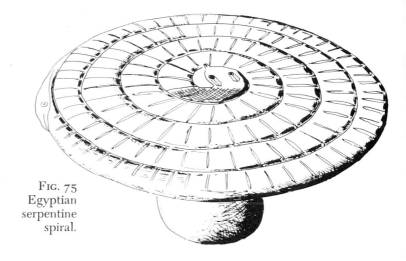

F<small>IG.</small> 75
Egyptian
serpentine
spiral.

ment a table top: the concentric windings of the pattern culmi-
nate in a snake's head. The Widow Merti's letter to her deceased
son, referred to earlier, is written in the form of a spiral on a
shallow bowl.

The Egyptians had a board game in which a flat stone in the
shape of a coiled snake represented the *mehen* or "king" of the
pieces. The game was played by two players on a board of thirty-
six squares. Twelve pieces were used, five simple ones, five with
knobs and two kings. This was not, however, a social game
played for mere amusement; what was at stake was nothing less
than bliss in the hereafter! Max Pieper has been able to trace this
ancient Egyptian board game through successive cultures to the
chess game played in India, from which our modern chess is
descended. A papyrus of the Twentieth Dynasty contains a
description of the complicated rules, and in addition a plea to
the gods and to the dead: "May you permit me to enter into the
Hall of the Thirty [Judges, located in square 7 on the board]
and let me become as a god, as the Thirty-first. . . ." When an
opponent was defeated, the phrasing was: "I place my pieces
firmly in the 'beautiful house' [Square 36]. I take [the opponent's
pieces] in the house 'beautiful back of the head.' My pieces are
in the van. My fingers are like a jackal who draws the boat. I
take his pieces, I throw him into the water. He drowns together
with his pieces. Your voice is true, says he, the *mehen*, to me. My
heart is glad (many) times." Here the spiral as the "king," as
the "snake" *mehen*, promises victory and hence happiness for
eternity.

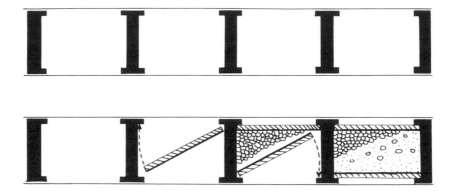

F_IG. 76 Many doors in Minoan buildings have double rabbets on either side of the jambs, such as this on the portico of Niru Chani (section shown in the upper picture). They could therefore be closed permanently, as the lower sketch shows. Two sets of slabs were fitted in for the inside and outside, and slid into the rabbets; the space between these sets was filled with rubble. Access was thereafter possible only by breaking the outer slabs. Ceremonial sealing of portals with masonry, which on festive occasions may occasionally be broken open, is not unknown in Christian ritual. Similar door openings have been found in Egyptian tombs.

All these spiral motifs and ornamental borders, including the Greek meander (which, as mentioned above, should be regarded as a broken spiral line), would seem to represent bliss in eternity, no matter whether they are found in the Cycladic culture, among the Minoans, Mycenaeans, Hellenes, or even later among the Romans, and even up to the present. But in the interval we moderns have lost awareness of the symbol's meaning. We therefore take it only as an ornament, no longer as a potent bit of magic.

This is the place to mention another and perhaps equally important parallel between Cretan buildings and Egyptian tombs. Some of the doors in the Cretan palaces are provided with rabbets in the jambs, which suggests that the doors could be firmly sealed. Once the slabs had been fitted into place, the door could no longer be opened from the outside. Where such rooms have no other entrances, they would thus be closed "for eternity." And the doors to the rock tombs of the Egyptian pharaohs were constructed on the same principle.

19

In the Sign
of the Bull

❁

Ever since the inception of the science of archaeology
there have been those who place their trust in the oral tradition as
set forth in myths and legends, and those who trust only what
the spade turns up. Oral traditions are too vague and uncertain, mythical notions too confusing and contradictory, legends
too fantastic, the latter argue. The traditions of the ancients
will at most serve for linguistic studies, they hold. On the other
hand the certified findings of excavation are free of subjective
distortions, can be reexamined at any time and are approachable
by modern scientific methods.

Others have been convinced of the accuracy of ancient tradition. Heinrich Schliemann owed two of his most astounding
triumphs in excavation—at Troy and Mycenae—to his absolute
faith in ancient texts, which undoubtedly recorded a long oral
tradition. At the very beginning of his scientific career he found
himself roundly berated (especially by German professors of
ancient languages) because he employed a measuring tape and
stopwatch to check Homer's descriptions of the site of Troy
against the actual measurements of Hissarlik. His later associate,
Professor Wilhelm Dörpfeld, recalled in 1932 how several German specialists ridiculed Schliemann's labors at Troy and Ithaca:
"This scorn, which a few great scholars later heaped upon my
own excavations at Homeric sites has always struck me as regret-

table. I regarded it as not only unfair but also unscientific."
Since Schliemann's feats could no longer be denied, the specialists
attacked the successful outsider for his faulty excavation methods
and for going at the work too fast.

We have already cited various passages from Homer as though
they were equivalent to historical evidence. Perhaps this assumption needs to be justified, for Homer's epics, after all,
are literature, and literature is by no means always to be taken
as documentary truth. Yet it seems evident that there is a good
share of realism in the Homeric lays. In the first place, the tales
were originally recited orally and to a particular audience. This
audience would have been intimately acquainted with both battle and seafaring, and would have had a pretty good sense of
the geography of the Aegean world. For the bard to have commanded the respect of his listeners he would have had to present an impressive amount of solid fact. Indeed, the wealth of
careful description, in both *The Iliad* and *The Odyssey*, of household gear, weaponry and customs testifies to this need. The fabulous element in the epics, therefore, is only one strand of the
whole and is associated with events on the border of time or
space, those set either in another age or on the fringe of the
ecumene, as the Greeks called the habitable world.

Thus when we read Homer we find ourselves face to face with
living human beings of his age, fixed in language and image
more vividly than any portrait offered us by archaeology. It is
an error to believe that we can animate the worlds of the past
through the finds of excavation alone. Many questions remain
unanswered even when the most advanced excavation techniques
have been used—because the found objects remain mute. Stones
cannot speak.

To be sure, the overemphasis on the results of excavation suits
our modern, technically oriented way of thinking, with its anta-
gonism to everything not immediately acceptable to the senses,
to everything that cannot be checked and double checked. But
it is even more dangerous to bring our "modern" habits of thought
to the *interpretation* of the finds, as if men of the Bronze Age
were the same as men of the present day.

Even if we do not seek to verify Homer with measuring tape
and stopwatch, he and he alone can reveal the mentality of hu-

man beings of those far-off times. Homer was almost three thousand years closer to the Aegean world than we are today. Surely he has something valuable to tell us about that world. To reconstruct a long-lost culture we must have some insight into its people, just as to decipher Linear B we must have some inkling of the purpose those texts may have served.

There is something fundamentally misleading about the dispute over whether to believe oral tradition or the results of excavation, as though one approach excluded the other. The archaeologist who carries out his field work with scientific rigor, but views his findings only through the lens of his own experience and the attitudes of his own day, will obviously go far wrong. He will derive at least as false a picture as the mythologist who sets out to interpret ancient traditions with sovereign unconcern for time, space and the yield of excavations.

By itself, neither tradition nor excavation is sufficient. Both must be combined to form a logical whole. But when we speak of logic, we do not mean to imply that, for example, it is necessary that the ancient rites for the dead or conception of the hereafter be logical in the modern sense. Any acquaintance with mythology should make us aware that the thought processes of the ancients were totally unlike our own. Once we have realized that, we should be very chary of imposing our cultural preconceptions on ancient peoples. Thus a large and complicated structure like Knossos is not inevitably a palace, especially when tradition has attached some sinister legends to it. A contradiction of this sort is a sign that there are lingering obscurities in the interpretation. The problem cannot be solved by rejecting the truthfulness of ancient myths and epics out of hand. There can be no doubt that the ancients thought in mythical terms, and it is a perfectly valid assignment for serious science to attempt to determine what facts lie hidden within the legends.

In this sense such works as those of Karl Kerényi (*Die Mythologie der Griechen* and *Die Religion der Griechen und Römer*) and Robert Graves (*The Greek Myths*) have a significant bearing on Minoan archaeology. At the risk of repetition, we shall have to review briefly what Greek mythology has to say about Crete.

We will recall the story of the Minotaur, half bull and half man, and how this monster claimed the lives of seven Athenian youths and seven maidens every nine years, or every year. Theseus, the heroic Athenian prince, overcame and killed the monster, then fled from the labyrinthine palce with the aid of Ariadne, the Cretan king's daughter. Thereafter the Athenians no longer had to pay the dread tribute to the Cretan ruler.

The scholars of the cold, logical north were not ready to believe this tale. They had their picture of an ideal humanistic world, and there was no room in it for fantastic beings of dual nature or for the practice of human sacrifice. Hence they explained the Minotaur legend as a symbol of the higher Hellenic culture's defeat of the non-Greek bull cult of the ancient Cretans. Human sacrifice could not have been practiced in reality; the Minotaur must be a symbol of the Cretan god Zeus Asterios; and the labyrinth in which the beast was kept was merely a fancy invented by Greek poets.

Despite the repeated representations of bulls that Arthur Evans's diggers brought to light in Knossos, despite the gold pendants with images of bulls from Schliemann's shaft graves at Mycenae, despite the pictures of Theseus' fight with the Minotaur which constantly recurred on vases, murals, reliefs, mosaics, gems and coins, the experts have refused to come to terms with what the bull betokened. Instead we find Minoan scholars like Friedrich Matz delivering such verdicts as this one:

> "There is nothing among the Minoan artifacts that points to a bull god or bull worship." This statement by the foremost authority on Minoan religion, the Swedish scholar Martin F. Nilsson, is incontestable. The very meaning of the bull sacrifice, in fact, should put an end to the many and constantly renewed efforts to demonstrate the existence of such a god. . . . But the bull games, which are one of the most remarkable and fascinating elements in Minoan art, cannot be understood altogether outside of a religious context.

Fig. 77
Bull fresco,
Knossos.

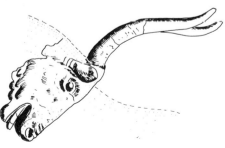

In other words, he insists there was no bull religion, merely athletic sports in a "religious context."

The Minoans sacrificed bulls; consequently they could not have worshiped a bull god. Does this conclusion follow? Certainly not. For the Egyptians also sacrificed bulls to their dead and simultaneously worshipped the cow goddess Hathor, Isis with the horns of a cow and the sacred Apis bulls. The Serapeum, near the resthouse of Sakkara, to which a burial chamber was added under Ramses II (1290–1223 B.C.) and a large gallery under Psammetich II (664–610 B.C.), still contains twenty-four mighty granite sacrophagi, each weighing over 65 tons, which enclosed the mummies of sacred bulls. Paintings from an Egyptian rock tomb, now in the Egyptian Museum in Turin, show the ritual slaughter of a bull being sacrificed to the dead. The blood of the offering was allowed to run off before the bull was killed. The Minoan sarcophagus of Hagia Triada likewise shows this method of ritual slaughter. The bull itself lies on an enormous altar. The blood was meant for the dead person (or the god) to whom the sacrifice was being made. Once the animal was dead, the blood coagulated in the veins and could no longer be obtained. In Orthodox Jewry this ritual slaughtering has continued to the present day. The process by which meat is rendered kosher goes back to ancient Mediterranean sacrificial rites.

FIG. 78
Bull's-head
rhyton,
Kato Zakro.

The sacrifice of bulls and the worship of bulls, therefore, are by no means mutually exclusive. To the tribes pressing into the Nile Valley the bull must originally have been a totem animal. It probably became, in the beliefs of the later period, a being of supernatural strength. In Memphis, Province I of Lower Egypt, the god Ptah's bull was elevated to the rank of sole local deity, as was Hathor's cow in Dendera, Province VI of Upper Egypt. But the symbols of other districts, such as the shield with the two crossed arrows of Saïs, Province IV of Lower Egypt, are crowned by a bull's head.

The Semitic sky god and weather god Baal (= Lord) also had a bull for his cult symbol. We still refer to this idol as the Golden Calf, and remember how Moses and the prophets fought to suppress its worship. Egyptian Hathor corresponded to the old Semitic goddess of love and fertility, Astarte, and to the Babylonian Ishtar, whose cult symbol was a cow. As Aphrodite, she is supposed to have entered Greece by way of Cyprus. As Venus, she was later venerated by the Romans.

Hathor, the fertility goddess, had a large following because of her temple prostitutes. Even at the lonely turquoise mines of the Sinai Mountains there was a temple of Hathor frequented by the miners isolated in the midst of the desert. Herodotus relates (I, 199) that before marriage every woman of Babylon was required to go to the temple of Mylitta (the Assyrian name for Astarte, Ishtar, Aphrodite) and lie with a stranger. It was a kind of *jus primae noctis* owed to the gods of fertility. In Babylon there was a god superior to Ishtar and all others. He was known as Marduk (the Merodach of the Hebrews) and dwelt on the upmost terrace of the seven-stepped ziggurat, the step pyramid in the center of the city known as the Tower of Babel. The uppermost chamber in this tallest of all temples was considered to be Marduk's connubial bed As Herodotus reports (I, 181 *f.*):

> On the summit of the topmost tower stands a great temple with a fine large couch in it, richly covered, and a golden table beside it. The shrine contains no image, and no one spends the night there except (if we may believe the Chaldeans who are the priests of Bel) one Assyrian woman, all alone, whoever it may be that the god has chosen. The Chaldeans also say—although I do not believe them—that the god enters the temple

in person and takes his rest upon the bed. There is a similar story told by the Egyptians at Thebes, where a woman always passes the night in the temple of the Theban Zeus. . . .*

From his tone it is plain that the enlightened Greek historian of the fifth century B.C. scarcely believed that the gods made such personal appearances. But he did not doubt the fact of temple prostitution; that was too well known. According to ancient belief, the god and goddess were living personalities who must be accorded, in the temple, their regular due in physical matters. It seems likely that in the temples of Marduk and of the Theban Zeus the priests performed the *hieros gamos,* the divine connubial rites, should the deity not deign to appear in person.

The children begotten in these encounters were not officially taken to be of divine descent, although the hetaerae performed their services in the temple and for the honor of the god. Ramses III in a papyrus boasts of his good works for the benefit of the wives of his divine father Ptah and Ptah's children:

> I made Thee mighty decrees with secret words, set forth in the hall of writings of Ta-Me-ri . . . to administer Thy venerable house [temple] to eternity and to maintain Thy pure establishment of women. I gathered together their children, who were scattered, because they sprang from men in slavery and from other [unknown] relations. I gave them to Thee for offices in the House of Ptah, and decrees were prepared for them for eternity.

From this it is apparent that the temple prostitutes were available to all and sundry, even to slaves and persons of unknown condition.

In Greece the children begotten in temples were not frowned upon. They were, in fact, formally taken to be the offspring of the gods of the particular temples. Although Europa had no less than three such "children of the god," she was taken to wife by Asterius of Crete and Knossos, who also adopted her sons, Minos, Sarpedon and Rhadamanthus. Hence the tribal mother of

---

* Herodotus, *The Histories,* p. 86.

our continent, as it were, was a *hierodule*, a temple prostitute, on whom the god had begotten thrice before she officially became Queen of Crete. Her daughter-in-law Pasiphaë, King Minos' wife, was of the same kind of parentage: she was a daughter of the god Helios. Of her seven children at least one, the Minotaur, was not her husband's; it was probably begotten "in the temple." Nor is it difficult to guess what temple, since the boy was given the name "Bull of Minos." In all probability Pasiphaë's son was sired in the temple of Ptah (or Baal), the supreme god of the Egyptians of Lower Egypt and of the Babylonians, who at various times was also worshiped in Phoenicia and Asia Minor.

Philo of Byblos, an ancient Phoenician city on the coast of the Mediterranean about 40 kilometers north of present-day Beirut, lived from A.D. 64 to 141. He wrote a voluminous history of Phoenicia, *Phoinikika*, of which only fragments have been preserved. Philo claims that his book is a Greek translation of a much older work from the hand of a Phoenician named Sanchuniathon, who wrote in the fourteenth to thirteenth centuries B.C., before the Trojan War. Hellenists long considered this statement a bit of literary hoaxing. However, this opinion was completely revised when, in 1929, C. F. Schaeffer began excavating the mound known as Ras es Shamra ("Cape Fennel"), some 10 kilometers north of the Syrian port of El Ladhaqiye (in Greek Laodikeia), and found Ugarit. The sprawling palace contained priceless ancient documents on the history and religion of Syria in antiquity. Ugarit, although considerably older than the first written notice of it, is mentioned in historical sources from 2000 B.C. on. At that time the port had trading links all over the known world. There is documentary evidence of its relations with the Egyptian Middle Kingdom. Around 1700 B.C. Ugarit also seems to have been in contact with Mari on the Euphrates. At about the same period a Middle Minoan trading post was established in Ugarit. Finds some four hundred years more recent give evidence of considerable immigration from the centers of Mycenaean culture. To a greater degree than other cities in the ancient Orient, Ugarit received cultural "imports" from the Aegean region. This is proved by the pottery; by the architecture (sets of tombs under corbeled vaults); by a palace labyrinthine in its planning and construction. The Aegean influence is above all apparent in the carved ivories and in the clay tablets with *Minoan* script. One of the greatest achievements of the Ugarites was the invention of an alphabetic cuneiform script, which was employed on quantities of clay tablets along with Akkadian cuneiform and hieroglyphs. The language of Ugarit was a Canaanite dialect. The Ugaritic documents are immensely valuable because they contain remnants of Canaanite mythology, which is even older than the Phoenician tradition.

But to return to Philo of Byblos: Among the Ugaritic clay tablets found at Ras es Shamra were some texts dealing with mythology that strikingly resemble what Philo had set forth in *Phoinikika* as deriving from Sanchuniathon. Philo, therefore, was not an oriental fabulist at all; he was indeed a translator who could be relied on.

Philo of Byblos relates (and this accords with what is written on the Ugaritic clay tablets) that Baal was worshiped as the supreme god. Baal's "sister" Anat, he says, was later displaced by Ishtar-Astarte. Ishtar, the most important goddess in the Sumerian-Akkadian pantheon, was venerated in an orgiastic cult. Since she was the mistress of sexual life, ritual temple prostitution was practiced in her honor. The sacred courtesans in the temple were regarded as embodiments of the mother goddesses Anat and Astarte. Young men as well as young women served in these erotic rites. The arrangement met the sexual needs of the populace and also provided the temples with a source of income, for those who availed themselves of the "priestesses" made offerings to the temples.

And Europa, we will recall, came from this very land of Phoenicia. She did not come voluntarily to Crete, but was forcibly carried away. In the familiar myth it is Zeus, in the engaging shape of the bull dedicated to Baal, who carried Europa across the seas to Crete, where she bore him three sons. A less well known and less "romantic" tradition is preserved by Herodotus (I, 2): "Later on some Greeks, whose name the Persian historians fail to record—they were probably Cretans—put into the Phoenician port of Tyre and carried off the king's daughter Europa. . . ."

This Asiatic version, in which the abduction of the princess is viewed as a rude kidnaping, seems to have prevailed for centuries over the Hellenes' prettified fable. At any rate, it is also to be found in the Byzantine historical chronicle of Johannes Malalas, written in the sixth century A.D. There it is stated that the people of Tyre long continued to commemorate in annual ceremonies of mourning that unfortunate evening when Agenor lost her daughter Europa and a Cretan commando raid provided our continent with its eponymous ancestor. Possibly it was Europa who introduced the Cretan freebooters to her native cult of Baal and Astarte. One thing, however, is clear about the story: it implies that close religious and familial ties existed between Phoenicia and Crete.

From the famous temple on Cythera, south of the Peloponnesus, the Ishtar cult, later assuming the form of the cult of Aphrodite, spread out on the Peloponnesus and the Greek mainland. Religious prostitution, native to Canaan, Syria and Asia Minor, spread to Cyprus and Crete. The Temple of Astarte had shrines decorated with serpentine motifs—which fits in well with the "snake priestesses" or "snake goddesses" of the Palace of Knossos. Zeus Kresios in the guise of a snake is regarded as the "protector" of storehouses, and seduces Persephone, the goddess of the underworld and spouse of Hades. Tombs would have been ideal lairs for snakes, who could prey on the mice attracted there by the goods set out for the dead. (The cats in Egyptian and oriental temples performed the same function.) The activity of rodents must have made it seem that the dead themselves were gradually consuming their stores and would soon face famine unless fresh offerings were provided. It seemed obvious that the snakes had something to do with all this. Apparently it was believed that the dead returned from the hereafter in the form of snakes in order to take food. Thus the Pelasgian creation myth refers to snakes as the reborn dead. In both Greece and Rome sacred snakes were kept to protect the temple supplies. Presumably they were fed on the offerings to the god, which consisted principally of those parts of an animal not palatable to men.

A dragonlike snake by the name of Python lurked along the roadside when young Apollo went from Delos to Parnassus. The god gravely wounded the monster with his arrow. Python slipped back into the womb of its mother, Earth, through the sacred crevasse in Delphi, which takes its name from the monster Delphyne, the Python's mate. Apollo pursued the snake and killed it at the sacred crevasse from which henceforth the mysterious vapors rose that inspired the prophetess of Delphi, the Pythia, to deliver her obscure oracular sayings.

Excavations have shown that Delphi was the site of an important cult dating from pre-Mycenaean times. The sacred meaning of the dolphin in Minoan Crete has already been commented on, and we have met the sportive sea animals on the great fresco in the Queen's Megaron at Knossos. From Crete the dolphin cult also reached Delphi. The priests known as *labryadai* ("double axe men"), who were active at Delphi into classical times, were in all probability of Cretan origin. There is a Cretan tradition that the Athenian maidens and youths were kept prisoners in the Knossos labyrinth for funeral games. Some were sacrificed at the grave, others were presented as slaves to the victors in the games. If we study the great bull-leaper fresco from the Palace of Knossos from this point of view, it becomes evident that human sacrifice is being carried out by the savage bull itself. The girl at the raging beast's horn is not swinging over the horns, but dangling helplessly from them—one of the sharp horns, which she clasps convulsively, has already passed through her chest instead of going by it on the side. The Spanish bullfighters were perfectly right when they told Arthur Evans that such a perilous leap over a bull was impossible. If an acrobat attempted to swing to the side of both horns, so that one horn passed safely under the armpit, he would acquire angular momentum that would inevitably cause him to fall askew on one horn. He would then be tossed into the air and trampled on the ground before he could pick himself up.

The figure of the girl behind the bull seems, in the reconstruction, to be offering aid. But her precise original position is not really known, since the fresco was found in fragments on the floor. It seems obvious, however, that this is no gay sporting event, but the sacrifice of three human beings. The instrument of death is a sacred bull dedicated to Ptah or Baal.

When a Delphic temple was being built it was customary to

bury twin brothers alive under the threshold at the entrance in order to fend off evil influences. This sacrifice replaced that of an original white bull. The bull cult and human sacrifice spread to Thrace, to Rome and even to the Celts. A "debased" form of this cult can be seen to this day in the arenas of the Iberian peninsula.

20

Zeus Meilichios: Of Death and Honey

❁

If we wish to understand an ancient civilization one of the matters we must inquire into is the basis of the economy. We must ask what products sustain a country's cultural institutions. We are not so much concerned with what the individual citizen lived on; but we do want to know what products yielded surpluses, for these alone would have been available for exchange.

In the Bronze Age the great majority of the population was engaged in either animal husbandry or tilling the soil, on Crete and elsewhere. In antiquity Crete was famous for its wine, its oil and its honey. Sphamia cheese is another product of Crete that enjoys a high reputation to this day. Clearly Cretan agriculture provided a good diet for the island's people. But Crete also maintained trade relations with the Near East and with Egypt. What did the Cretans have to offer on the world market that would have made distant and rather dangerous voyages worth the risk? Small images of ships have been found at various Minoan excavation sites. They have always been cited as evidence for the high development of Cretan seafaring. But an objective visitor to the Herakleion Museum comes away with the impression that these little boats were fitted out very simply and can scarcely be regarded as equipped to sail the high seas. In fact they rather resemble the little funeral barges we are familiar with from Egyptian tombs. There they served as symbolic vessels for crossing the river into the hereafter—a concept that had a literal counterpart, for the land of the dead lay on the other side of the river Nile. The conception of a frontier river that has to be crossed into the land of the dead passed into Greek thought as Acheron; the idea remained even when the dead were no longer actually carried across a river. Even in Roman times a coin was placed under a corpse's tongue for paying Charon, the ferryman who conveyed the dead across the rivers of the underworld.

But even if we may not regard these Minoan barks as models of the Cretan merchant marine, proofs do exist that the Minoans visited the Greek mainland, Phoenicia and Egypt. They must once have known more about shipping than the surviving models reveal. Prospects of some day finding an actual Minoan ship are not so bad when we consider the geologically recent subsidence of the Cretan coasts. Giving the dead entire vessels to take with them into the grave is a common custom among ancient peoples. The Scandinavians practiced it, and so did the Egyptians; seaworthy ships of the dead have been found buried in the immediate vicinity of the pyramids. Palaces near the sea, like those of Mallia, or the buildings around Amnissos and Niru Chani, might produce similar finds, especially if the search were extended to those parts of the coastal plain that have subsided since Minoan times and now stand under water.

We have reason for assuming that the Minoans crossed the seas to pursue trade. But what could they offer their customers? Wine, oil, honey, cheese? Were these profitable wares for merchants?

Wine, unfortunately, spoils easily; at least that is true of ordinary Mediterranean country wines. It spoils especially under conditions of prolonged transportation, as we find out if we take an opened bottle with us in a train or car and do not drink it up promptly. It can be resined or acidulated. Then it keeps better but has a pungent taste that may not please all customers. Resinous wine was probably what was shipped. But most amphorae would have contained water. Water is needed on board a vessel; wine would have been used only for mixing, to improve the taste of slightly rank ship's water. There is, however, one difficulty with the hypothesis that the Minoans exported

wine overseas. All the other countries bordering on the Mediterranean can grow their own wine grapes and therefore would not
have been dependent on imported wine.

The olive, too, is and was grown throughout the Mediterranean
region. Olive oil keeps better than wine, but the cost of shipping
it any great distance would have severely curtailed profits. The
same is true for cheese. Wine, oil and cheese might be sold in
small quantities, for the sake of variety; but such commodities
would not be big business in any of the Mediterranean countries
whose own crops would have been in and on the market before
the cargo vessel from Crete had a chance to dock.

I do not mean to undervalue these three indubitably precious
and desirable products, but I cannot think that the Minoans
could have used them to finance the cultural expenditures of
their country and to exchange for rather considerable imports.
On the basic principle that small weight plus high commercial
value equals big sales and big profits, there must have been
other things on Crete that her trading partners did not have, or
at least did not have in sufficient quantity. Such wares would
have justified the effort and risk involved in shipping because
they promised a high margin of profit.

The Cretans, for example, were interested in incense and myrrh
from southern Arabia, and in gold and other metals, because
these things were not to be found on their island. What could
they offer in return? Certainly "balsamic plants" and their products, such as ladanum; possibly also cedar oil and other unguents, which had a high commercial value and which the
Keftiu healers had introduced throughout the Mediterranean
world of the period.

Greek mythology puts us on the track of another such "principal product." Zeus was hidden immediately after his birth in
the cave of Dikte on Crete to save him from his murderous father
Cronos. The divine child's nourishment was *honey*. And Karl
Kerényi speaks of the "honeyed" Zeus of the dead who receives
the veneration of the living in the form of a serpent. Nectar and
ambrosia make up the traditional food of the gods on Olympus.
The opinions of scholars differ on the nature of ambrosia, but
there is no question as to what was meant by nectar.

We have noted earlier that Crete was famous for its honey. The

fact figures interestingly in the myth of Glaukos, the story of the
death and revival of the small son of Minos and Pasiphaë. We
will recall that a Cretan named Polyeidos performed this mira-
cle:

> Polyeidus wandered through the labyrinthine palace until he
> came upon an owl sitting at the entrance to a cellar, frighten-
> ing away a swarm of bees, and took this for an omen. Below in
> the cellar he found a great jar used for the storing of honey,
> and Glaucus head downwards. Minos, when this discovery was
> reported to him, consulted with the Curetes [priests of Rhea],
> and followed their advice by telling Polyeidus: "Now that you
> have found my son's body, you must restore him to life!" Polyei-
> dus protested that, not being Asclepius, he was incapable of
> raising the dead. "Ah, I know better," replied Minos. "You will
> be locked in the tomb with Glaucus' body and a sword, and
> there you will remain until my orders have been obeyed!"
>
> When Polyeidus grew accustomed to the darkness of the tomb
> he saw a serpent approaching the boy's corpse and, seizing his
> sword, killed it. Presently another serpent, gliding up, and find-
> ing that its mate was dead, retired, but came back shortly with
> a magic herb in its mouth, which it laid on the dead body.
> Slowly the serpent came to life again.
>
> Polyeidus was astonished, but had the presence of mind to
> apply the same herb to the body of Glaucus, and with the same
> happy result.[*]

Thus Robert Graves relates the mythological tradition.

Honey was undoubtedly employed for embalming in antiquity.
According to Strabo, the Assyrians laid corpses in honey to preserve them. The Spartan kings Agesipolis and Agesilaos, as well
as Alexander the Great, were embalmed with the aid of honey.
Honey was likewise used for the preservation of fruit. Plato
writes that offerings for the gods originally consisted of fruit
coated with honey—in other words, a type of candied fruit.
When we discussed Herakleion's old name of Candia, we spoke
of Crete as the island of candied fruit. Honey may have been
served to the gods pure or in its fermented state as honey wine
(mead). In either case it was divine provender. Ambrosia and

---

[*] Robert Graves, *The Greek Myths* (Penguin Books, 1955), pp. 304 f.

nectar seem to have consisted of candied fruit and honey (wine). The food for the gods was, it would seem, produced in Crete.

In Cretan "houses" the bodies of children have been found in jars; supposedly they were buried under the floors of their own houses. More likely these were burials of children in their parents' vaults. Quite often, apparently, the children's bodies were preserved in honey, just as the bones of Trojan heroes after cremation were placed in oil and honey to be taken home.

On Minoan gems Hermes may be seen summoning the dead from jar burials while their ghosts, in the form of bees, hover above the scene. From the necropolis of Mallia in northern Crete comes a gold pendant with two wasps or bees at a honeycomb.

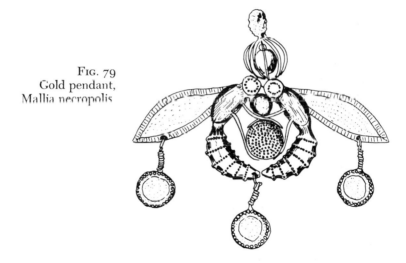

FIG. 79
Gold pendant,
Mallia necropolis

Nectar and ambrosia were needed in all the temples and sanctuaries dedicated to the rites for the dead, needed as urgently as sacramental wine is in Christian churches—but in vastly greater amounts. Thus we read in the papyrus listing Ramses III's donations for the god Ptah in Memphis:

> I gave Thee troops and beekeepers and gatherers of incense. I established inspectors to force these to come here and to bring the work of the year to Thy venerable treasury, and to fill the storerooms of Thy house with many things, and to double Thy offerings, and to present them to Thy *ka* [immortal soul].

The Egyptian Prince Sheshonk, providing for the death services of his father Namirt, likewise lists beekeepers first of all: "Beekeepers, five men, each one 6⅔ *kite* pay; makes 3⅔ *deben* of silver."

Prince Sheshonk later became the first ruler to be called pharaoh, and reigned from about 950 to 929 B.C.; he is the same pharaoh we encounter in the Bible under the name of Shishak (Kings I, 14:25–26). After the death of King Solomon he took away the treasure of the king's house (Solomon's tomb) and all the golden ritual shields it contained. By this time grave robbing had generally become an affair organized on military lines.

Egyptian reliefs show kneeling male figures with hands raised before large numbers of bees. It is difficult to say whether these represent the beekeepers so often mentioned, or pious mourners showing reverence to the souls of the dead symbolized by the bees. In any case bees were highly important in the Egyptian cult of the dead.

But could not other nations of the ancient world have kept bees and obtained honey? Undoubtedly they could have, but there is one important factor in beekeeping that should be stressed here. If the honey that the bees gathered for the winter,

FIG. 80
Bee relief,
tomb of
Pubês, Thebes.

for after the harvest or for the time of the Nile flood were removed, the bees would have starved. Nowadays they could be
given sugar to subsist on because cheap beet sugar or cane sugar
is available. But in ancient times the only source of sweet was
honey, and most of what the bees gathered was needed by themselves unless—and this is the point—unless the climate permitted
the bees to fly out in search of nectar all year round, unless some
flowers were always blooming. Crete has a particularly good
climate for beekeeping and favorable vegetation. Thus obtaining honey and manufacturing candied fruit was a profitable business as long as the custom of embalming in honey was widespread.

That probably was the traditional mode of Greek embalming,
at any rate for important personages such as the Spartan kings
or Alexander the Great. We know that the body of the latter
was preserved in honey when the conqueror died in Babylon in
323 B.C. His attendant physicians took charge of the process, thus
making it possible for the body to be brought to Alexandria where
it could be buried with all the honors due to a pharaoh and ruler
of the entire known world. Perhaps Egyptian *taricheutes* also
assisted in preparing the corpse so that it could be treated like
Late Egyptian mummies.

21

Visit in the Underworld

❁

We cannot help being struck by the repeated references to the underworld in the tales of the Greek heroes. Sometimes the reference seems oblique and arbitrary, as in the story of Perseus, who was conceived and borne by Danaë in the tomb where Zeus had visited her as a divine shower of gold. There are Theseus and Peritous, who tried to snatch away Persephone from the underworld and whom Hades punished by fixing immovably to death seats ("chairs of forgetfulness") at the entrance to his dark realm. There is Heracles, who frees Theseus and in addition slays the water serpent, the Hydra of the Lernaean Swamp, guardian of the gate to the underworld. Heracles is more deeply involved with underworld imagery than most, for he also captures Cerberus, another guardian of the lower world, and steals the bull of King Minos of Knossos from the underground labyrinth. Eurystheus, King of Mycenae is so frightened when Heracles returns with the bull that he plays dead. He hides himself in a pithos, obviously a funerary jar. And then there is Orpheus, who attempts to recover his deceased wife from the realm of the shades. Finally there is the well-known story from Homer of the descent into hell by Odysseus.

A sealing from Knossos shows a dog-headed Hecate, goddess of the underworld, threatening a man in a boat. This would seem to be someone recently deceased who has just begun the journey

to the hereafter in his death ship. The dog-headed Hecate of
ancient Crete takes the place of the dog- or jackal-headed Egyptian god Anubis, god of the dead and of embalmers. Jackal-
headed helmets and masks have been found; these were worn
by priests, wizards or actors impersonating the god in the funeral
ceremony. Similar masks for the other gods must have been worn
in mystery plays and in sacred acts. The conception of a human
being with an animal's head, such as the bull-headed Minotaur
of Greek legend or the many comparable Egyptian gods, might
have had such a genesis.

Other hybrid creatures of the Egyptian and Mesopotamian
cults of the dead found their way into Greek mythology. One
example is the Chimaera, a fabulous being with the head of a
lion, the body of a goat and the tail of a snake. Images of such
creatures have been turned up by the spade throughout the
entire eastern Mediterranean region. Possibly the dragons of
Nordic sagas derive from these monsters; in northern mythology
dragons likewise appear closely associated with the underworld
and hidden treasures hoarded there.

A considerable portion of the underworld myths, especially the
adventures of Greek heroes in the nether regions, may perhaps
be explained as veiled descriptions of penetration into tombs for
the purpose of plundering the treasures contained there. No
doubt the fabulous beasts depicted in paintings on the walls of
the tombs would have been terrifying when illuminated only by
the faint, flickering light of torches. We need only recall those
life-size paintings of griffins in the "Throne Room" of the Palace
of Knossos. A windowless corridor more than 50 meters long,

Fɪɢ. 81 Egyptian Anubis
(jackal) mask for priests.
Length 50 centimeters.
Hildesheim 158.5.

running in perplexing zigzags, with strange figures portrayed in fresco along its sides, it must have been a far cry from the present-day appearance of the place, flooded with sunlight. What was involved was not treasure alone; the grave robbers were equally intent on stealing cult images and mummies with magical properties, which, like Persephone, were "recovered" from the underworld. The priests in charge of the burial place must have welcomed the eerie paintings and the tortuous passageways. Effects of this sort made the vaults of the labyrinth safer for them. They, too, must have done their best to frighten away undesirable visitors.

Even the dead, as we have mentioned earlier, were not admitted into the underworld until they overcame some obstacles and passed through the Judgment. To this day the belief persists in some parts of Europe that the dead who have not expiated their sins will not be able to find peace in the grave.

Significantly, the underworld judges of the dead in Greek mythology are Minos and Rhadamanthus. Minos is said to have died on an expedition to Sicily and to have been buried there in the Temple of Aphrodite until Theron, the tyrant of Acragas (Agrigento), had his body translated to Crete. The story goes that Minos was pursuing the runaway builder of the labyrinth, Daedalus. To identify him Minos asked that a thread be threaded through a triton shell. Only Daedalus, he reasoned, would have the ingenuity to carry out such a feat. Daedalus tied the thread to the leg of an ant, smeared one end of the shell with honey and let the ant make its way through the shell. In fact, genuine and man-made triton shells have been found in large numbers in Minoan buildings.

Later on the labyrinth was represented as a maze for a ritual dance, laid out by Daedalus for Princess Ariadne on the Egyptian model. Thus we read in Book XVIII of *The Iliad,* at the end of the famous description of the shield:

> And the renowned smith of the strong arms [Hephaestus]
>   made elaborate on it
> a dancing floor like that which once in the wide
>   spaces of Knosos
> Daidalos built for Ariadne of the lovely tresses.
> And there were young men on it and young girls,
>   sought for their beauty

with gifts of oxen, dancing, and holding hands
      at the wrist. These
wore, the maidens long light robes, but the men wore tunics
of finespun work and shining softly, touched with
      olive oil.
And the girls wore fair garlands on their heads,
      while the young men
carried golden knives that hung from sword-belts of silver.
At whiles on their understanding feet they would
      run very lightly,
as when a potter crouching makes trial of his
      wheel, holding
it close in his hands, to see if it will run
      smooth. At another
time they would form rows, and run, rows crossing
      each other.*

This labyrinth dance apparently constituted one of the funeral
ceremonies that had already been practiced in the Egyptian labyrinth and remained the custom in Knossos, in Troy and in Italy
(as Pliny relates). Mazes, possibly constructed for a similar labyrinth dance, are known in Cornwall, Scandinavia and northern
Russia.

Thetis had made her children immortal by burning them. She
sent their mortal husks, converted into ashes, to Olympus. Peleus,
the father, was able to snatch the seventh son, Achilles, out of
the flames when every part of him had been burned—that is,
made immortal—except for his heel (the well-known Achilles'
heel). This myth apparently records the transition from inhumation to cremation around the twelfth century B.C. Oddly enough,
in spite of his supposed invulnerability Achilles needs a shield
for the battle with Hector—that magnificent shield the god
Hephaestus forges for him. Incidentally, we find the name Achilles already mentioned in Linear B tablets of the Mycenaean
period, together with Theseus, Ajax, Glaucus and such gods as
Dionysus.

Nowadays we tend to think of the underworld as a figurative
place, an abstract notion of the realm of the dead that rose in

* *The Iliad,* translated by Richmond Lattimore (University of Chicago
Phoenix Book, 1970), p. 391.

the minds of ancient peoples. In taking this view we too easily
forget that for thousands of years, in certain parts of the eastern
Mediterranean and elsewhere, caves were used as burial places,
generally in conjunction with underground shrines or temples.
Such was the case with the extensive caves in the Dikte and Ithi
mountains of Crete, where myth situates the birth and early life
of Zeus. In other words, the dead were not taken to the world
of the hereafter in imagination alone; they were in a very real
sense conducted into the underworld of funerary caves to be laid
to rest. The physicians, priests and priestesses of the underground
temples received the dead, prepared them for their eternal sleep
and carried out the prescribed religious rituals. As possessors of
traditional medical and psychological knowledge, they also
exerted considerable influence upon the world of the living. Since
they managed the oracles which were supposed to hold the secrets
of the future, they could directly affect the daily life of the times.

Quite often, no doubt, the services at the mortuary temples
were performed by old women and physically misshapen though
intellectually superior persons—giving rise to fear of witches and
of the misshapen. Old women might be considered representatives of the Fates (the Roman Parcae, the Greek Moirae), who
belonged to the underworld but secretly guided the lives of those
in the upper world. But the temple servitors of this "underworld"
did not devote themselves solely to the cult of the dead. Births

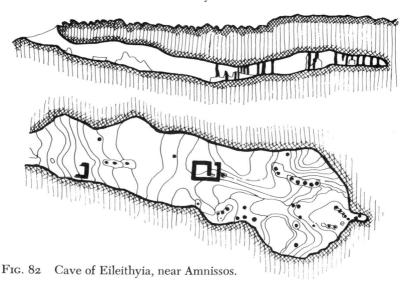

FIG. 82   Cave of Eileithyia, near Amnissos.

FIG. 83 Leaping *phersu* (masked man), Tomba degli Auguri, Tarquinia (Etruria).

are also recorded in such shrines, as they were in the above-ground temples of worship. The familial circumstances were probably similar in both cases. The children who came into the world in cave sanctuaries were quite often considered "children of the god."

The power of the Moirae, sustained by witchcraft and oracles, gained such an ascendancy that fear of the underworld became almost unbearable. Some relief was required, and it took the form of the myth of Persephone, the daughter of Demeter—one of Zeus's "children of the god." A virgin, she was abducted while picking flowers, and in the underworld at the side of Hades she was able to acquire power over the Fates.

An important part of the ancient Greek religious dramas or mystery plays dealt with the theme of Persephone overcoming the Fates. The Fates in these plays were depicted by actors on high *cothurni* wearing grotesque masks. The audience would have been properly impressed by the fearsome power of the Fates before they were driven away by Persephone. Underworld masks were also worn at the time of the winter solstice, as part of the cult ceremony for redeeming the sun from the darkness. Subsequently, in the ecclesiastical year of the Christian church, the time for donning these masks was set at a later season. The

-custom survives to this day in the masks and disguises worn at carnival time in Catholic countries.

In order to counter the power of the underworld Persephone herself had to suffer death. The same motif recurs in the death of the Saviour on the cross. Here, too, we have a sacrifice that brings about redemption from death. Belief in the might of the underworld, and the possibility of overcoming it, has remained strong and deeply rooted in the subconscious mind of the human race. Eventually the use of masks, which was associated with classical tragedy, was taken over by comedy, its antithesis. Many humorous effects depended on the drubbing meted out to masked characters. We still have an example of this type of infraculture in the Punch and Judy show. By infraculture in this context we mean those elements of vanished oligarchic cultures that are unconsciously adopted and continued by the broad masses of the people who do not themselves recognize the significance of such modes of behavior. Vestiges of this sort—which tend to be more cult than culture—live on within the common people after the tiny oligarchic upper class has died out. The persistence of such infracultural traditions proves that peoples cannot be ethnically destroyed. But where the essential culture is the exclusive property of the upper class, and the masses at best engage in cult games whose meaning they do not understand, we cannot properly speak of a true culture.

Now and then trivialities demonstrate how amazingly durable are some aspects of long-since-forgotten cults. The Punch and Judy show mentioned above provides a good example. The figure of the "traditional" devil wears the mask of the Etruscan messenger of death, Charun, who can be found complete with hooked nose, goat's beard and horns in Etruscan tombs (for instance, the Tomba dell' Orco in Tarquinia, from the third century B.C.). Charun is none other than the Greek ferryman Charon, but he has been equipped with wings and with a bird's head over his shoulder, evidently in an allusion to the ancient tradition of birds of death. The horns are an attribute borrowed from the ancient Mediterranean bull cult.

Another related element has persisted down the ages. Our theater devils are red. Not black, brown or olive green, but red, as red as Minoan men on the frescos in Knossos or as Etruscan

FIG. 84
Charun, Tomba
dell'Orco,
Tarquinia.

mourners wearing the makeup proper to the funeral ceremonies. These mourners are red even when they blow flutes or dance. That was the prescribed body color for men engaged in cult activities. (Women reddened their bodies only when they replaced men in music making or the dance.) A similar practice would explain why the Philistines of the Bible were given the name "red men," Puresatoi. In childhood we used to read stories about the American Indians, and the term *redskin* had all kinds of exciting connotations for us. Indians are actually light brown in complexion. Their ruddy hue came from the dye with which they rubbed their bodies before going to war or engaging in religious ceremonies. The copper-skinned Minoans of the frescos may actually have been olive-complexioned, as Mediterranean people are to this day, but they also rubbed their skins with coloring matter for ritual purposes. In their part of the world the dye might have come from the kermes insect which lives on the kermes oak (our word *carmine* is derived from its name).

That time-honored expletive, "The Devil take you!" would thus mean essentially: "May Charon take you across the river into the netherworld." This underworld was originally the realm of burial caves, rock tombs, labyrinths and mortuary temples— the general area under the earth where the dead rest unless they venture on a visit to the upper world in the form of snakes, birds or bees.

The dead (as a rule mummified) lived on in their graves, although in a state of separation of body and soul not easily grasped by reason. Evidently they took nourishment, for were

not the offering stones and bowls sooner or later emptied? The
concept of the underworld as an imaginary realm of the shades
arose comparatively late. It came into being along with the
changeover to cremation, which abolished the real underworld.
Once the belief had taken hold that the underworld was unreal,
Greece abruptly moved far from the original notions of the
Minoan-Mycenaean Age, and from earlier reminiscences of Egyptian and Mesopotamian religious views.

The idea of a link between veneration of the dead and a fertility cult runs counter to our modern ways of thinking. But there

FIG. 85 Rock tombs, Bay of Matalla, southern Crete. The deepest tombs, directly above the beach, at the lower left end of the picture are partly flooded by sea-water, sign of a recent subsidence on this part of the Cretan south coast. Further to the west, on the steep coastal cliffs to the south of the Levka On, water-level marks at a considerable height indicate recent elevation of these parts of the island.

is a close connection, so close that we might almost speak of the cult of the dead as a form of fertility magic. Telling proof of this may be seen at the museum of Paestum, where among the examples of grave finds we are struck by the terracotta torso of a pregnant woman and similar symbols. To the early inhabitants of Paestum there was no incongruity between birth and death— rather the opposite. Earlier Stone Age pyknomorphic female figures were probably also intended as symbols of fertility. The Greek legend of conception and birth in the tomb—as in the story of Danaë—is not, after all, lacking in logic. It is based on an ancient belief that the dead know the future. Ancestors are also responsible for providing for the continuance of the race. In this sense culture signifies the sum of everything connected with the preservation and increase of fertility. Originally fertility referred not only to man, but also to domestic animals and domesticated plants. The cult of the dead was central to this concern with being fruitful and multiplying. In the Stone and Bronze ages man was obsessed with concern for his life after death.

It may seem to us that this is no longer so, and that civilized man has altogether other concerns. Yet when we give the matter deeper thought, does not this question take on another cast? Is not our present-day cultural life, whether it be defined in terms of literature, theater, music or the visual arts, designed to form a bridge between the past and the future, to preserve, to carry on, to fructify? To be sure, we now prefer to ignore the world below and do not like to think that our proud cultural achievements had their origin in the provision for and veneration of the dead. Here again, a new view of Knossos may cause us to revise some of our basic attitudes.

22

Linear B Decipherment—
Sense or Nonsense?

The Minoan world extends from a prehistoric period without writing into an early historical period of which we possess literary remains. It was generally expected that the decipherment of Minoan scripts would cast great light on Minoan history and life, but so far, in spite of sensational initial successes and the further labors of many scholars, the decipherment has produced two grave disappointments.

1. The texts evidently are not historical or literary, but consist of various lists and seem to be records of duties or possibly taxes.

2. The tablet texts are full of terms for curious professions and strange objects whose place within a Minoan system of taxation is hard to fathom. We have already discussed this problem in connection with Palmer's coinage of the vivid phrases "ghost occupations" and "ghost forms."

In the readings so far achieved a good many of the texts are so ambiguous, not to say nonsensical, that some philologists have seriously wondered whether the decipherment of Linear B can really be regarded as successful. Among the skeptics who question the Ventris-Chadwick decipherment, Werner Ekschmitt lists W. C. Brice, M. S. F. Hood (director of the present excavations in Knossos), J. Sundwall, E. Grumach, H. Bengtson, H. Berve,

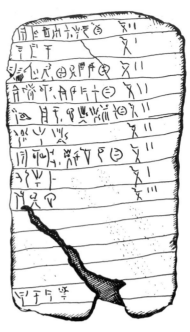

FIG. 86
Linear B Tablet
My An 102.

E. Kunze and others. Klaffenbach, who at first accepted the decipherment (1957), later changed his mind somewhat and argued:

> Although we agree on the basis of the archaeological indications that the language of Linear B is indeed early Greek, we are not at all sure that the path of decipherment Ventris and (after his untimely death) his associate Chadwick have marked out is correct. The right way remains to be found. It is also noteworthy that after the first wave of general enthusiasm, in which we ourselves were carried away, a pall of quiet has descended. The earnest efforts of the linguists of many countries to make further progress along the new path are altogether disproportionate to the results.

What can be the reason for this? The difficulties are inherent in the nature of the texts. Imagine that during a telephone conversation you have noted down a few key phrases, together with some figures, because you know by experience that such items are hard to remember. What you have is a kind of shorthand text in the form of a list, without any sentences to link the context. The next person who reads these lines will scarcely know what the telephone conversation was about. Were deliveries or orders involved or were those figures from a balance sheet or an income tax form? Was the subject under discussion donations for a charity or aid to a developing country? The two persons who talked knew what the discussion was all about. An outside third party cannot know. In Knossos, Pylos and Mycenae everybody who had to do with the tablets naturally knew perfectly well what they were all about. Today we do not know the context— we are in the position of the outside third party.

Faced with extremely terse summaries, for the most part consisting only of fragments of sentences, we can translate them intelligibly only if we know their purport. Texts and keys to decipherment alone do not unlock the actual meaning of something written. Completely different versions can be produced, depending on what picture the translators have of the writers' way of life and mode of thought.

As an example of the problem of multiple readings let us have a look at Pylos Tablet An 607. It is plain that several notations on this tablet concern women, for there is the ideogram for a woman at the end of the line, preceded by numerals. When Ventris and Chadwick translated the tablet in 1953 they rendered the women as female slaves. However, in 1956 the translation was revised and the women were represented as pickers, reapers or gleaners of grain. Finally a decision was made in favor of "barley reapers." However, by 1963 Palmer felt so dissatisfied with this reading that he declared he wanted to drop it. The women, he decided, were an association of religious women in the service of a goddess. Moreover, he noted that a word in the first line (*kerimija*) is associated with cloth manufacture and that the women may therefore have had something to do with weaving. He proposed that they be called "clothworkers." It is odd, however, that the lines in question also included the phrases *mate patede* or *pate matede*, generally rendered as "mother and father" and "father and mother." Werner Ekschmitt remarks: "It is intriguing to speculate what special interest the Pylian palace administration could have in the parentage of clothworkers. All this is as interesting as Ventris' and Chadwick's barley reapers."

But two years later disaster overtook these unfortunate women. In a paper on the "Pylos tax register" L. Deroy and M. Gérard read the term as *keeimijai doquejai* and believed it meant "prison wardresses." And there were no less than twenty-six of these ladies! Pylos, then, turns out to have been one of the first penitentiaries on the continent of Europe. Nor was it any consolation that the first word, *metapa,* was construed as a geographical name, so that the institution was located in "Metapa, District of Pylos"—which puts this ominous Bronze Age women's prison not far from the palace of King Nestor.

Thus twenty-six Bronze Age women have been assigned four different occupations within a span of twelve years. First they were slaves, then barley reapers, then clothworkers, and finally prison wardresses. Surely there is something wrong with the interpretation of Linear B.

In order to arrive at a "sensible translation" we can approach the material in various ways.

1. The texts can be fiddled with; this or that reading can be tried, and a more or less plausible interpretation put together, depending on the current picture of historical conditions.

2. We can completely abandon the previous method of decipherment and seek another method. So far, however, there seem to be no other possible approaches to Linear B.

3. We can venture the assumption that Knossos, Pylos and Mycenae were not entirely extraordinary, that at the period there were similar places in other parts of the eastern Mediterranean which produced comparable texts that we may be better able to penetrate. Granted, we will then be depending on analogy. But the previous translations have been depending all along on linguistic or experiential analogies. Of course we are not going to find precisely the same texts elsewhere to serve as, so to speak, finished translations. But possibly we will discover that such abbreviated texts were used elsewhere; for it seems likely that other ancient cultures in other places set down similar "shorthand" notes.

Perhaps the new interpretation of the Minoan palaces offered in this book will provide a hint that might help clarify certain obscurities in the Linear B texts.

Let us proceed on the assumption that Knossos was in communication with Phoenicia and Egypt as well as with Pylos and Mycenae, since this is sustained by historical tradition and archaeological finds. In these other regions there must have been similar lists, institutions and shorthand texts. After what we have said in earlier chapters it seems quite reasonable to look to Egyptian records, for there we have texts whose interpretation is no longer in doubt. Thus, for example, on a granite block of the tenth century B.C. excavated at Abydos in 1860 by Auguste Mariette we read:

> Aside from this is what will replace the 50 *setat* which are situated in the vicinity of the plateau south of Abydos, which is called Wah-nisur: 12 silver: 6 *deben*, and what is to the west in the irrigated area of the canal in Abydos: fields, 50 *setat*, makes silver 4 *deben*. Sum: fields of the citizens of both places in the vicinity of the plateau south of Abydos together with the vicinity of the plateau north of Abydos: fields, 100 *setat*, makes silver: 10 *deben*.
>
> Farmer Pa-wer, son of . . . , his servant Arbok, his servant Bup-Amon-haa, his servant Na-senu-meh, and his servant Denit-en-Hor: sum 5 men, makes silver: 4 *deben*, 1 *kite*. Cattle, 10 head, makes 2 *deben*.
>
> Garden which is in the vicinity of the plateau north of Abydos, makes silver: 2 *deben*.
>
> Gardener Hor-mose, true in voice, son of Pen-mouth, makes silver: 6⅔ *kite*.
>
> The fowler Ni-mer-ju, true in voice, son of Meh-Hor-n-pa-aref, true in voice, whose mother is Ta-kenet, true in voice, makes silver: 6⅔ *kite*.
>
> Beekeepers, 5 men, each one 6⅔ *kite* payment per man, makes silver 3⅔ *deben* [a mistake; should be 3⅓].
>
> Transmitted to the silver house of the Osiris.
>
> Half of a *hin* [liter] of honey is to go to the silver house of the Osiris as a daily delivery to the divine offering to the Osiris, the mighty great one Mashwesh, Namirt, true in voice unto eternity and infinity. As for the work of these 5 beekeepers, their silver was transmitted to the silver house of the Osiris. Let them not die and let them not cease!
>
> Carriers of incense, 5 men, each 6⅔ *kite*, makes silver: 3⅔ *deben* transmitted to the silver house of the Osiris [incorrect; should be 3⅓ *deben*].
>
> 5 *kite* of incense are to go to the treasury of the Osiris as a daily delivery to the divine offering of the Osiris, the mighty great one Mashwesh, Namirt, true in voice until eternity and

infinity. As for the work of the 5 carriers of incense, their silver is to be transmitted to the silver house of the Osiris. Let them not die and let them not cease!

Gatherer of myrrh, a single man, makes silver 6⅔ *kite*, transmitted to the silver house of the Osiris.

The half of a *hin* of oil for burning is to go to the silver house of the Osiris as a daily delivery for the lamp of the Osiris, the mighty great Mashwesh, Namirt, true in voice, whose mother Mehit-em-wesechet, true in voice, is unto eternity.

As for the work of the myrrh collector, his silver is to be sent to the silver house of the Osiris. Let him not die and let him not cease! A single man shall be given.

Brewers, 2 men, each one 6⅔ *kite*.

Kneaders of cake, ¼ man, makes silver 1 *kite* [incorrect; should be 1⅔ *kite*], sent to the treasury of the Osiris.

This barley and wheat shall go as a daily delivery of bread and beer from the stores of the Osiris' granary, together with the brewery of the Osiris, the mighty great one of Mashwesh . . . etc.

As for the labors of this brewer and of the kneader of cake, their silver shall be transmitted to the silver house of the Osiris . . . together with the grain of this field up to the 100 *setat* that go to the granary of the Osiris as the due of one year. Let them not die and let them not cease!

Sum of the silver, these men, that is transmitted to the silver house of the Osiris. Silver: 8 *deben*, 7⅔ and ⅔ *kite* [correct sum] makes 12¼ men [incorrect: should be 13¼ men].

Here we have Palmer's "ghost occupations": fowlers, beekeepers, incense carriers and gatherers, gatherers of myrrh, brewers, kneaders, grain reapers together with their fathers and mothers true in voice (the Egyptian way of saying "the honorable so and so").

Were it not for the constant references to "the Osiris," the whole thing might be taken for a bill of lading or a tax list. Since there are also mentions of property changes and of farmers and gardeners, we might think we were dealing with the land register of Abydos. From what we have already said about Egyptian customs, however, it is evident that "the Osiris" refers not to the god but to one of his particular personifications, namely Namirt. The list in fact deals with the measures undertaken by Pharaoh

Sheshonk I (*ca.* 950–929 B.C.) to provide for the funerary services for his father Namirt. Sheshonk's provisions were far more elaborate than those of his Minoan fellow rulers, but then we have come a few hundred years closer to the present and Sheshonk had much more capital at his disposal to realize his wishes impressively "in stone." In Knossos, Pylos and Mycenae things had to be done a good deal more cheaply; clay tablets instead of granite were considered good enough. But the idea of listing a bequest for the cult of the dead was precisely the same.

From a funerary papyrus of Ramses III (1181–1150 B.C.) we learn of his generous donations of honey, incense, barley and wheat for the cult of his father Ptah. He gave heaps of grain "that reached the sky." The exaggerations are no more to be taken seriously than the arithmetic errors in Sheshonk's lists; good intentions were more important than good bookkeeping. Ramses III's lists are evidence of his good deeds and meant as a letter of recommendation to the "western ones" in the realm of the dead across the Nile.

As late as the days of Ptolemy II Philadelphos (285–246 B.C.) such lists read much the same:

List to let the king know, as summary for his father.
They say concerning this:

Fruit (flour?) doubly good	148 *hin*
Fruit in pots	13 pots
A third of duties	
Cattle	400
A flock (?) of fowl	
Wine, doubly good, from Charu, Syria	1 *hin*
Fruit juice (?), good	1 *hin*
Cider	
Honey	8 *hin*
?	13 *hin*
Milk	148 *hin*
Fruit juice (?), liquid, strong	6 *hin*

The inventory goes on, mentioning figs, cream, cooked cheese (?), melted lard, oil, fresh incense, tree oil (cedar oil?), lotus, crushed fruits, fruit and dates "whose like has not been picked," combs of honey, dried fruit, ivory, a thousand bundles of reeds, clothes, a thousand royal bandages, "wrappings and bandages and stuff. . . ."

In the Linear B clay tablets we seem to have a list of the same goods, together with their makers and the various foodstuffs generally provided for the dead. Evidently it was a fairly luxurious life-style on "the other side" (of the Nile or wherever).

Here is a scattering of items selected from various Minoan-Mycenaean clay tablets (we must remember that the readings are still tentative):

Pylos, maidservants of the priests on account of sacred gold: 14 women (PY Ae 303).

Thinwasijai: women 9, girls 3, boys 3, overseer 1, female overseer 1 (PY An 689).

Pylos: Thinwasijai: women 9, girls 4, boys 1: wheat 3/0/0, figs 3/0/0 (PY Ab 190).

Of the *telestai*, from so much seed: wheat 1800 liters.

Domain of the war-leader: wheat 600 liters.

Of the *telestai*, from so much seed, wheat 1800 liters.

So many *telestai*: men 3.

Camp district, empty

of so large a seed: wheat 360 liters (PY Er 312).

Slave the father, but the mother *kutereupi*.

Slave the father, but the mother divine slave.

Slave the mother, but the father smith (PY An 607).

Knossos: to all the gods honey amphora 1 to the Mistress of the Labyrinth honey amphora 1 (KN Gg 702).

Stana to the Mistress . . . 1

enuwarijo 1 *pajawo poseda* (one) 1 (KN V 52).

To the Mistress Sito (Demeter) (?) 190 (x) [ideogram unknown]

poropoi (?) 190 10

diwonusojo [the god Dionysus?]

Mare 5 stallion 4 foal x

Mare 3 foal 2 stallion 4 (KN CA 895).

Wool 2, goat 4 (?) 3 wine 10 figs 4 (KN An 35).

Awaso/quamo ram 90   ewe 10 (KN Db 1099)

So many swords sword 50 (KN Ra 1540).

dose wheat 4 wine 3   bull 1

ram 2 Tu+Ro₂ 5 A+Re+Ro 0/0/2 hide+Ko 1

ram 2 flour 0/6 wine 0/2 . . . (KN Un 718).

sinito/rukito (? Sinitos from Lyktos) ram 39 ewe 11
ram 10   ram 40 (KN Dg 1280).

The Linear B notations are far less elaborate than the circumstantial texts of a world power like Egypt. The style of the Mycenaean and Cretan tablets is, in fact, distinctly telegraphic. However, the extreme brevity becomes quite comprehensible if we grasp the purpose of these notations. The tablets were kept in the vicinity of the deceased's tomb in order to prove in the hereafter that he had been a godfearing man and a good son of those who had preceded him into the other world, since during his life he had donated to them so many hecatombs of animals (ram 39 + ewe 11 + ram 10 + ram 40 = 100—a hecatomb), as well as honey, fruit, grain and servants. Undoubtedly some of this was boasting and some of the arithmetic is awry, as Werner Ekschmitt has shown, just as it sometimes was in Egypt. The gods would forgive that, all the more so since they read only the final sum with the ideograph especially intended for them. When addressing the gods, the Cretans wrote in the old-fashioned way, using the venerable hieratic ideograms (analogous to the use of Latin in the Christian Church).

We encounter this dual method of writing to an even greater extent in Egypt. There whole "books of the dead" were prepared in triplicate, so to speak: a top strip of pictures; below that a text in the old hieratic script for the gods; and along the bottom the same text in demotic script for the human beings on "the other side." In the light of this, the readings of "foal FOAL" and "cheese CHEESE" of the Minoan tablets, which Ekschmitt pokes fun at, are not at all ridiculous.

We have already spoken of the lists of grave goods and the donations of property. The data are somewhat uncertain because difficult to translate, but the meaning is surely recognizable:

Jug for the queen's priest, bull's head form, ornamented with seashells.
Jug ornamented with chariot driver and battle scene.
Jug ornamented with goddess, women with bull's head, spirals (PA Ta 711).

At the end of each of the lines there is always the ideogram for JAR (by convention, the ideograms in these texts are always given in capital letters in the translations).

Tripods, goat handles, Cretan workmanship.
Tripod, with one foot, with ear handles.
Tripod, Cretan work, legs burned off.

Jar 3   jar, large, four-handled,
jar, small, four-handled,
jar, small, three-handled
jar, small, without handles (PY Ta 641)

After the tripods comes the ideogram TRIPOD, after the jars the appropriate ideogram with the number of handles plainly shown and the numbers of the item indicated on the extreme right edge of the tablet.

More complicated texts, the details of which are by no means certain, run about as follows:

The district governors and *dumate* and the vice-governors and the keepers of the keys and the overseers of figs and the ships' captains shall deliver temple bronze, arrow and spear-heads . . . (PY Jn 829).

As follows Arxotas (Alxoitas?) gave Thyestas, the unguent boiler, ingredients for unguent to be boiled:

coriander seed	360 liters	liquid 288 liters
cypress seed	360 liters	dry ingredient (?) 960 liters
fruit (?)	150 liters	wine 360 liters honey 36 l.
(?)	36 liters	cider (?) 36 liters
		(PY Un 267).

The total amount of unguent, 1680 liters, was a quantity that struck Werner Ekschmitt as quite excessive. Yet considering the size of the "bathtubs" and funerary pithoi, such an amount would scarcely have sufficed for more than twenty to thirty corpses. Perhaps the figures were inflated, perhaps understated.

This approach by no means solves all the problems of the Linear B texts. But with this new view, the work may be given fresh impetus. Once we know what purpose the lists served, translation should prove to be a good deal easier, and a good many erroneous notions can be corrected.

The tablets, then, were shorthand notes given to the dead to take with them into the hereafter. In some cases they were messages to the dead of the mortuary palace. Possibly the Phaistos Disc was one of these telegrams to the "living dead."

23

From the Parian Marble
to Radiocarbon Dating

✦

Along with discovering, rescuing and preserving the finds, the aim of every archaeological project is to establish a chronological succession and, if possible, an absolute dating. The further back into early history or into scriptless prehistory the archaeologist goes, the more difficult this task becomes. How can we really tell how old an object is, and what datings do we have for the Minoan world?

It was early recognized that at many excavation sites several strata of finds of different ages lay one on top of the other. Along the coastline of northern Germany mounds have been built in the mud flats to protect houses from high water. Since the coastline has been slowly sinking for centuries, every generation or two it has been necessary to pull down houses and barns, build up the mound by a meter or so and erect new buildings. In the rubble that is heaped up all sorts of artifacts of the inhabitants of the time may be found—broken pottery, utensils, kitchen refuse, remains of wood and so on. Through the centuries "cultural strata" have heaped up one on the other like the leaves of a book. The archaeologist speaks of a stratigraphic succession, the obvious principle of which is that the oldest layers are toward the bottom of the heap, the most recent toward the top.

By comparison of finds—say, the incidence of similar pottery in other mounds nearby—it is possible to determine how a stratum in mound A relates to a stratum in mound B. The strata above and below can then likewise be compared, at least approximately. This method of determining ages, which of course yields no specific dates, is termed the method of relative chronology. The development of pottery in particular has proved to be an excellent standard of comparison.

A simple measurement of the depth of strata is of little use, since from case to case the amount of rubble heaped up may differ enormously. Sometimes, too, severe storm tides follow in quick succession, forcing the inhabitants to raise the level of their houses repeatedly. At other times there will be no threat for a considerable period and the mounds will build up very slowly.

In the Valle di Comacchio Etruscan remains have been found at a depth of up to 12 meters below the present surface of the ground, from which an average rate of increment of half a meter per century has been calculated. At other places the rate is considerably less, sometimes only a few centimeters per century.

In addition, the archaeologist cannot always count on the normal stratigraphic succession of finds. Cellars and tombs may have been dug into the heaped-up rubble later on, so that more recent parts of a building will be found on a level consisting chiefly of older layers. Similar confusions may be created by the digging of walls, cisterns and offering shafts, as well as by foundations of all sorts. In laying the foundations for the heavy baldachino at the crossing of the nave and transepts in St. Peter's, Rome, Bernini found it necessary to dig into the catacombs under the church. The sarcophagi stood so thickly there that they could not be moved aside. According to the Urbaldi report of 1626 on these old "excavations," the sarcophagi that were in the way had to be opened. Bodies were found embalmed and swathed "like children," some in long garments. After the bodies and wrappings had been exposed to the air for some time, they disintegrated into dust, except for a few scraps of cloth. The ancient custom of the Egyptians and the Mycenaeans of covering the corpse's face with a mask was used in the embalming of eminent personages down to the seventeenth century. Queen Christina of Sweden, who was buried in St. Peter's in 1689, was given a mask of silver (rather than of the gold worn by the pharaohs and the heroes in the Mycenaean shaft graves).

If the stratigraphic succession has been relatively undisturbed and if there is sufficient pottery for comparison of finds, relative chronologies can yield good results. But dates will still be needed. For early history there are clues in oral and written tradition, but such clues must be weighed with the greatest care.

Starting in 1615, Thomas Howard, second Earl of Arundel and Surrey, began establishing a collection of ancient Greek finds. An agent of his obtained the items in Greece and the Levant. Among the numerous gems, statues, busts, sarcophagi and inscribed tablets was a marble fragment from the island of Paros with an inscription listing events in Greek history from the year 1581 or 1580 to 264 B.C. This Parian Marble, as it is called, has provided many clues to chronology. Among other things, it gives the genealogy of the families that are well known to us from Greek mythology. The *Marmor Parium* mentions two rulers of Crete named Minos: a Minos I who reigned or lived from 1462 to 1423 B.C., and Minos II who ruled around 1294 B.C.

The latter's grandson Idomeneus, as commander of the Cretan contingent, took part in the expedition against Troy. And here might be the place to consider what *The Odyssey* is really about. For when we look at the time-honored tale anew we become aware of many elements that throw a different light on the story of "wily Odysseus." We will remember how Odysseus ended the long siege of Troy by a nefarious trick. First he had a huge wooden cult image made in the shape of a horse and dedicated it to the Trojan supreme deity. Then the Achaeans pretended to withdraw. But Odysseus was hidden in the interior of the horse. When the horse was drawn into the Trojans' hill sanctuary, Odysseus succeeded in entering the fortified temple and opening its gates to his own forces. While the Trojans and the Achaeans were locked in combat, Odysseus made off with the temple treasures. He quarreled over the loot with Idomeneus' son and killed him out of hand. The robbed Trojans and the cheated Achaeans alike cursed Odysseus. For ten years he did not dare show his face at home. Most of this time he spent amusing himself abroad with a young beauty who so enchanted him that for a long time he did not think of returning to Ithaca. But after he had used up the treasure and Circe was some years older, he began to suffer from homesickness. After further adventures, in the course of which he had to be careful never to mention his name, he reached Ithaca by way of the mysterious land of the Phaeacians. Once home, he escaped the long arm of the law only by murdering en masse all the notables of his kingdom. All in all, the man about whom the oldest work of literature revolves was a highly dubious character!

But let us continue with the chronicle given by the Parian Marble. It assigns to the Trojan War the dates 1218–1209 B.C. Idomeneus was evidently already a mature man with a grown son. Perhaps he was around fifty, which would surely not be too old for a reigning prince and commander of the Cretan forces. Thus he would have been born around 1260 B.C., thirty years after the date of his grandfather Minos II's reign. Minos I therefore must have been an early ancestor of the family. The names of the rulers who came between these two have not been handed down. Presumably they would also have been named Minos, so that we may consider Minos II as Minos the Last.

We owe a somewhat divergent chronology to Eratosthenes of Cyrene (born *ca.* 295–280 B.C., died toward the end of the third century). He was a mathematician, astronomer, geographer and librarian of the University of Alexandria in Egypt. His dating of the Trojan War is 1194–1184 B.C., twenty-four years, or a whole generation, after the dates given by the Parian Marble. In historical times such a deviation would be an inexcusable lack of precision, but considering the general vagueness of our chronologies for early history, the data given by these two sources are in striking agreement. A twenty-four-year discrepancy is nothing within a period of nearly a thousand years, during which the transmission of historical facts was almost entirely oral. In fact, we might say that the agreement is quite astonishing.

However much the material was subjected to literary reworking and "alienation" effects, there can be no doubt about the historical fact that Greeks once upon a time sailed against Troy. The expedition took place in an age in which religion alone no longer protected mortuary temples from being robbed. As early as 1300 B.C. grave robbers had penetrated into the rock-cut chambers of Tutankhamen in the Valley of the Kings, without, however, succeeding in disturbing the eternal rest of "the august mummy of this god." A century earlier the tomb of Thutmosis IV had been visited by grave robbers and heavily pillaged. By around 1200 B.C. grave robbery, even in rigidly governed Egypt, assumed such proportions that there are—as we have already seen —records of the trials of such robbers.

We may assume without question that the ancient Cretan mortuary palaces likewise succumbed to the assaults of these grave robbers, who shrank from no sacrilege. It is ironic that the selfsame beliefs that prompted the ancients to heap up treasures for the dead to use in the hereafter led the tomb robbers into crime and sacrilege. The poor had no claim to an eternal life in the bliss of the world to come; they were doomed to vanish without a trace in the gloomy realm of the shades. Consequently they had nothing to lose, but everything to gain—prosperity in this world and eternal life in the next. Commander Sheshonk, not being rich, rifled the treasures of King Solomon's tomb in order to be able to pay for the expensive funeral donations for his father Namirt.

In Egypt it did not occur to anyone to protect tombs from robbery by fortifications. Instead the principle of concealment was adopted—sham graves, sham doors, traps, rock tombs whose *dromos* (entrance) was filled with earth—but it was no use. Most of the time the grave robbers found what they were looking for, which is hardly surprising, since they were the workmen who had helped in building the tombs or were related to such workmen by blood or marriage. Since the robbery usually benefited their own fathers, the floodgates to total corruption were wide open. Workmen in the necropolises could not face the reproach: "Do you mean to let our poor father be deprived of eternal life? Is he alone among those who have 'gone west' to have nothing?" The workmen would betray the secrets of their calling, close relations would carry out the necessary actions, and the profits of tomb robbery returned to the embalmers and the priests. Making mummies and caring for the dead was a profession that paid off.

In Troy, Mycenae and Tiryns, and in many other hill sanctuaries on the mainland, another course was taken. At first only a few bold individuals ventured into the treasure chambers of the underworld, and for their daring they were hailed as heroes. But when tomb and temple robbery became too widespread, the recourse of fortifying the sites was taken. The walls originally thrown up around necropolises to keep in the ghosts naturally served also to keep out external enemies. A few additional out-posts turned a hill sanctuary into a hill citadel. Now individual grave robbers no longer had a chance. The would-be robber had to overpower such an *acrotyrsis* (hill sanctuary) by military action if he wished to get at the treasure within. The story of the Trojan War shows how difficult this was to do against a powerful garrison. Even after a siege of years the Achaeans did not succeed in capturing Troy's sacred seat of the gods. There was food for the dead aplenty in there, and even water. The stores intended to feed the dead Trojans in the hereafter pro-vided well for their defenders. Thus the Greeks made no real progress until Odysseus hit on his trick of constructing a cult image.

Since Troy had adequate fortifications by 1200 B.C., the age of individual grave robbers was evidently over by this time. That earlier age had produced Theseus and Heracles, the solitary heroes. Once Theseus had escaped alive from the labyrinth (through Ariadne's treachery), the news spread that someone had emerged alive from the underworld and the tomb robbers could no longer be frightened off. Knossos and other sanctuaries of the same type were thoroughly ransacked before they could be turned into walled fortresses. This pillaging undoubtedly took place before the Trojan War. The details are not known; we can only make deductions from the myths. According to tradition, Theseus was a generation older than those who fought at Troy, but the pillaging may have taken place still earlier. Leonard Palmer, the British scholar, believes that Knossos was still fully able to function as late as 1200 B.C. The identity in character of the Linear B tablets from Knossos, Pylos and Mycenae bears out his theory of a close temporal and functional connection among these "palaces."

The archaeologist John Boardman has taken strong exception to this view. M. S. F. Hood, the present director of the excava-tions in Knossos, dates the destruction of the site around 1350 B.C., even before the last Minos of the Parian Marble and almost five generations before the Trojan War according to the dating

of Eratosthenes. What is this opinion based on? Chiefly on comparison of finds in Egypt and the Euphrates Valley.

In the third century B.C. an Egyptian priest named Manetho
wrote a history of Egypt in Greek from the beginning of the Old
Kingdom (*ca.* 2900 B.C.) to historical times, dividing the pharaohs into thirty-one dynasties. He was able to base his account
—an opportunity unique in history—on the lists of kings chiseled
into the stone of the Egyptian mortuary temples. Because the
Nile flood began annually between the 17th and the 19th of
July, the Egyptian year had been precisely defined from very
ancient times. Simultaneously with the onset of the flood the
fixed star Sirius (the Dog Star) appears in the morning sky. This
"heliacal rising" was first observed on July 19 of the year 2769
B.C. This date was selected as the beginning of the Egyptian
calendar; the basis of the calendar is a cycle of Sirius that takes
1460 years. Sirius was dedicated to the goddess Isis, the spouse
of Osiris and mother of Horus, who in the form of pharaoh seized
power and would die as Osiris in order to be born again. As
goddess of the star Sirius, Isis was also called Sothis, for which
reason the period from heliacal rising to heliacal rising was also
known as a Sothis period.

With the year precisely divided by the Nile flood, whose
height (measured by the Nilometer at Assuan) decided whether
a year would be fat or lean, and with the larger division of the
Sothis period, the Egyptian calendar was the first relatively precise calendar in the world. There were some difficulties because
of a few interregna in which the succession to the throne was
somewhat irregular, and there were cases in which the reigns of
rival kings coincided. But if there is any history with more or less
assured dates in ancient times, it is the history of Egypt. Practically the entire early history of the eastern Mediterranean region is based on it or keyed into it. If we compare Egyptian finds
in Crete and Cretan finds in Egypt with dates of reigns in the
Egyptian calendar (there are cartouches on the objects or names
mentioned in tomb inscriptions), we arrive at the following chronology:

The similarities between the labyrinth of Knossos and that of
Hawar suggest that Knossos was built in a similar form around

1850–1800 B.C., or already existed at that time. Pharaoh Chian, whose name is found on a diorite statuette and on the lid of a box dug up in Crete, belongs to the Second Intermediate Period (1700–1555 B.C.).

Pictures of Keftiu processions are found in the tombs of the Eighteenth Dynasty (1580–1350 B.C.). Thutmosis III, whose name is recorded on an alabaster vase from a tomb in the port of Knossos, reigned between 1500 and 1450 B.C. But the decisive factor for the archaeological interpretation is the presence of Minoan Postpalatial vases in Tell Amarna, that is, in a site associated with Ikhnaton, whose reign began in 1364 B.C. Thus the end of the Minoan palaces (Postpalatial period) must be dated *before* 1364 B.C.

This definitely does not mean that Minoan culture as such was annihilated. There are many "Postpalatial" sites that show more and more agreement with Mycenaean styles. Nicolas Platon explains that the intruding Achaeans abandoned all the palaces after their destruction by the eruption of the Santorin volcano around 1450 B.C.—all except Knossos, that is, which survived under Achaean rule until 1380 B.C. This theory is necessary to account for the Greek language of the Linear B tablets and their general similarity to Mycenaean tablets. Egyptian finds in the palaces of Phaistos, Mallia, Kato Zakro and Akrotheri (on Santorin) continue only until the end of the reign of Thutmosis III in 1436 B.C. Consequently, the period around 1450 B.C. is considered by many Minoan archaeologists to be the date of the catastrophic eruption of Santorin. Pieces of lava and pumice found at Kato Zakro have strengthened Platon in his view that this palace in eastern Crete was destroyed by the same volcanic eruption that buried the Minoan site of Akrotheri under ashes. Supposedly the other palaces were destroyed by the earthquake that accompanied the eruption, and Knossos alone was rebuilt.

We can at any rate state with confidence that neither the earthquake nor the eruption of Santorin around 1450 B.C. totally annihilated Knossos, and certainly the natural disaster did not destroy Minoan civilization. Evidently there was a more or less smooth transition into the Postpalatial and Mycenaean ages, in the course of which the palaces were gradually abandoned— Knossos last of all, it would seem.

At this point we must mention another method of determining age that has been applied with increasing frequency in the past few decades. This is radiocarbon dating, developed by the Nobel Prize–winning American physicist W. F. Libby and his associates E. C. Anderson and J. R. Arnold.

In 1911 the Austrian physicist V. F. Hess discovered a type of radiation entering the earth's atmosphere from outer space that had unusually intense penetration, far more intense than the gamma radiation produced by radioactive decay. Instrument-laden unmanned balloons and rockets have found that this "cosmic radiation" increases up to an altitude of about 20,000 meters and then diminishes to a constant value. Cosmic-ray bombardment of the nitrogen in the air produces a radioactive isotope of carbon known as carbon-14. Because of the respiration of animals and plants and the effects of the food chain, a minute quantity of this carbon-14 replaces some of the stable, nonradioactive carbon-12 in all living organisms. But when an organism dies, the constant intake of carbon-14 from the atmosphere ceases. Nothing is added to the amount of radiocarbon in the body; instead, that amount slowly diminishes as a consequence of radioactive decay, and diminishes at a fixed rate independent of external influences. After the passage of 5568 ± 30 years only half of the original radiocarbon content is left. This period is what physicists call the "half-life" of the element. After another half-life of 5568 years only a fourth is left, then an eighth and so on.

If the exact initial value is known, and if the remaining proportion of radiocarbon to normal carbon can be determined, it is possible to calculate the time that has passed since the death of the organism.

Thus the investigator can select fragments of building lumber, bits of charcoal from fires, bones and similar organic materials, and have the carbon-14 remaining in them determined. The fragment of organic matter serves as a radiometric clock which was started at the very moment that life ceased in the organism. But unfortunately this clock, like all others, has certain inherent flaws. There is the possibility that the material may have been contaminated. The results are not precise. Wood from a ship of the dead found in the tomb of Sesostris III, whose age according to the Manetho Chronicle would be 3750 years, has been dated

by the C-14 method (the mean of three measurements) at an
age of 3621 ± 180 years.

When the method is applied to Minoan sites the destruction of
the Palace of Knossos is put closer to 1200 B.C. (which tends to
support Leonard Palmer's datings) than to the 1450 B.C. date
accepted by most Minoan archaeologists. The difficulty is that
the margin of error is so great; the radiocarbon method is not
much more accurate than historical dating with the aid of the
Parian Marble or by comparisons with Egypt. The method, however, is of great value where written sources or datable finds are
not to be had.

To sum up, we may say that the Cretan palaces were deserted
during the Egyptian Eighteenth or Nineteenth Dynasty. They
were not deserted all at once, however, nor did their abandonment mean that Minoan civilization as a whole collapsed. The
Minoans did not all die out, taking a uniquely high culture and
the knowledge of great civilized achievements with them. Rather,
they gradually merged into later cultures. Thus Minoan culture
became Mycenaean; that in turn developed into Post-Mycenaean
and Protogeometric, that into Geometric and ultimately Hellenic.

Certainly the island suffered from earthquakes now and again.
It must also have felt the distant effects of volcanic eruptions on
Santorin and elsewhere. But the great geological catastrophe at
the end of the Minoan Age that supposedly dealt the death-blow
to an entire culture never really happened.

24

A Peaceful End

From time immemorial man has been terror-stricken by the forces of nature. Hence upheavals in the natural world have repeatedly been held responsible for the extinction of species, nations and civilizations. Yet we know of no nation in history that has been wiped out by an elemental catastrophe. On the contrary, man himself has been the source of far more terror and devastation than nature. "Much there is in the world that is terrible," the famous chorus in Sophocles' *Antigone* begins, "but nothing so terrible as man." Let us not accuse nature of what man in his fanaticism, his ideological rigidity, his pollution of the environment, has done. "Catania at the foot of Europe's highest active volcano has more often been destroyed by wars than by volcanic eruptions or earthquakes." These words by A. Rittmann, the great volcanologist who has been studying Vesuvius and Etna for half a century, should give us pause.

It was no mighty natural disaster that brought about the cessation of life in the Minoan palaces. The Minoans lodged in them were already dead when the buildings were erected, and no less dead when the walls fell to ruin. All that could be snatched from them was their life in the underworld. And that undoubtedly was taken away not by earthquakes or eruption, but by men in their greed for treasures consigned to the dead.

There was no security from tomb robbers. The embalmed

body in its feudalistic eternal dwelling, provided with adequate provisions for the hereafter, could no longer be assured eternal rest. Ritual shields, curses, dark, twisting corridors with frightening fresco figures that seemed to move in the dimness, were no longer any use. It seemed better to follow the ancient custom of warriors and burn the dead with all their possessions, smashing unburnable grave goods so that no tomb robber would find anything useful.

The adoption of that course meant the end of the Minoan culture of labyrinthine buildings, for that culture had been essentially an elaborate cult of the dead. Today we must express our agreement with the intuition of Oswald Spengler, which we referred to at the beginning of this book, though his idea that the buildings were mortuary temples must be modified. Temples in the strict sense are not found in the Minoan buildings (aside from later Hellenic additions). The Minoans built genuine tombs for the preservation and care of the dead. These tombs were allowed to decay when the old cult of the dead was superseded by the new "heroic" method of cremation with its built-in insurance against grave robbing.

Historians and archaeologists naturally must regret the change, for it meant the destruction of valuable evidence of cultural development from the era between Mycenaean and Hellenic times. Aside from the Geometric funerary urns, the tombs are as empty as they would have been after pillaging. Everything the dead formerly received in usable form was now given to them burned. The urns, moreover, no longer needed to be placed in eternal dwellings or mortuary palaces; they could be simply interred in graveyards.

In answer, then, to the crime of grave robbing the practice of cremation spread over large parts of Eurasia. Only poor people without grave goods to attract robbers, and without money for expensive funeral pyres, continued to be inhumed without cremation.

Thus the Geometric period appears to be a time of culturelessness, a Dark Age between Minoan-Mycenaean civilization, with its mortuary palaces, and the rise of the Hellenic culture of temple-building.

Along with the abandonment of the old cult of the dead, the writing used in the mortuary palaces was forgotten. The earlier hieroglyphs and the later Linear A and B scripts were, after all, not intended for everyday use. They were the secret signs of an initiated priesthood and of a few somewhat less well educated members of the undertaking establishments. Trade and ordinary life went on, largely without the need for writing; it sufficed for buyers and sellers to strike a bargain in the traditional way, by shaking hands. And the ruler's bailiffs collected taxes "in kind," by force if necessary. The tax collectors did not need to know how to read and write. Only when the complexities of long-distance commerce were developed by the Phoenicians did it become essential to have a secular script for everyday life. One was then created to take the place of a script used only for shorthand messages to the dead in the hereafter. The old script fell totally into disuse. From Phoenician writing evolved the script used by the Greeks, Romans and Etruscans. Our present alphabet is, of course, its lineal descendant.

As we learn from the Linear B texts, the priests who moved through the labyrinth did not speak of kings named Minos, but of a Mistress of the Labyrinth. She was none other than Sito, the Great Mother Demeter, whose cult continued on into Hellenic times, although the labyrinth had long since been abandoned. We will recall that the daughter of Zeus and Demeter was Persephone, whom Hades dragged off into the underworld and made his wife, but who by order of Zeus was annually permitted to return to the upper world during the summer. Even Zeus could not win her back completely into this world because she had already shared a pomegranate with Hades. The Persephone cult as a symbol of resurrection developed into the Eleusinian Mysteries of classical Greece. In these Mysteries Persephone would be called Kora ("Maiden") or Despoina ("Mistress"), the same title that had been given to her mother as Mistress or Lady of the Labyrinth of Knossos.

Cretan communities of priests, the "double axe men," carried on their cult traditions in Delphi well into the Classical Age. Thus we have a certain continuity in cult, although not in funerary practices.

FIG. 87 How a Cretan in ancient Egypt earned his bread. The above is an advertisement found in the Serapeum at Sakkara. It reads: "I interpret dreams, for I am entrusted to do so by the god, with good fortune. It is a Cretan who interprets." Ptolemaic period, Cairo 27, 567.

Secular Cretans likewise had to emigrate in the course of the following centuries, and did so in large numbers. They turn up as the Philistines of the Bible (*Puresatoi*, or *red men*) in the vicinity of the Israelites. Others hired out as Cretan archers; they are the Cherethites of the Bible (Sam. 2: 8,18), as the Pelethites are the Philistines. There was no question of extinction of any population, neither at the end of the Bronze Age nor earlier.

Let us quote Robert Graves once more: "Despite differences of race and climate, the religious system of the neolithic and Bronze Ages in Europe seems to have been remarkably homogeneous. . . ." ° The same may be said of habitation patterns and architectural continuity, so that in Orchomenos and Knossos Neolithic and Bronze Age structures can be excavated at the selfsame sites. Throughout the Neolithic and the Early and Middle Bronze ages the same kind of agriculture was practiced, utilizing the same technical methods in the same areas, that is, in the river valleys and coastal plains that could be worked with wooden plows. Where clay or stony soil was encountered, the area of settlement ended and the extensive realms of wooded pasture and waste began. Not until the transition from the Middle to the Late Bronze Age did the available tillable land, plus the forested pasturelands, become so divided up that the country could be said to be overpopulated. "Overpopulation" is, of

° *The Greek Myths* (Penguin Books, 1955), p. 11.

course, a relative term. Where agriculture is technologically underdeveloped, a given land area will support a far smaller population than it might under conditions of intensive exploitation of the soil by modern methods—as the recent past has forcefully shown.

Behavioral research has demonstrated that overpopulation produces certain deleterious effects: breakdown of social cooperation, more and more violent individual clashes, ultimately social violence. We have every reason to assume that the Late Bronze Age witnessed the first such epoch of overpopulation in considerable areas of then inhabited Eurasia. Even Egypt did not escape the consequent migrations, the "wandering of the sea-peoples," although within Egypt a central government, strict control of property and, in all likelihood, population planning made possible control of population growth. The story of Moses—a "surplus" child exposed and found among the reed thickets of the Nile delta suggests one measure applied in ancient Egypt to regulate the population. (*Mose* means "the begotten." Begotten by whom? Properly speaking, a father's name should precede: A-mose, Thut-mose, Ptah-mose. Use of *mose* without a patronymic indicates that the father is unknown, that the child is a foundling.) Another measure must have been ritual sacrifice. Perhaps we may attribute the obvious stagnation in the long development of ancient Egypt to such smoothly functioning population planning. Good management of this sort established an equilibrium between population and natural resources and thereby fended off the negative consequences of population growth. But it also destroyed certain positive consequences, for the dynamism of a society is to a considerable degree a response to the strains on it. Necessity is the mother of invention, and invention thrives particularly in times of war and unrest. This was appreciated by the ancients, so that Heraclitus hailed war as the father of all things.

It is difficult to choose between peace and order at the price of infanticide, or rising population with the alternation between technological breakthroughs and such byproducts of density as war, epidemics and pollution. Ancient Egypt went one way; Europe followed the Greek example and went the other. The one way has in the past led to a static and servile society, the other to Western civilization, but also to a still unknown destination in the near or distant future. Where will it take us?

In the Late Bronze Age at any rate, around 1200 B.C., the capacity of the usable land to sustain the existing population density appears to have been overstepped. Throughout the known world there were quarrels, migrations, wars. In the Aegean area the most familiar of such movements are the Trojan War and the Dorian Migration, but these occurred at the same time as the above-mentioned migration of the sea-peoples and similar movements in Asia Minor and Mesopotamia. The times became so unruly that even the dead no longer had peace in their graves. Pillaging the eternal dwellings, which had become virtual treasure chambers, was the simplest way to achieve an "equalization of property relationships." All one had to do was to overcome traditional Stone Age and Early Bronze Age ideas, banish from one's mind the deeply rooted dread of tombs, liberate oneself from the notion of their inviolability—and one would be a made man. In some cases, moreover, the corpses of personal, political or military enemies were no doubt deliberately routed from their rest in order to do harm to them even after death.

The old population on the land was not annihilated when new migrants entered the country. As in the period of the Great Migrations after the end of the Roman Empire, the actual number of persons participating in such wanderings was relatively small. Even 100,000 invaders (the estimated number of the Vandals before they crossed the Straits of Gibraltar) can in the long run scarcely affect the ethnic composition of a country the size of North Africa. The local population of millions, which often has a higher civilization, absorbs the influx of fresh blood and assimilates the new arrivals to such an extent that after a few generations the old stock and the new are indistinguishable.

Aside from political developments, what was the effect of the tribes of the Great Migrations, of the conquests or settlements of the Normans in the Mediterranean region, in Russia and even in remote North America, of the Franks in the eastern part of the Mediterranean and of the numerous immigrant populations in Cretan history? Masters changed, but in general the people remained the same, except for slight changes in their language, dress and customs—charges that the course of history has brought to regions without immigration.

The Late Bronze Age was a thoroughly restless period of world history, but it was also a time of epoch-making technological advances, especially in metallurgy. Out of the age's restlessness came the crucial invention of smelting and working iron. Long preliminary experimentation with the new metal eventually came to fruition; it could be introduced into the production process. The result was, in the Iron Age that followed, an expansion of the terrain susceptible to tillage, an increase in the food supply and hence a period of calm and cultural evolution. The light of the later Helladic culture, then, would not have been possible without the preceding darkness.

As soon as the iron plowshare appeared, hitherto unavailable regions were opened up to agriculture, settlement and more intensive exploitation in general. That is true particularly for the Celtic West, for central Europe and northern Italy; but the agricultural prosperity was felt elsewhere, as for example in the expansion of the Etruscan iron industry and the burgeoning of Greek commerce. The Greeks established commercial colonies in distant areas of the Mediterranean. Some of these outposts were meant for trading with Gaul, as the foundation of Massilia (Marseilles) indicates. The Iron Age expansion of the area of settlement deep into previous wastelands can be regarded as a genuine cultural revolution—all the more so since the concomitant intensification of trade at the same time laid the economic basis on which Greek cultural wealth could develop.

Interestingly enough, there seems to have been a trend away from urn burial during this period. In Etruria and in the area occupied by the Celts we once more encounter expensive vaults for the dead and inhumations or mound graves containing a wealth of grave goods. (Hallstatt period, between 800 and 500 B.C., and the La Tène period between 500 and 50 B.C.). It is somewhat amusing to see how the Greeks disseminated their heroic mythology by exporting vases handsomely decorated with illustrations of their epics. In the vast Etruscan and Celtic necropolises we find such pottery, some of it obviously imitated by non-Greek traders trying to worm their way into a profitable business. The fact that most of these vessels were used as grave goods

suggests that the business dealt in death, that is, in the appurtenances of funerals: spices, embalming oils and similar substances.

While the Etruscans, Celts and even the Germans of the age
returned to elaborate funeral architecture and filled their tombs
with goods eagerly supplied by Greek trading posts, the Greeks
themselves channeled their religious feelings less into private
funeral monuments and more into lavish and permanent temples
for the worship of the gods. The individualistic cult of the dead
for the benefit of a few great families gave way to general veneration of the gods of the city or the nation. Unifying common
worship replaced family ceremonies for the dead. In this way
the Greeks, probably alone among the peoples of the Late Bronze
and Early Iron ages, were able to develop a sense of the common bonds of nationhood, while the Etruscans, Celts and the
Germans were still far from any such feelings. Thus the Romans
could gradually conquer all of Etruria and Gaul without en-
countering any effective alliances of the subject peoples or
common defense efforts on a large scale. Etruscan, Celtic and German resistance to Roman expansion was generally based on temporary tribal alliances that were easily undermined or smashed.
Thus the southern Etruscans had no help from the north to fend
off Roman attacks, and the northern Etruscans were similarly
exposed to the Celtic invasion. And just as there had been no
national sense of unity among the twelve Etruscan city-states,
there was also no feeling for nationhood among the tribes affected by the Roman conquests in Gaul and in Germany.

It is amazing, however, that Etruscan and Celtic funerary
architecture at this period developed forms quite similar to the
tombs of the Middle Bronze Age. Along with simple inhumation
we find rock tombs, large barrows, stone chamber tombs and
even labyrinthine structures. Originally these were closely associated with the cult of the dead, but later they became castles
of refuge (*oppida*), to which the populace inhabiting the plains
fled from attackers.

During the Hallstatt and La Tène periods these funerary citadels largely continued to serve their original functions. The lands
inhabited by the Celtic tribes remained fairly quiet, although increasing population density from 500 B.C. on impelled young

Celtic immigrants to expand southward into Upper Italy and into the Balkans and Asia Minor (the Galatians). For a time this emigration scarcely affected the Celtic homeland, any more than the settlement of the New World by European emigrants in later centuries at first affected Europe. The emigration later brought new imports from the conquered lands, but the Gallic expansion of the fourth century B.C. rather resulted in a shutting off of foreign imports from the homeland of the Celts. This change marks the beginning of the La Tène period, the culture of which seems more coherent and native than that of the preceding Hallstatt culture with its innumerable Greek and Etruscan imports. Celtic conquests abroad had severed old trade relations with the Celtic homeland.

en the Romans set about conquering all of Gaul during the la .wo centuries B.C. the old funerary citadels frequently offered the sole ready defense. These citadels could be used for a last desperate resistance to the Roman cohorts. This shift in function of what had been ancient structures dedicated to the cult of the dead deceived the Romans of the Imperial Age, so that they were confused about the former uses of the *oppida*. They did not know that the walls rising up from some lofty pinnacle above the plain had once been erected not for defense against the outside but for protection from within, that is, to keep the deceased safely for all eternity. That is why the skulls at the doors of such *oppida* led Diodorus Siculus to report that the Celts had been headhunters.

25

The Origin of
Western Civilization

❁

Have you ever reflected on how our advanced European civilization developed? What gave rise to that current of intellectual life that has been flowing in Europe for more than two thousand years, has brought forth such staggering achievements, and for some five hundred years has been the most important export of this small but amazingly dynamic continent?

It is well known that we are the heirs of Rome, by way of the Christian Middle Ages, and, through Rome, ultimately Greece. But what caused the ancient Greeks to develop their remarkable intellectual abilities? Was their culture a product of borrowings, or did they create it afresh out of themselves? Did they build upon the simple earlier stages of Stone Age culture?

On the whole, the nineteenth century accepted Greek civilization as something given, without reflecting closely on its origins. It seemed sufficient to begin every treatise of any consequence with the words: "The ancient Greeks had already . . ." —much as every fairy tale still begins: "Once upon a time . . ."

Our own century was at first disposed to believe that the ancient Greeks simply belonged among that small but select band of peoples who possessed superior intellectual capacities and therefore brought culture to all mankind. This tenet of the superior natural endowment of certain tribes or races became a favorite theme of a nationalistic era. Many confusions sprang from public misunderstanding of scientific ideas, many from deliberate political misuse of such ideas to the detriment of humanity as a whole.

By now we know that all the human beings of this earth, from the Tierra del Fuegan to the Eskimo, belong to a single biological species and genetic community—to a common gene pool. There are no basic differences in intellectual abilities among the peoples of the earth; there are only differences in education. The offspring of other continents can, despite linguistic obstacles and other barriers, quickly take possession of European ideas and modes of thinking, and their accomplishments will be and are equal to those of Europeans.

In spite of this knowledge the notion of "culture carriers" dies hard. After all, it is flattering for Westerners to think that they perform such a role *vis-à-vis* the developing countries. The idea is particularly pervasive in archaeology. Thus Doro Levi attributes the beginning of Minoan culture to the sudden invasion of new peoples into Crete, or Werner Keller maintains that the Etruscan lit the lamps of civilization in the area of the western Mediterranean. Over the last few decades things have improved in one respect: scholars no longer credit every cultural current within a vast periphery to some shadowy Indo-Europeans. On the other hand we should not fall into the opposite error and conjure up vanished high civilizations everywhere, even when there is virtually no evidence for them.

Major cultural achievements do not appear suddenly out of nothingness, like meteors, and then vanish again into unhistorical obscurity. In spite of wars and natural disasters it is slow growth and continuity that give rise to culture. Western civilization was carried from people to people, from nation to nation, for more than two millennia. Each group that received the heritage expanded it. The downfall of the Greek city-states did not put an end to that heritage, nor did the decline of Rome, of the Goths and Lombards, of the states of medieval Europe, of Byzantium and the Holy Roman Empire. It has survived many vicissitudes.

Why then, was Greece the cradle of European civilization? Why not Etruria, Gaul, North Germany or elsewhere? Why did not the Egyptians or Mesopotamians, ancient civilized nations of great stature and striking architectural prowess, display comparable or greater intellectual and spiritual creativity? Surely it is not an adequate explanation to say that the great Greek heritage only chanced to come down to us, whereas the cultural and intellectual achievements of all other nations were wiped out by ethnic or natural disasters. Etruscan culture did not vanish suddenly; it was gradually absorbed into Roman life, to such an extent that many Roman and Etruscan families became linked by marriage and friendship. Thus Livia, Emperor Augustus' wife, was a close friend of Urgulania, of an old Etruscan family, whose daughter Urgulanilla became the wife of the future Emperor Claudius. Claudius himself wrote a twenty-volume history of the Etruscans. It is now lost, but was read at least during his reign, and was quoted by Pliny the Elder and Tacitus. If there had been a preeminent Etruscan culture, the Romans—and thus we—would certainly have been its heirs.

Similarly, the culture of the Gauls was gradually adapted to that of the Romans during the Gallo-Roman period around the beginning of the Christian era; and apparently no unique intellectual achievements were lost forever in the course of that adaptation. Whatever was of value in the culture of the North Germans has come down to us in written monuments.

As we have seen, there were close ties between the Greeks and the Egyptians from the Minoan period to the time of Alexander the Great (who himself held the title of pharaoh), and on into the period when Roman governors ruled Egypt and the University of Alexandria was one of the great centers of Hellenistic learning. As for the Land of the Two Rivers, the Western world early became acquainted with it through the Bible.

The idea of the cometlike rise and decline of cultures, though popular and seemingly confirmed by our experience with two catastrophes of such proportions as the world wars of the twentieth century, cannot really be sustained—not in its original version as conceived by Oswald Spengler nor in the more moderate form given to it by Arnold Toynbee. Occidental civilization, whose beginnings go back to the Minoan and Mycenaean heritage, has already lasted for more than thirty-five hundred years, and is at present expanding to become the uncontested global civilization. Its downfall now would be the equivalent to the end of the human race.

Strangely enough, this European civilization, which has otherwise penetrated into almost all the realms of mind and nature, has been unable to work out any hard-and-fast conception of its own orgins. Since the idea of "culture carriers" does not solve the problem but merely displaces it in one or another geographical direction, scholars nowadays tend merely to state that in antiquity Greece lay at the crossroads of various influences, which combined to bring about a cultural blossoming. But cannot it be said that Egypt or Mesopotamia also lay at crossroads? Moreover, there were in those lands tightly organized states, administrations and voluminous written archives, all of which might have fostered tremendous intellectual developments.

At the risk of bringing down upon my head the wrath of philosophers of history, I should like to pose a number of hypotheses that seem to me worth considering.

First Hypothesis

The flourishing culture of the ancient Greeks was neither delivered to them ready made by other "culture carriers" nor did it spring full-blown from the head of a hero, as it were, because of the Greeks' superior faculties. Rather, their superb cultural achievements had to be built up stage by stage over a long succession of generations.

Second Hypothesis

The process of cultural development was not initially based upon writing but on language spoken and listened to. Through the use of speech in theater, an entire nation learned to sharpen its intellectual capacities. Intelligence is not preexistent. Intelligence is learnable; it can be honed by speech. We know today how handicapped the children from underprivileged circumstances are because they have not, from earliest childhood on, been able to test and strengthen their intellectual capacities by talk.

Third Hypothesis

The starting point for the early Greek development of language was the cult of heroes, originally a cult of the dead. A wealth of stories about heroic deeds was intended to keep alive among the people a living memory of the men of the past. The festivals held at regular intervals in honor of the dead heroes were partly occasions for training the bodies of young men for physical feats, partly for another, moral purpose. Following the stories of heroes would make the audience identify with those exemplary figures and imitate them. The heroic narratives performed in the theater, with the participation of the chorus and, at one time, of the whole people, must be counted among the roots of European culture. We are very wrong if we relegate *The Age of Fable* or similar works to children's reading.

Fourth Hypothesis

In spite of its epoch-making triumphs the Greek theater was basically a makeshift institution, although one thoroughly Greek and utterly brilliant. In Egypt and Mesopotamia mighty mortuary palaces preserved the life stories and the death rites of deceased great men in architecture, sculpture, reliefs and writing. A petrified immortality could be achieved in those countries. In Greece, on the other hand, countless legends of the lives and deaths of heroes and kings were passed from mouth to mouth. The small, relatively poor country, split up into many islands and valleys, would not have had the wealth to erect, for each of its hundreds of great men, a mausoleum that would bear witness to his deeds. Instead the Greeks invented a form of cult-building suitable to the veneration of all heroes; the principle was an empty frame into which any picture may be fitted. On the stage of the Greek theater actors could reawaken to life any of the venerated dead. Instead of a pantheon a panheroön. And how paradoxically it all turned out! The oriental potentates immortalized in the lavish but intellectually sterile mortuary palaces were forgotten. But the spoken words about the Greek heroes keep green their memory down to the present day.

Fifth Hypothesis

Thus the ancient Greeks alone were able to convert the old, expensive and fundamentally unproductive cult of the dead into something throbbing with life, intellectually stimulating and forward-looking. Not that they could have been aware in advance of the consequences. The energies that other peoples devoted to the veneration of the dead were in Greece redirected toward life. Whereas the others had to write off enormous expenses as a total loss, the Greeks found that their expenditures more and more paid off in the training of the young and in the sharpening of the general intelligence. They invented the humanistic principle of education: exercise of language using examples of classical writers to shape the growth of the mind. We know today that such growth need not be based specifically upon Homer or Tacitus. But practice in language and sustained verbal contact with elders are indispensable—which should not be forgotten in this age of audiovisual teaching aids.

One argument that has been raised against my thesis is that I have misunderstood the psychology of the Minoans, who were more concerned with their daily reality than with any cult. The argument itself shows how far modern man has come from the attitudes of the ancients. And as I have said above, we are indebted to the Greeks for this change, which has colored the whole subsequent history of thought. Today we are perhaps beginning to free ourselves of that fear of the beyond that obsessed the Minoans and their contemporaries (although even today very few persons are completely free of such fear). It is very hard for us to put ourselves into the frame of mind of an ancient people, for whom the welfare of the departed was a far more important matter than the needs of the living. Yet we know that this was the attitude of the Egyptians, and Egypt is only one especially dramatic and instructive example of this orientation. National unity was achieved early there, making enormous economic and technological resources available to some individuals. Moreover, the static Egyptian way of life and governmental order preserved living fossils, as it were: Stone Age and Bronze Age modes of thought were perpetuated until the Hellenistic and Roman spirit finally displaced them. Then again, we simply know a great deal about Egypt because Egyptian archaeology developed relatively early, and because so many Egyptian monuments, cult objects and written records have come down to us.

I have established, I think, that the Minoans did not all succumb to natural disasters, taking with them into the grave a unique civilization comparable in no way to the cultures of other countries. On the contrary, they survived and continued to contribute to Greek cultural development. The very knowledge that the ancient Cretans, as part of the Greek stock, once practiced a Stone Age and Bronze Age cult of the dead resembling that of the Egyptians, but subsequently moved away from that cult, provides an explanation for the later intellectual development that so profoundly influenced the future. I am in no way denigrating the Minoan buildings when I interpret them as funerary architecture, nor am I thereby undervaluing Minoan civilization. When all the arguments are weighed objectively, it should be apparent that this new view throws a more positive light upon the evolution of Greece and Europe than any vague notions about an irrecoverably lost paradise. We now see clearly that thirty-five hundred years ago a new way of thinking germinated in Crete. Far from disappearing in some imaginary catastrophe, the Minoans found a way to break out of the rigid conventions of a fundamentally Stone Age religion. They and the Mycenaeans began overcoming the cult of the dead, began to turn toward the requirements of a genuine life of the mind.

But then, if the Egyptians and the Cretans originally subscribed to an essentially kindred cult of the dead, a religion of the hereafter, how do we account for the different directions their development took later on?

The difference was in fact already prefigured at the time of the unification of Upper and Lower Egypt in the Old Kingdom, nearly five thousand years ago. This united state was then the biggest in the world; several millions of human beings in the fertile Nile Valley lived under a single unified command. Probably that unification was geographically inevitable, for the welfare of all Egypt depended on the same flood. The country had a single economic fate; it became unitary in its feelings and thinking; ultimately it was united in administration under a centralized power. All contradictory efforts and divergent tendencies were repeatedly smothered until, after three thousand years of history, the land froze into immobility, an easy prey to dynamic conquerors.

By ancient tradition it was the duty of relatives, friends and subordinates to use the period of mourning between death and burial to erect a funeral monument. Tumulus graves were bigger the more friends and dependents of the deceased there were to share in making them. Such monuments therefore became status symbols more or less scaled (for there was always exaggeration) to the departed's importance. Some hundred thousand workmen are supposed to have labored for twenty years building the pyramid of Cheops. Though we were long given to understand that individual monarchs, obsessed with pride, had pyramids built for themselves by wringing the labor from their oppressed people, such an explanation now strikes us as naive and moralistic. Since the dead pharaoh was the earthly embodiment of Osiris, god of the dead and of vegetation, he was entitled to a funeral monument consistent with the creative powers of the entire nation. It was firmly believed at the time that failure to bury a dead king with due honors would bring down dire punishment upon the whole country. Above all, it might mean a failure of the Nile flood and hence the end of vegetation, which was directly dependent on Osiris and his earthly representative. Of course the masses of the people had to be guided, but force was not involved. The inner coercion of religion was effective enough.

Naturally such a vast undertaking could not wait until the period of mourning began, that is, until the pharaoh had actually died. The dimensions of the task required long preparation, paid specialists and above all an elaborate organization. The task of directing such projects and guiding the masses belonged to a few highly-placed personages who stood close to the pharaoh, and who, like the pharaoh, were for the most part a nobility of birth. The *fellahin*, on the other hand, had their role in life marked out from the start. They passed their days and years in mute submissiveness, without any chance to rise in the world. Egyptian civilization was thus characterized by an insuperable contrast between a tiny upper class of cultivated potentates and their advisers, and the totally uneducated masses who bowed to their fate as god-given and made no effort to escape from it.

Geographically and politically the Greek world presented a totally different picture. The land, divided into innumerable islands, bays, lowlands and mountain valleys, hindered all efforts at political unification, all initiatives toward achieving power on a large scale, all attempts at intellectual regimentation. By the time the antithesis between Sparta and Athens was at last settled in favor of Athens, and Greece was finally united under Macedonian rule, Greek culture had long since (to its and our good fortune) been developed to the full. The Hellenistic period was the heir, not the creator, of that culture.

In that somewhat chaotic world there was room for great and small, for striving for political influence and intellectual development. Importance was not accorded by birth alone; it could be gained at any time by personal vigor and commitment. The Greek heroes were the exact opposite of pharaoh, although both were "of divine origin." In Greece divine descent meant something quite different from what we generally understand by the term, and from what ancient Egypt meant by a legitimately born scion of a pharaoh. As we have explained, the "children of the god" were not the offspring of a regular marriage, but were born in the temple of a god (frequently Zeus or Apollo) because the young mother did not yet have a house of her own or was not yet married in keeping with her station. Many highborn young ladies brought children into the world in this way; the infants were ascribed to the god in whose sanctuary these women had been temple servants or whose medical men had taken care of the parturient. The sanctuaries of the time included not only temples and burial places, but also what we would now call hospitals. Illegitimate birth was no stain, and most of these mothers later entered into quite proper marriages.

A later, less matter-of-fact age subsequently wove around the many tales of "illegitimate" confinements in Greek sanctuaries, especially when these concerned the birth of heroes, fables of the personal fatherhood of Zeus or Apollo. Thus Zeus (to whom most sanctuaries were dedicated) acquired the reputation of an incorrigible rake and adulterer.

For many of the heroes birth out of wedlock was a stimulus

to make their way in life without the protection of an influential father. They strove for power, tried to win rich heiresses (frequently by abduction) and tested their courage in all sorts of adventures. The people, who identified with these heroes in the recurrent funeral games, were moved to imitate great men in enterprise, in intuition and even in wiliness. The Greek heroic epics give the highest palm to success; the means to that end need not have been of the purest.

Whereas in Egypt education was the privilege of a tiny minority, in politically divided Greece it became, by way of the cult of heroes, the property of the people. And it was such universal education that led to true culture.

But when, we must ask, did this separate development begin? When was the Stone Age cult of the dead overcome by the Greek world and replaced by the tradition of the heroic epics? From what point on can the specifically Greek form of cult festival games be demonstrated?

First let us inquire how long the ancient Mediterranean cult of the dead followed parallel lines in Egypt and in the Aegean region.

To archaeologists and philosophers of history it has long seemed evident that Egypt and Greece had little in common. For Egypt had that most characteristic monument, the pyramid, which was noticeably absent from the Greek world. However, this factor is highly misleading. Essentially the pyramid was nothing but a dwelling for the dead, or rather, a heaping up, one upon the other, of a number of burial chambers, each one diminishing in size toward the top. Originally there had been one chamber or layer for each part of the country the pharaoh ruled. The step pyramid of Pharaoh Djoser, of the beginning of the Third Dynasty, shows more plainly than most the development of the form out of the stepped *mastaba*. Hence we can expect to find pyramids only where a kingdom with centralized power has been formed out of the union of several more or less equal provinces. For a local prince, chief of a province or ruler of an island, bay or valley, a pyramid consisting of several tombs piled one atop the other would be pointless.

By the time of the Fourth Dynasty Egyptian centralism had developed the step *mastaba* into the true pyramid; quite possibly the building of the pyramid contributed to the unity of the kingdom and was thus a political necessity.

The parallelism between the development of Egypt and of the Aegean region appears most plainly during the Middle Kingdom. For then the Egyptians under Amenemhet III, the colonizer of the Fayum, developed the labyrinth, which was imitated by the Cretans, by the people of Lemnos and later by the Etruscans.

The paths of development begin to separate perceptibly during the New Kingdom, just about the time of the important Eighteenth Dynasty, contemporary with the later palaces of Crete. Along with a rock tomb hidden in the slopes of the Valley of the Kings, from now on every pharaoh has a special funerary temple dedicated to his cult. The decoration of these structures, some of them on an enormous scale, serves the personal glorification of the dead king. His life and deeds are depicted in words and pictures, and due attention is paid to the ceremonies the cult requires. Just as the churches of the Middle Ages showed the lives and works of the saints or the Saviour in paintings and inscriptions, the temples of the pharaohs recorded (though often in magnified form) the history of these rulers in stone. Once such stone cult monuments were built, the ritual obligation was satisfied and popular adoration fastened upon the succeeding pharaoh, who was the new incarnation of the same god, Osiris.

The Aegean world did not follow Egypt in this petrified glorification of individuals by means of vast mortuary temples (unless we wish to see something analogous in the sanctuaries of the gods). No man in ancient Greece would have had the wealth, or after death the horde of relatives and dependents, to commission such mortuary temples as were constructed for the Egyptian kings. But the dead were by no means forgotten. Memorial ceremonies at regular intervals kept the lives of significant men of the past ever-present in the memories of the living. At intervals of four years (half of a "Great Year") the inhabitants of a given community met with foreign venerators of the dead hero for a ritual repetition of the funeral. On such occasions there were theatrical representations of the hero's life and death, and athletic competitions such as had been celebrated from very ancient times in honor of the dead. These "games" had originally been a very serious business in which, quite often, the penalty for defeat was death. For the dead man was entitled to companions on his journey into the hereafter, and these companions were frequently the losers in the match.

Part of the Olympic chariot races, for example, would be a reenactment of the flight of Pelops (whose name is preserved in Peloponnesus) with Hippodamia, pursued by King Oenomaus, who would have run his lance through his daughter's suitor if he had been able to catch him. The ritual acts, the plays and games, took place in the vicinity of the former burial sites, where

FIG. 88 Theater scene fresco, Palace of Knossos.

the sanctuaries to the gods had also been erected: in Olympia, Dodona, Delphi, Eleusis or Corinth (where the Isthmian Games took place).

Instead of huge mortuary temples for individuals, the Greeks needed theaters and arenas, so that the life of the dead could be shown on the stage or imitated on the race track. The first representation of such Greek ritual games is a fresco in the Palace of Knossos. It has hitherto been interpreted as a garden party, probably because three tall trees with ample crowns separate the stage from the spectators' area. Instead of "young girls dancing," as Nicolas Platon calls them, we are in reality looking at part of the chorus of a Greek tragedy. There are fourteen (preserved) figures of women, all in the same dress and pose, with exposed breasts (they have "rent their garments," as the Bible puts it) and arms raised in mourning. The portion depicting the left side of the stage has not come down to us, but this would have been the place for the individual actors who portray the life of the hero. The stage, like the viewing area, is rectangular; it has not yet attained the famous semicircular form of the classic Greek theater. In Knossos, and on an even more generous scale in Phaistos, such early theaters have been excavated: large rectangular areas with places for the audience rising like steps on two adjacent sides. These theatral areas are located in the immediate vicinity of the mortuary palaces. A long road paved with slabs, the Sacred Way, leads directly into the theater, terminating in and becoming an organic part of the theatral area. This paved way suggests the cult processions depicted in frescos and on vases, processions that evidently reached the palace area at this point. We also find the frescos showing the contests in honor of the dead, the bull games in which youths and maidens pitted their agility against the clumsy fury of the beast.

To see nothing but gaiety and playfulness in all that is to misunderstand ancient religion. Comedy was the product of a much later age; in the beginning these games and contests were as "deadly" as could be. Tourists in Spain today, knowing nothing of a tradition thousands of years old, and steeped in the modern idea of protecting animals, ought to consider that the age-old bullfight (like the horse race, which came later) once upon a time constituted an important link in the evolution of Western civilization.

But then, we must ask, why did not Celtic Iberia or southern Gaul, where bullfights are held to this day, become the nucleus for Western civilization? In this region, too, there were isolated islands, bays and valleys; in this region, too, political unity was achieved late, only under Roman occupation.

In Egypt and in the Near East generally rulers possessing unlimited power, together with a small circle of their advisers, monopolized culture. In Gaul, in the other areas inhabited by

FIG. 89   Phaistos: theatral area with steps serving as seats for spectators.

Celts (the British Isles, South Germany, Upper Italy) and in Etruria culture was in the hands of another elite minority, the priesthood. In the Near East writing began early, but it was used solely for the benefit of the upper class and the glorification of the potentates. In Etruscan and Celtic western Europe knowledge was passed on orally from generation to generation of priests. No outsider was allowed access to the secret doctrines. For the Druids committing anything to writing was equivalent to betraying mysteries. That is why we find such sparse written records in both Celtic and Etruscan graves, although there is often a wealth of grave goods. Celtic and Etruscan history is known to us only to the extent that the Romans reported it. In Minoan Crete, too, there was obviously some trepidation about setting down knowledge of any importance on the clay tablets.

Oral tradition functioned amazingly well from the times of Minoan Crete on. The genealogies of the Agenorides, the descendants of King Agenor of Phoenician through his daughter Europa, and of the Asterides, the descendants of King Asterios of Crete, are well known to us from the Greek heroic legends. The tradition was handed down orally for approximately a thousand years before being committed to writing on the Parian Marble and in the chronology of Eratosthenes.

Between the mystifications of the priesthood in the West and the pretensions of the potentates in the East, both equally hostile to intellectual development of other classes of the population, there remained only a comparatively narrow strip where untrammeled cultural evolution was permitted: Greece and Greece's window to the southeast, Crete. Like Europa, the first Cretan queen to be enrolled in the heroic legends, important cultural influences came from the Near East as well as Egypt. But Europa had to move to Crete to become the ancestress of Greek and thus European heroes. Similarly it was in Crete that the Afro-Asiatic cultural heritage was transformed into the foundations of Western civilization.

With the development of the first theatral areas and dramatic frescos Minoan Crete showed that it had put behind it the ancient Mediterranean cult of the dead, and thus created the basis for further intellectual evolution. In the cultural sense theater

Fig. 90 Pithos storeroom, Phaistos. Right front, a "footstool," perhaps merely a stand on which offerings were placed.

and painting raise Minoan Crete far above Egypt and Mesopotamia, although those areas were far advanced in architecture, written tradition and political power. Thus Crete was the land that gave birth to Western culture, and with it Greece, while the kingdoms of the oriental monarchs passed away, leaving little of their glory to posterity. What traces there are of them have come down indirectly, through Greece.

But in what does this culture consist? Obviously not in mighty structures that proclaim the pride of their builders, nor in the accumulation of vast material treasures, nor in military victories or political triumphs. Culture is not manifested by a social order in which a small band of "knowers"—whether they be born masters with inherited power or an elite caste of priests initiated into sacred traditions by virtue of their office—directs the lives of the great masses of ignorant *fellahin* as they see fit. Culture is cultivation of the people, is intellectual ability on the broadest scale; it is thought operating in breadth as well as depth. In this sense Greek culture seems to have been the first that was worthy of the name.

Epilogue and
Acknowledgments

◈

For more than five decades the prehistory and early history
of Crete suffered from the tensions of a patent internal contradiction. On the one hand Minoan Crete was more and more
acknowledged as the cradle of European civilization. But on the
other hand, according to the postulates of Minoan archaeologists,
that early efflorescence of civilization in the Late Bronze Age
was almost totally annihilated, wiped out so thoroughly that
only vague memories in myth and legend were left, little more
than a remote and distorted reflection of the first isolated emer-
gence of culture on the soil of Europe.

There may have been many who felt this contradiction, but
few commented openly on it, let alone solved it. How could the
Minoan world have been the starting point of occidental culture
if the whole of Cretan civilization had almost completely vanished long before Classical Greece could take over the heritage?
In that case the Hellenes must have produced their much later
cultural explosion wholly on their own; it must have been a
new creation without any inner connection to the long since
forgotten Minoan culture. The author's principal concern in this
book has been to make a contribution toward resolving this
paradox. Perhaps the contradiction itself strikes him, from his
geologist's vantage point, more strongly than it does many of his
colleagues in the liberal arts.

Future generations of historians will examine without bias which of the two hypotheses is more fruitful: the idea I have here suggested, for the first time, of a distinct discontinuity in burial rites at the point where the "Palace period" ends and is succeeded by the era of predominant cremation; or the idea deriving from Evans, and much elaborated by his followers, of a catastrophic end to the Minoans and their culture. The Evans thesis robs early Crete of precisely what to my mind distinguishes it: its claim to be the land in which European culture and civilization originated. To put the point at issue in another way: I see discontinuity in burial rites only; the Evans school sees discontinuity in the whole culture.

Scholars trained in the traditional view, who have presented that view in lectures and publications for many years, will probably need a long time to think over the thesis offered here. The case is different with the younger generation. The young tend to be less burdened by tradition and to seize upon whatever appears to them logical. Scholarly disputes of this sort cannot really be settled by more or less cogent arguments of authorities, or by a vote among the specialists. Given a reasonable time for opinions to form, the better position will ultimately be accepted. I do not fear the outcome.

In all probability a good many of the ideas presented here will have to be modified. Further study will suggest new approaches, and specialists with more detailed knowledge than an outsider in the fields of prehistory and early history can possess will want to correct and refine various points. I shall always be glad to hear from those who know more than I do. But I doubt that it will be possible to present the theories of Evans and his successors as if this book had never been written. When something is untenable from the geological viewpoint, it cannot be made tenable from the archaeological viewpoint.

I am deeply indebted to all who have aided my work on this book by references and factual contributions. Foremost among these are D. B. Ascher, Haifa; W. D. Bach, Mannheim; G. Bauer, Stuttgart; W. Baur, Stuttgart; Dr. G. J. Boekschoten, Groningen; Frau R. Briner, Bern; Professor Dr. K. Brunnacker, Cologne; Frau Dr. H. Friese, Bietigheim; Professor Dr. R. Hachmann,

Saarbrücken; Professor Dr. S. Haussühl, Cologne; Dipl. Biol. B. Herrmann, Berlin; Frau H. Hinze, Celle; Professor Dr. K. Jeremias, Stuttgart; Dr. B. Kern, Stuttgart; Herr W. Kollmar, Hamburg-Blankenese; Dr. U. Kull, Stuttgart; Dr. J. Kunsemüller, Stuttgart; Dr. -Ing. E. Lang, Aachen; Dr. J. Lehmann, Stuttgart; Frau E. Mann, Meersburg; Professor Dr. C. Oftedahl, Trondheim; Dr. G. Prause, Hamburg; Dr. E. Rall, Göppingen; Dr. Z. Silberstein, Haifa; Professor Dr. H. Thierfelder, Münster; and Frau L. Wunderlich, Erfurt.

My warm thanks go to my associates at the Institute for Geology and Paleontology of the University of Stuttgart for the patience with which they have tolerated their chairman's prolonged preoccupation with matters other than the earth sciences. Herr Akad, Dr. Behmel and Herr Seligmann by their comments in our discussions, Herr Frech by his valuable assistance with the photographic work and Herr Karrasch by his drawings have made signal contributions to the success of this work. It is a testimony to their industry that nevertheless the current work of the Institute was not neglected.

. . . To all of the Rowohlt staff I want to express my cordial thanks.

Finally I must mention my family, who from the first observations on Crete through the collecting of material, the writing of the manuscript, the choosing and reproduction of the illustrations, on down to the correction of the proofs, lent their aid in every way.

H. G. Wunderlich

Bibliography

GENERAL

World Archaeology

Alkim, U. Bahadir. *Anatolia*. Translated by James Hogarth. Cleveland: World Publishing Co., 1968.

Gryaznov, Mikhail P. *The Ancient Civilization of Southern Siberia*. Translated by James Hogarth. New York: Cowles Book Co., 1969.

Hatt, Jean Jacques. *Celts and Gallo-Romans*. Translated by James Hogarth. Geneva: Nagel, 1970.

Karageorghis, Vassos. *Cyprus*. New York: Cowles Education Corp., 1969.

Margueron, Jean Claude. *Mesopotamia*. Translated by H. S. B. Harrison. Cleveland: World Publishing Co., 1965.

Platon, Nicolas. *Crete*. Translated from the Greek. London: Muller, 1966.

Bederke, Erich, and Wunderlich, Hans-Georg. *Atlas zur Geologie*. Map legends in German, English, French, Spanish, and Russian. Mannheim: Bibliographisches Institut, 1968.

Caesar, C. Julius. *War Commentaries: De Bello Gallico and De Bello Civili*. Edited and translated by John Warrington. ("Everyman's Library," Classical, No. 702) New York: Dutton, 1965.

Ceram, C. W. [Kurt W. Marek] *Gods, Graves, and Scholars*. 2nd rev. and enlarged ed. Translated by E. B. Garside and Sophie Wilkins. New York: Bantam, 1972.

———— *The March of Archaeology*. New York: Knopf, 1958.

———— *The First American*. New York: Harcourt, 1971.

Champollion, Jacques. *The World of the Egyptians*. Translated by Joël Rosenthal. Geneva: Minerva, 1971.

Graves, Robert. *The Greek Myths.* New York: Penguin Classics, 1955.

Herodotus. *The Histories.* Translated by Aubrey de Sélincourt. New York: Penguin Classics, 1971.

Homer. *The Iliad of Homer.* Translated by Richmond Lattimore. Chicago and London: The University of Chicago Press Phoenix Books, 1970.

——— *The Odyssey of Homer.* Translated by Robert Fitzgerald. New York: Doubleday Anchor Books, 1963.

Keller, Werner, *Denn sie entzündeten das Licht.* Munich: Droemer/Knaur, 1970.

Kerényi, Karl. *The Gods of the Greeks.* Translated by Norman Cameron. New York: Grove Press, 1960.

——— *The Heroes of the Greeks.* Translated by H. J. Rose. New York: Grove Press, 1960.

Roeder, Günther. *Die Ägyptische Götterwelt.* Zurich and Stuttgart: Artemis-Verlag, 1959.

——— *Kulte, Orakel und Naturverehrung im alten Ägypten.* Zurich: Artemis-Verlag, 1960.

——— *Mythen und Legenden um ägyptische Gottheiten und Pharaonen.* Zurich: Artemis-Verlag, 1960.

——— *Zauberei und Jenseitsglauben im alten Ägyten.* Zurich and Stuttgart: 1961.

Schliemann, Henry, *Mycenae.* New York: Scribner, Armstrong and Co., 1878.

——— *Ilios.* New York: Harper and Brothers, 1881.

——— *Troja.* New York: Harper and Brothers, 1884.

——— *Tiryns.* New York: C. Scribner's Sons, 1885.

Schwab, Gustav. *Gods and Heroes; Myths and Epics of Ancient Greece.* New York: Pantheon, 1946.

Spengler, Oswald. *The Decline of the West.* Authorized translation by Charles Francis Atkinson with notes. New York: A. A. Knopf, 1926–28.

——— *Zur Weltgeschichte des zweiten vorchristlichen Jahrtausends.* Munich: 1935.

Toynbee, Arnold Joseph. *A Study of History.* 12 vols. New York: Oxford University Press, 1948–61.

Vacano, Otto-Wilhelm von. *Die Etrusker.* Stuttgart: Kohlhammer, 1955.

——— *The Etruscans in the Ancient World.* Translated by Sheila Ann Ogilvie. New York: St. Martin's Press, 1960.

Valentin, Veit. *Illustrierte Weltegeschichte.* 2 vols. Munich: 1959.

Woldering, Irmgard. *The Art of Egypt; The Time of the Pharaohs.* Translated by Ann E. Keep. New York: Greystone Press, 1963

Wolf, Walther. *The Origins of Western Art, Egypt, Mesopotamia, the Aegean.* New Hyde Park, N.Y.: University Books, 1971.

Wunderlich, Hans-Georg. *Einführung in die Geologie: Exogene Dynamik und Endogene Dynamik.* 2 vols. Mannheim: 1968.

——— "Das Geheimnis der minoischen Paläste Altkretas," *Naturwissenschaft und Medizin* 8, Nr. 36 Mannheim (1971).

——— "Keine Brandkatastrophe im Palast von Knossos?" *Umschau im Wissenschaft und Technik* 71, Heft 16, Frankfurt/M. (1971) 599.
——— "Knossos—eine Totenstadt." *Bild der Wissenschaft.* Stuttgart: 1972.

ARCHAEOLOGICAL LITERATURE ON CRETE

Banti, L., Pugliese Carratelli, G., and Levi, D. "Arte Minoica e Micenea." *Enciclopedia dell'Arte Antica Classica e Orientale,* Vol. V, p. 42 ff.

Bossert, Helmuth. *The Art of Ancient Crete.* London: Zwemmer, 1937.

Charbonneaux, Jean. *L'Art égéen.* Paris: G. van Oest, 1929.

Childe, V. Gordon. *The Dawn of European Civilization.* New York: Vintage Books. 1964.

Demargne, Pierre. *La Crète dedalique.* Paris: E. de Boccard, 1947.

——— *The Birth of Greek Art.* Translated by Stuart Gilbert and James Emmons. New York: Golden Press, 1964.

Dussaud, René. *Les civilisations préhelléniques dans le bassin de la mer Égée.* Paris: P. Geuthner, 1914.

Evans, Arthur J. *The Palace of Minos.* 4 vols. London: Macmillan, 1921–35.

Fimmen, Dietrich. *Die kretisch-mykenische Kultur.* Leipzig-Berlin: B. G. Teubner, 1924.

Forsdyke, J. "Minoan Art," *Proceedings of the British Academy* 15. London (1929).

Glotz, Gustav. *La Civilisation égéenne.* Paris: A. Michel, 1952; also *The Aegean Civilization.* Reprint of 1925 edition. New York: Barnes and Noble, 1968.

Graham, James Walter. *The Palaces of Crete.* Princeton, N.J.: University Press, 1962.

Hall, H. R. *The Civilization of Greece in the Bronze Age.* London: Methuen, 1928.

Hutchinson, R. *Prehistoric Crete.* London: Penguin Books, 1962.

Karo, Georg Heinrich. "Kreta," *Pauly-Wissowa Realencyclopädie.*

——— *Greifen am Thron, Erinnerungen an Knossos.* Baden-Baden: B. Grimm, 1959.

Marinatos, Spyridon. *Crete and Mycenae.* With photographs by Max Hirmer. New York: Abrams, 1960.

Matz, Friedrich. "Die Ägäis," *Handbuch der Archäologie* II (1950) 179 ff.

——— *Kreta, Mykene, Troja.* Stuttgart: G. Kilpper, 1958.

——— *The Art of Crete and Early Greece.* Translated by Ann E. Keep. New York: Crown Publishers, 1962.

——— *Minoan Civilization.* Cambridge: University Press, 1962.

Montelius, O. *La Grèce préclassique.* 2 vols. Stockholm: 1924–28.

Pendlebury, J. D. S. *The Archaeology of Crete.* London: 1939.

Platon, N. "Cretese-Miceneo," *Enciclopedia Universale dell'Arte* IV, p. 70 ff.

Praschniker, Camillo. *Kretische Kunst.* 1921.

Schachermeyr, F. "Die prähistorischen Kulturen Griechenlands," Pauly-Wissowa Realencyclopädie 22. 1954.

———— *Die ältesten Kulturen Griechenlands.* Stuttgart: 1955.

———— *Die minoische Kultur des alten Kreta.* Stuttgart: Kohlhammer, 1964.

Schweitzer, B. "Altkretische Kunst," *Antike* II (1926) 191 ff.

Snijder, G. A. S. *Kretische Kunst.* Berlin: Gebr. Mann, 1936.

Thompson, G. *The Prehistoric Aegean.* London: 1954.

Zervos, Christian. *L'art de la Crète néolithique et minoenne.* Paris: Editions "Cahiers d'art," 1956.

REPORTS ON EXCAVATIONS

Knossos

Evans, Arthur J. *The Palace of Minos.* 4 vols. London: Macmillan, 1921–35.

———— "Prehistoric Tombs of Knossos," *Archaeologia* LIV, London (1914).

Evans, J. "Excavations in the Neolithic Mound of Knossos," *Bulletin of the Institute of Archaeology* 4 (1964).

———— "Excavations in the Neolithic Settlement of Knossos," *British School Annual* 59 (1964) 152 ff.

Furness, Ozanne, "The Neolithic Pottery of Knossos," *British School Annual* 48 (1953) 94 ff.

Phaistos

Levi, D. "Eine Reihe von Aufsätzen über die neuen Grabungen seit 1951," *Annuario della Scuola Italiana di Atene;* also in *Bolletino d'Arte et Parola del Passato.*

Pernier, Luigi. *Il Palazzo Minoico di Festòs.* I. Rome: Libreria dello Stato, 1935.

———— and Banti, L. *Il Palazzo Minoico di Festos.* II. Rome: 1951.

Mallia

Interim reports since 1928 in the series entitled *Etudes Cretoises* by F. Chapouthier, P. Demargne, H. Gallet de Santerre, J. Deshayes, A. Dessenne, and H. and M. van Effenterre.

Messara

Xanthoudides, S. *The Vaulted Tombs of Messara.* Liverpool: 1924.

See also in the reports on other sites in the writings of Hogarth, Bosanquet, Dawkins, Seager, Boyd, Hall, Hood, Hutchinson, Boardman, Hazzidakis, Xanthoudides, Marinatos, Platon, Alexiou.

AGE DETERMINATIONS

Aberg, Nils. *Bronzezeitliche und früheisenzeitliche Chronologie*. (*Griechenland*, IV) Stockholm: 1933.

Evans, Arthur J. "Essai de classification des époques de la civilisation minoenne," Congrès d'Archéologie, 1906.

Hutchinson, R. "Notes on Minoan Chronology," *Antiquity* XXII (1948) 61 ff.

———— "Minoan Chronology Reviewed," *Antiquity* XXVIII (1954) 155 ff.

Levi, D. "Classificazione della civiltà minoica," *Bolletino d'Arte et Parola del Passato* (1960) 81 ff.

Libby, Willard F. *Radiocarbon Dating*. 2nd ed. Chicago: University of Chicago Press, 1965.

Matz, Friedrich. "Zur ägäischen Chronologie der frühen Bronzezeit," *Historia* I (1950) 173 ff.

Platon, N. "Chronologie minoenne," p. 509 in Zervos *op. cit.*

Smith, Sidney. "Middle Minoan I and Babylonian Chronology," *American Journal of Archaeology* (1945) 1 ff.

Stubbings, Frank. "Chronology of the Aegean Bronze Age," *Cambridge Ancient History*. Vol. I, Chap. VI, Cambridge [Eng.]: University Press, 1962.

Weinberg, S. "Relative Chronology of the Aegean in the Neolithic and the Early Bronze Age," *Relative Chronologies in Old World Archaeology* (1954) 86 ff.

MINOAN CULTURE IN ITS CONTEMPORARY CONTEXT

Burn, A. *Minoans, Philistines and Greeks*. New York: A. A. Knopf, 1930.

Kantor, H. I. *The Aegean and the Orient in the Second Millennium B. C.* Bloomington, Ind.: 1947.

Marinatos, Spyridon. *The Minoan and the Mycenaean Civilization and the Influence on the Mediterranean and Europe*. VI. Congrès des Sciences pré- et protohistoriques I. 1961.

Pendlebury, J. *Aegyptiaca*. 1930.

———— "Egypt and the Aegean in the Late Bronze Age," *Journal of Egyptian Archaeology* 16 (1930).

Vercoutter, J. *L'Egypte et le Monde égéen préhellénique*. Le Caire: 1956.

———— *Essai sur les Relations entre Égyptiens et Préhellènes*. Paris: A. Maisonneuve, 1954.

MINOAN LANGUAGE AND SCRIPT

Chadwick, John. *The Decipherment of Linear B*. New York: Random House, 1957.

Ekschmitt, W. *Die Kontroverse um Linear B*. Munich: 1969.

Myres, John Linton. *Who Were the Greeks?* Berkeley: University of California Press, 1930.

Palmer, L. R. *Mycenaeans and Minoans*. New York: Knopf, 1961.

—— and Boardman, J. *On the Knossos Tablets*. Oxford: Clarendon Press, 1963.

Stella, Luigia. *La civiltà Micenea nei documenti contemporanei*. Rome: 1965.

Ventris, Michael, and Chadwick, John. *Documents in Mycenaean Greek*. Cambridge [Eng.]: University Press, 1959.

—— "Evidence for Greek Dialect in the Mycenaean Archives," *Journal of Hellenic Studies* (1953).

DESTRUCTION OF THE MINOAN CULTURE

Andronikos, M. "The Dorian Invasion and Archeology," Ἑλληνικά 13 (1959) 45 ff.

Desborough, Vincent Robin d'Arba. *The Last Mycenaeans and Their Successors*. Oxford: Clarendon Press, 1964.

Marinatos, Spyridon. "The Volcanic Destruction of Minoan Crete," *Antiquity* XIII (1939) 425 ff.

MINOAN RELIGION

Evans, Arthur J. "Mycenaean Tree and Pillar Cult," *Journal of Hellenic Studies XXI* (1901) 99 ff.

Guthrie, William Keith. "The Religion and Mythology of the Greeks," *Cambridge Ancient History*. Vol. II, Chap. 40. Cambridge [Eng.]: University Press, 1961.

Matz, Friedrich. "Göttererscheinung und Kultbild im minoischen Kreta," *Abhandlung der geistigen und socialwissenshaftlichen Klasse*. Mainz: Akademie der Wissenshaften und der Literatur (1958).

Nilsson, M. *The Minoan-Mycenaean Religion*. Lund: 1950.

—— "Geschichte der griechischen Religion," I. *Handbuch der Religionswissenschaft* V. 1950.

Persson, Axel Waldemar. *The Religion of Greece in Prehistoric Times*. ("Sather Lectures," XVII) Berkeley and Los Angeles: University of California Press, 1942.

Picard, Charles. *Les Religions préhelléniques (Crete et Mycènes)*. Paris: 1948.

MISCELLANEOUS (SEALS, STYLISTIC ELEMENTS)

Biesantz, Hagen. *Kretisch-mykenische Siegelbilder*. Marburg: N. G. Elwert, 1954.

Kenna, Victor. *Cretan Seals*. With a catalogue of the Minoan gems in the Ashmolean Museum. Oxford: 1960.

Lorimer, Hilda. *Homer and the Monuments.* London: Macmillan, 1950.

Marinatos, Spyridon. "La Marine crétomycénienne," *Bulletin Correspondence Hellénique* 57 (1933) 170 ff.

Matz, Friedrich. *Die frühkretischen Siegel.* Berlin-Leipzig, 1928.

——— "Torsion," *Abhandlungen der gestigen und socialwissenshaftlichen Klasse,* No. 12. Mainz: Akademie der Wissenshaften und der Literatur (1951).

CULTS OF THE DEAD, BURIAL CUSTOMS, MUMMIFICATION

Andronikos, M. "Totenkult," *Archaeologia Homerica.* Bd. III, Kapitel W. Göttingen (1968).

Dörpfeld, W. "Uber Verbrennung und Bestattung der Toten im alten Griechenland," *Zeitschrift für Ethnologie* 37, Berlin (1905) 538–41.

Hörmann, K. "Vorgeschichtliche Leichendörrung, die Mittelstufe zwischen Bestatten und Verbrennen," *Schumacher-Festcrift.* S. 77-79. 1930.

Küchenmeister, F. "Die verschiedenen Bestattungsarten menschlicher Leichname vom Anfang der Geschichte bis heute," 4 Folgen. *Zeitschrift für gerichtliche Medizin.* Vierteljahresschrift für gerichtliche Medizin und öffentliches Sanitätswesen. Bd. 42-44. S. 1885 f.

Robinson, D. M. *Necrolynthia—A Study of Greek Burial Customs and Anthropology.* Baltimore: 1942.

Zehetmaier, Josef. *Leichenverbrennung und Leichenbestattung im alten Hellas.* Leipzig: 1907.

GUIDEBOOKS, MAPS, DESCRIPTIVE GUIDES, PICTURE BOOKS

Crete and Greece

Blauer Führer Griechenland, 1963. Large section on Crete.

Bowman, John Stewart. *Crete. (An Albatross Guide.)* London: Secker and Warburg, 1962; also *A Guide to Crete.* New York: Pantheon Books, 1963.

Bradford, Ernle. *The Companion Guide to the Greek Islands.* 1st ed. New York: Harper and Row, 1963.

Bryans, Robin. *Crete.* London: Faber, 1969.

Burian, Christian. *Polyglott Reiseführer Griechische Inseln.* Cologne and Munich: 1969. (Multilingual)

Christoforakis, J. M. *Kreta—Grosse Autokarte* 1:300,000. Iraklion, 1970.

Cresti, Carlo. *Forma e colore: Il Palazzo di Cnosso.* Florence, 1965.

Crete and Its Treasures. Text by Olivier Reverdin. Preface by N. Platon. 88 color photos by Rudolf Hoegler, N. Platon, and N. Creutzburg. Translated by Eric and Mary Peters. New York: Viking Press, 1961.

Marinatos, Spyridon. *Crete and Mycenae.* Photos by Max Hirmer. New York: Abrams, 1960.

Mathioulakis, C. Landkarte von Kreta, 1:300,000. Athens: 1969.
———— *Knossos. Führer durch das Ausgrabungsgelände.* Athens: 1970.
Merian—Kreta. 16 Jg. Heft 12, Hamburg. (1963).
Miller, Henry. *The Colossus of Maroussi.* New York: New Directions, 1958.
Münster, Thomas. *Kreta hat andere Sterne.* Munich: 1960.
Pars, Hans. *Göttlich aber war Kreta. Das Erlebnis der Augrabungen.* Olten: Walter-Verlag, 1957.
Schneider, Toni. *Kreta.* Zurich.

Egypt

Brunner-Traut, E. and Hell, V. *Ägypten—Studienreiseführer mit Landeskunde.* Stuttgart: 1966.
Grieben—Reiseführer Ägypten. Munich: 1970.
Strelocke, Hans. *Reiseführer Ägypten.* Cologne-Marienburg: 1966. (Multilingual)
Voss-Gerling, Wilhelm. *Bertelsmann—Reiseführer Ägypten.* Gütersloh: 1966.

Rome—Campania

Maiuri, Amadeo. *Herculaneum.* (Ministero della Pubblica Istruzione, Nr. 53) Rome: 1963.
———— *Pompeii.* (Ministero della Pubblica Istruzione, Nr. 3) Rome: 1955.
———— *Pompeii.* Bailey, 1960.
Romanelli, Pietro. *Palatine.* (Ministero della Pubblica Istruzione, Nr. 45) Rome.
Sestieri, Pellegrino Claudio. *Paestum.* (Ministero della Pubblica Istruzione, Nr. 84) Rome.

GEOLOGICAL LITERATURE (CRETE, SANTORINI, EASTERN MEDITERREAN)

Boekschoten, G. J. "Some geological observations on the coasts of Crete," *Geologie en Mijnbouw* 42 (1963) 241–47.
———— "Quaternary tephra on Crete and the eruptions of Santorin volcano," in "Evolution in Aegean," Edited by A. Strid. *Opera Botanica* 30. (1971) 40–48.
Evans, J. D. "Summary and Conclusions" in "Knossos Neolithic," *Annals of the British School of Archaeology at Athens* 63 (1968) 267–76.
Finley, M. I. *Early Greece: The Bronze and Archaic Ages.* London: 1970.
Hedervari, P. "International scientific congress on the volcano of Thera," *Geological Newsletter I. U. G. S.* (1969) 399–403.
Marinos, G., and Medionis, N. "On the amplitude of the tsunami originating from the prehistoric eruption of Santorini," *Etaira Greek Geological Society* 4 (1961) Athens, 210–18. (In Greek)
Mellis, O. "Volcanic ash-horizons in deep-sea sediments from the eastern Mediterranean," *Deep-Sea Research* 2 (1954) 89–92.

Ninkovich, D., and Heezen, B. C. "Santorini tephra," *Colston Papers of the Bristol University* 17 (1965) 413–53.

——— "Physical and chemical properties of volcanic glass from Thera island and ash layers in eastern Mediterranean deep sea sediments," *Nature* 213 (1967) 282–84.

Olausson, E. "Description of sediment cores from the Mediterranean and Red Sea," *Report of the Swedish Deep Sea Expedition* 8 (1960) 286–334.

Papastamatiou, J. "Le gites de gypse et d'anhydrite dans l'île de Crète," *Geological Society of Greece* III, Nr. 1 (1958) 146–56.

Popham, M. R. "The destruction of the palace of Knossos and its pottery," *Antiquity* XL (1966) 24–28.

Reck, H. *Die Geologie der Ring-Inseln und der Kaldera von Santorini.* 3 vols. Berlin: 1936.

Thorarinsson, S. "Toxic hazard to sheep from Hekla's eruption," *New Scientist* 47 (1970) 175.

Index

Numbers in italics indicate an illustration of the subject mentioned.